Optimized Cloud Resource Management and Scheduling

T0076716

Optimized Cloud Resource Management and Scheduling

Theories and Practices

Wenhong Tian
Yong Zhao

AMSTERDAM • BOSTON • HEIDELBERG • LONDON
NEW YORK • OXFORD • PARIS • SAN DIEGO
SAN FRANCISCO • SINGAPORE • SYDNEY • TOKYO

Morgan Kaufmann is an imprint of Elsevier

Morgan Kaufmann is an imprint of Elsevier
225 Wyman Street, Waltham, MA 02451, USA

British Library Cataloguing-in-Publication Data
A catalogue record for this book is available from the British Library.

Library of Congress Cataloging-in-Publication Data
A catalog record for this book is available from the Library of Congress.

ISBN: 978-0-12-801476-9

For Information on all Morgan Kaufmann publications
visit our website at www.mkp.com

Working together
to grow libraries in
developing countries

www.elsevier.com • www.bookaid.org

Transferred to Digital Printing in 2014

Contents

Foreword   ix
Preface   xi
About the Authors   xv
Acknowledgments   xvii

1   An Introduction to Cloud Computing   **1**
    1.1 The background of Cloud computing   1
    1.2 Cloud computing is an integration of other advanced
         technologies   3
    1.3 The driving forces of Cloud computing   **8**
    1.4 The development status and trends of Cloud computing   **8**
    1.5 The classification of Cloud computing applications   **10**
    1.6 The different roles in the Cloud computing industry chain   **12**
    1.7 The main features and technical challenges
         of Cloud computing   **13**
    Summary   15
    References   15

2   Big Data Technologies and Cloud Computing   **17**
    2.1 The background and definition of big data   **17**
    2.2 Big data problems   **20**
    2.3 The dialectical relationship between Cloud computing
         and big data   **26**
    2.4 Big data technologies   **28**
    Summary   46
    Acknowledgments   46
    References   47

3   Resource Modeling and Definitions for Cloud Data Centers   **51**
    3.1 Resource models in Cloud data centers   **51**
    3.2 Data center resources   **51**
    3.3 Categories of Cloud data center resources   **54**
    3.4 Constraints and dependencies among resources   **69**
    3.5 Data modeling of resources in a Cloud data center   **70**
    3.6 Conclusion   **75**
    Appendix 1: The UML Relationship of Resources   **76**
    References   77

4   Cloud Resource Scheduling Strategies   **79**
4.1 Key technologies of resource scheduling   79
4.2 Comparative analysis of scheduling strategies   80
4.3 Classification of main scheduling strategies   85
4.4 Some constraints of scheduling strategies   90
4.5 Scheduling task execution time and trigger conditions   90
Summary   91
Appendix: Some elementary terms   91
References   92

5   Load Balance Scheduling for Cloud Data Centers   **95**
5.1 Introduction   95
5.2 Related work   96
5.3 Problem formulation and description   96
5.4 OLRSA algorithm   101
5.5 LIF algorithm   106
5.6 Discussion and conclusion   113
References   113

**6   Energy-efficient Allocation of Real-time Virtual Machines
      in Cloud Data Centers using Interval-packing Techniques**   **115**
6.1 Introduction   115
6.2 GreenCloud architecture   117
6.3 Energy-efficient real-time scheduling   120
6.4 Performance evaluation   127
6.5 Related work   132
6.6 Conclusions   132
References   132

**7   Energy Efficiency by Minimizing Total Busy Time of Offline
      Parallel Scheduling in Cloud Computing**   **135**
7.1 Introduction   135
7.2 Approximation algorithm and its approximation ratio bound   140
7.3 Application to energy efficiency in Cloud computing   146
7.4 Performance evaluation   149
7.5 Conclusions   155
References   156

**8   Comparative Study of Energy-efficient Scheduling in Cloud Data
      Centers**   **159**
8.1 Introduction   159
8.2 Related research   161
8.3 Comparative study of offline scheduling algorithms   162

8.4 Online algorithms 167
8.5 Summary 177
References 177

9   Energy Efficiency Scheduling in Hadoop 179
9.1 Overview 179
9.2 Scheduling algorithms 182
9.3 Energy control 186
9.4 Energy-efficient scheduling for multiple users 188
9.5 Performance evaluation 195
9.6 Summary 202
Questions 203
References 203

10   Maximizing Total Weights in Virtual Machines Allocation 205
10.1 Introduction 205
10.2 Problem formulation: WISWCS 206
10.3 WISWCS 209
10.4 An exact SAWISWCS 211
10.5 Applications of WISWCS 213
10.6 Related work 215
10.7 Conclusions 215
References 215

**11   A Toolkit for Modeling and Simulation of Real-time Virtual
      Machine Allocation in a Cloud Data Center** 217
11.1 Introduction of the cloud data center 217
11.2 The architecture and main features of CloudSched 220
11.3 Performance metrics for different scheduling algorithms 225
11.4 Design and implementation of CloudSched 229
11.5 Performance evaluation 234
11.6 Conclusions 240
References 242

12   Toward Running Scientific Workflows in the Cloud 245
12.1 Introduction 245
12.2 Related work 247
12.3 Integration 248
12.4 Experiment 254
12.5 Experiment on Amazon EC2 259
12.6 Conclusions 264
References 265

Foreword

Cloud computing has become one of driving forces for the IT industry. IT vendors are promising to offer storage, computation, and application hosting services and to provide coverage on several continents, offering service-level agreements-backed performance and uptime promises for their services. They offer subscription-based access to infrastructure, platforms, and applications that are popularly termed Infrastructure-as-a-Service (IaaS), Platform-as-a-Service (PaaS), and Software-as-a-Service (SaaS). These emerging services have reduced the cost of computation and application hosting by several orders of magnitude, but there is significant complexity involved in the development and delivery of applications and their services in a seamless, scalable, and reliable manner.

One of challenging issues is to have efficient scheduling systems for cloud computing. This book is one of a few books focusing on IaaS-level scheduling. Most of data centers currently only implement simple scheduling strategies and algorithms, there are many issues requiring in-depth system solutions. Optimized resources scheduling, mainly faces the fundamental questions such as optimal modeling, allocation, and dynamic live migration. This book addresses these fundamental problems, and takes multidimensional resources (CPU, storage, networking, etc.) with load balance, energy efficiency and other features into account, rather than just considering static preset parameters.

In order to achieve objectives of high performance, energy saving, and reduced costs, cloud data centers need to handle the physical and virtual resources in dynamic environment. This book aims to identify potential research directions and technologies that will facilitate efficient management and scheduling of computing resources in cloud data centers supporting scientific, industrial, business, and consumer applications.

This book offers excellent overview of the state of the art in resource scheduling and management in cloud computing. I strongly recommend the book as a reference for audiences such as system architects, practitioners, developers, new researchers, and graduate-level students.

Professor Rajkumar Buyya
Director, Cloud Computing and Distributed Systems (CLOUDS) Laboratory,
The University of Melbourne, Australia
CEO, Manjrasoft Pty Ltd., Australia
Editor in Chief, IEEE Transactions on Cloud Computing

Preface

Optimized resource scheduling can be a few magnitudes better in performance than simple or random resource scheduling.

Cloud computing is a new business model and service model that composes tasks across a large number of different computer data centers, so that all applications can obtain necessary computing power, storage space, and information services. The network or data center that provides services is often called a "cloud." Cloud computing is treated by researchers as the fifth public resource (the fifth public utility), in addition to water, electricity, gas, and oil. Following the personal computer revolution and Internet changes, cloud computing is seen as the third wave of IT and is an important strategic component of the world's emerging industries that will bring profound changes to life, production methods, and business models.

Web searches, scientific computing, virtual environments, energy, bioinformatics, and other fields have begun to explore the applications and relevant services of cloud computing. Many studies have predicted "the core of future competition is in the cloud data center." Cloud data centers accommodate equipment resources and are responsible for energy supply, air conditioning, and equipment maintenance. Cloud data centers can also be placed in a separate room within other buildings, which can be distributed across multiple systems in different geographic locations. A cloud brings together resources: multi-tenant mode services for large-scale consumers. Physically, the sharing of distributed resources exists, and a single overall form is presented to the user logically.

There are many different types of resources. The resources involved in the book include:

Physical machines (PMs): are the compositions of physical computing devices in a cloud data center; each PM can host multiple virtual machines, and can have more than one CPU, memory, hard drive, and network cards.
Physical clusters: consist of a number of PMs, necessary networks, and storage facilities.
Virtual machines (VMs): are created by the virtualization software on PMs; each VM may have a number of virtual CPUs, hard drives, and network cards.
Virtual clusters: consist of a number of VMs, necessary networks, and storage facilities.
Shared storage: high-capacity storage systems that can be shared by all users.

The resource scheduling of a Cloud data center is at the core of cloud computing; advanced and optimized resource scheduling is the key to improving efficiency of schools, government, research institutions, and enterprises. Improving the sharing of resources, improving performance, and reducing operating costs are of great significance and deserve further systematic study and research.

Resource scheduling is a process of allocating resources from resource providers to users. There are generally two levels of scheduling: job-level scheduling and facility-level scheduling. Job-level scheduling is a program-specific operation; the system is assigned specific jobs. For example, some require more computing resources, independent and time-consuming procedures, or high-performance parallel processing procedures; these procedures often require large-scale, high-performance computing resources (such as cloud computing) in order to be completed quickly. Facility-level scheduling refers primarily to the underlying infrastructure resources as a service (Infrastructure as a Service, abbreviated as IaaS) available to users, based on actual use of these resources. For example, PMs (including CPU, memory, and network bandwidth), VMs (including virtual CPU, memory, and network bandwidth), and virtual clustering are types of infrastructure computing resources.

This book focuses on facility-level scheduling. Most data centers currently only implement simple scheduling strategies and algorithms; there are many issues requiring in-depth system solutions. Optimized resource scheduling concerns the following three fundamental questions:

1. Scheduling objectives: What are the optimization objectives for the allocation of a virtual machine?
2. Allocation problems: Where should resources be allocated on a virtual machine? (e.g., What is the criteria for allocating the resources in a virtual machine?)
3. Migration issues: How can a virtual machine be migrated to another physical server when overloads, failures, alarms, and other exceptional conditions occur?

When addressing fundamental problems, dynamic scheduling takes into account multidimensional resources (CPUs, storage, and networking), load balance, energy efficiency, utilization, and other features, rather than just considering static, preset parameters.

Cloud data centers need to handle physical and virtual resources in this new dynamic scheduling problem, in order to achieve the objectives of high performance, less energy usage, and reduced costs. The current resource scheduling in cloud data centers tends to utilize traditional methods of resource allocation, so it is difficult to meet these objectives. Cloud data centers face scheduling issues challenges, including: dynamic flexibility in overall performance in the distribution and migration of VMs and PMs, the overall balance (CPU, storage, and networks), and other resource factors, rather than a single factor; the resolution of inconsistencies in specifications related to system performance; energy-efficiency, and cost-effectiveness.

This book aims to identify potential research directions and technologies that will facilitate the efficient management and scheduling of computing resources in cloud data centers supporting scientific, industrial, business, and consumer applications. We expect the book to serve as a reference for larger audiences, such as systems architects, practitioners, developers, new researchers, and graduate-level students. This area of research is relatively new, and—as such—has no existing reference book to address it.

This book includes: an overview of Cloud computing (Chapter 1), the relationship between big data technologies and Cloud computing (Chapter 2), the definition and modeling of Cloud resources (Chapter 3), Cloud resource scheduling strategies (Chapter 4), load balance scheduling (Chapter 5), energy-efficient scheduling using interval packing (Chapter 6), energy efficiency from parallel offline scheduling (Chapter 7), the comparative study of energy-efficient scheduling (Chapter 8), energy-efficient scheduling in Hadoop (Chapter 9), maximizing total weights in virtual machine allocations (Chapter 10), using modeling and simulation tools for virtual machine allocation (Chapter 11), and running practice scientific workflows in the Cloud (Chapter 12).

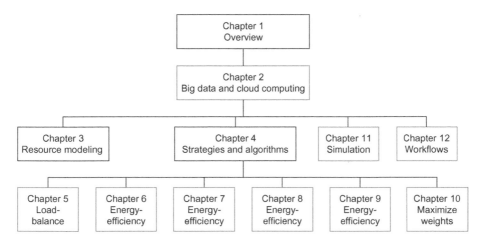

Thanks go to the following people for their editing contributions: Yaqiu Jiang for Chapter 3; Minxian Xu for Chapters 4, 5, and 11; Qin Xiong and Xianrong Liu for Chapters 6, 7, and 8; Yu Chen and XinYang Wang for Chapter 9; Jun Cao for Chapter 10; Youfu Li and Rao Chen for Chapters 2 and 12.

This book aims to be more than just the editorial content of a small number of experts with theoretical knowledge and practical experience; you are welcome to send comments to CloudSched@gmail.com.

About the Authors

Dr. Wenhong Tian has a PhD from computer science department of North Carolina State University. He is now an associate professor at University of Electronic Science and Technology of China (UESTC). His research interests include dynamic resource scheduling algorithms and management in Cloud data centers, dynamic modeling, and performance analysis of communication networks. He published about 30 journals and conference papers in related areas.

Dr. Yong Zhao is an associate professor at the School of Computer Science and Engineering, University of Electronic Science and Technology of China. He obtained his PhD in Computer Science from the University of Chicago under Dr. Ian Foster's supervision. He worked 3 years as a design engineer in Microsoft USA. His research areas are in Cloud computing, many-task computing, and data intensive computing. He is a member of ACM, IEEE, and CCF.

Acknowledgments

First, we are grateful to all researchers and industrial developers worldwide for their contributions to various cloud computing concepts and technologies discussed in this book. Our special thanks to all the members of Extreme Scale Computing and Services (ESCSs) Lab of the University of Electronic Science and Technology of China (UESTC), who contributed to the preparation of associated theories, applications and documents. They include Dr. Quan Wen, Dr. Yuxi Li, Dr. Jun Chen, Dr. Ruini Xue, and Dr. Luping Ji, and their graduate students.

We thank the National Science Foundation of China (NSFC) and Central University Fund of China (CUFC) for supporting our research and related endeavors.

We thank all of our colleagues at the UESTC for their mentorship and positive support for our research and our efforts.

We thank the members of the ESCSs Lab for proofreading one or more chapters. They include Jun Cao, Min Yuan, Xianrong Liu, Siying Zhang, Yujun Hu, Minxian Xu, Yu Chen, Xinyang Wang, Qin Xiong, Youfu Li, and Rao Chen.

We thank our family members for their love and understanding during the preparation of the book.

We sincerely thank external reviewers commissioned by the publisher for their critical comments and suggestions on enhancing the presentation and organization of many chapters in the book. This has greatly helped us improve the quality of the book.

Finally, we would like to thank the staff at Elsevier Inc. for their consistent support and guidance during the preparation of the book. In particular, we thank Todd Green for inspiring us to take up this project and Lindsay Lawrence for setting the process of publication in motion.

Wenhong Tian
University of Electronic Science and Technology of China (UESTC)

Yong Zhao
University of Electronic Science and Technology of China (UESTC)

An Introduction to Cloud Computing

Main Contents of this Chapter

- Background of Cloud computing
- Driving forces of Cloud computing
- Status and trends of Cloud computing
- Classification of Cloud computing applications
- Main features and challenges of Cloud computing

1.1   The background of Cloud computing

The world is entering the Cloud computing era. Cloud computing is a new business model and service model. Its core concept is that it doesn't rely on the local computer to do computing, but on computing resources operated by third parties that provide computing, storage, and networking resources. The concept of Cloud computing can be traced back to 1961 in a speech on the centennial of MIT, when computer industry pioneer John McCarthy said: "The computing may one day be as common as the telephone resources (public utility), ... the computer resources will become an important new industrial base." In 1966, D. F. Parkhill in his classic book "The Challenge of the Computer Utility," predicted that computing power would one day be available to the public in a similar way as water and electricity. Today, the industry says that Cloud computing is the fifth public resource ("the fifth utility") after water, electricity, gas, and oil.

People often use the following two classic stories to describe Cloud-computing applications [1].

In the first story, Tom is an employee of a company; the company sends Tom to London for business. So, Tom wants to know the flight information, the best route from his house to the airport, the latest weather in London, accommodation information, etc. All of the above information can be provided through Cloud computing. Cloud computing is connected to a wide variety of terminals (e.g., PC, PDA, cell phone, TV) to provide users with extensive, active, highly personalized service.

In the second story, Bob is another employee of the same company. The company does not send him on a business trip, so he works as usual at the company. Arriving at the company, he intends to manage recent tasks, so he uses Google Calendar to manage the schedule. After creating his work schedule, Bob can send and receive mail through Gmail and contact colleagues and friends through GTalk. If he then wants to start work, he can use Google Docs to write online documents.

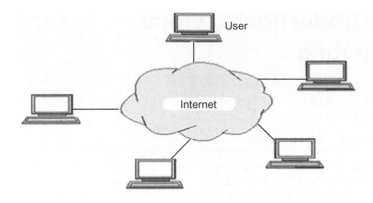

Figure 1.1 Internet depicted as a cloud.

During the process, if he needs access to relevant papers, he can search through Google Scholar, use Google Translate to translate English into other languages or vice versa, and even use Google Charts to draw diagrams. Bob can also share logs via Google Blogger, share video through Google's YouTube, and edit and share pictures through Google Picasa.

A popular argument to explain why "Cloud computing" is called "Cloud" computing: during the rise of Internet technology, people used to draw a cloud when describing the Internet, as shown in Figure 1.1, because when people access the Internet through a web browser, they may need to go through several intermediate transfer processes, which are transparent to them. Therefore, when choosing a term to represent this new generation of Internet-based computing services, "Cloud computing" is used, which does not reference the network's forwarding processes, but relates to client services and applications. This interpretation is very interesting and trendy, but it can confuse people. Especially in Chinese, many words associated with the word cloud are derogatory terms, so it is necessary to give a clear definition of Cloud computing.

There are many definitions of Cloud computing. Wikipedia's definition is: "Cloud computing is a computational model and information services business model. It distributes tasks to different data centers that consist of a number of physical computer servers or virtual servers, so that all kinds of applications can obtain necessary computing power, storage space and information services [2]." A Berkeley white paper defines Cloud computing as "includ[ing] various forms of Internet applications, services, and hardware and software facilities provided by data center [3]." We integrate the characteristics of Cloud computing and define it as: "a large-scale, distributed computing model driven by economies of scale, which provide the abstract, virtualized, dynamically scalable, and effective management of computing, storage, the pooling of resources and services, and an on-demand model via the Internet to external users [4]." It is different from the traditional computing model in that: (1) it is large scale, (2) it can be encapsulated into an abstract

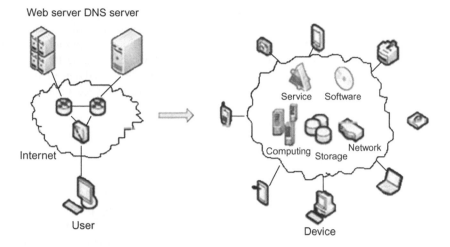

Figure 1.2 Cloud computing services and applications.

entity and provide users with different levels of service, (3) it is based on economies of scale, and (4) the service is dynamically configured and on-demand.

Cloud computing can provide network computing and information services and applications as shown in Figure 1.2, including computing, storage, networking, services, and software, among others.

In 1966, D. F. Parkhill, in his classic book "The Challenge of the Computer Utility," predicted that computing power would one day be available to the public in a similar manner to water and electricity. Many computer scientists constantly explore and innovate to achieve this goal, however, a successful widely accepted approach by industry and users has not been found. Many approaches have been proposed, but have been overthrown or have not been used widely [5]. With the continuous improvement of network infrastructure, and the rapid development of Internet applications, Cloud computing is accepted by more and more people. People have called Cloud computing the "the fifth utility"—the fifth public resource after water, electricity, gas, and oil. Some people call it the "poor man's supercomputer" because users no longer need to purchase and maintain large computer pools, they only need to use computing resources through the network on demand.

1.2 Cloud computing is an integration of other advanced technologies

In the history of computer science and technology development, often landmark technologies appear and change the landscape dramatically.

These technologies have a tremendous impact on the world's IT applications and service models. These include parallel computing, grid computing, utility computing, virtual computing, and software as a service (SaaS) [1]. Cloud computing gradually evolved from these techniques, but not in a simplistic manner. The industry generally believes that Cloud computing is a synthesis (integration) of other advanced technologies. Figure 1.3 shows a few key technologies in the evolution of Cloud computing.

1.2.1 Parallel computing

Parallel computing divides a scientific computing problem into several small computing tasks, and concurrently runs these tasks on a parallel computer, using parallel processing methods to solve complex computing problems quickly. Parallel computing is generally used in the fields that require high computing performance, such as in the military, energy exploration, biotechnology, and medicine. It is also known as High-Performance Computing or Super Computing. A parallel computer is a group of homogeneous processing units that solve large computational problems more quickly through communication and collaboration. Common parallel computer architecture includes a shared memory symmetric multiprocessor, a distributed memory massively parallel machines, and a loosely coupled cluster of distributed workstations. Parallel programs to solve computational problems often require special algorithms. To write parallel programs, one needs to consider factors other than the actual computational problem to be solved, such as how to coordinate the operation between the various concurrent processes, how to allocate tasks to each process, and so on.

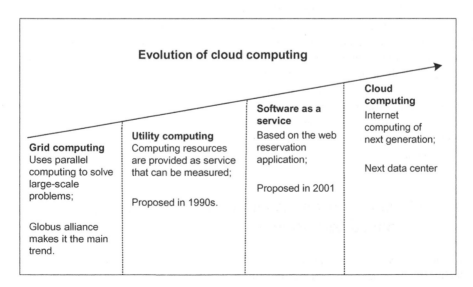

Figure 1.3 Major evolution process of Cloud computing.

Parallel computing can be said to be an important part of the Cloud environment. Similar to the idea of Cloud computing, the current world has been built on a number of supercomputing centers that serve parallel computing users in contiguous regions and charge in a cost-sharing way. However, there are significant differences between Cloud computing and traditional parallel computing. First of all, parallel computing requires the use of a specific programming paradigm to perform single large-scale computing tasks or to run certain applications. In contrast, Cloud computing needs to provide tens of millions of different types of applications with a high-quality service environment, to improve responsiveness based on user requirements, and to accelerate business innovation. In general, Cloud computing doesn't limit the user's programming models and application types: users no longer need to develop complex programs, they can put all kinds of business and personal applications in the Cloud computing environment. Second, Cloud computing puts more emphasis on using Cloud services through the Internet, and it can manage large-scale resources in the Cloud environment. In parallel computing, the computing resources are often concentrated in the machine or in a cluster in a single data center. As noted above, Cloud computing resources are distributed more widely, so they are no longer limited to a data center, but can extend to a number of different geographic locations. At the same time, the use of virtualization technology effectively improves Cloud computing resource utilization. Thus, Cloud computing is the product of the flourishing of the Internet and information technology industry and completes the transformation from the traditional, single-task-oriented computing model to a modern, service-oriented, multi-computing model.

1.2.2   Grid computing

Grid Computing is a distributed computing model. Grid computing technology integrates servers, storage systems, and networks distributed within the network to form an integrated system and provide users with powerful computing and storage capacity. For the grid end users or applications, the grid looks like a virtual machine with powerful capabilities. The essence of grid computing is to manage heterogeneous and loosely coupled resources in an efficient way in this distributed system, and to coordinate these resources through a task scheduler so they can complete specific cooperative computing tasks.

We can conclude that grid computing focuses on managing heterogeneous resources connected by a network and ensures that these resources can be fully utilized for computing tasks. Typically, users need a grid-based framework to build their own grid system, and to manage this framework and perform computing tasks on it. Cloud computing is different. Users only use Cloud resources and don't focus on resource management and integration. Cloud providers provide all of the resources and the users just see a single logical whole. Therefore, there are big differences in the respective relationships of resources. We can also say that in grid computing, several scattered resources provide a running environment for a single task, but in Cloud computing a single integrated resource serves multiple users.

1.2.3   Utility computing

Utility computing is based on the premise that IT resources like computing and storage resources are provided based on user requirements: users only pay according to their actual usage. The goal of utility computing is for IT resources to be supplied and billed like traditional public facilities (such as water and electricity). Utility computing allows companies and individuals to avoid the large one-time investment, and to still have huge computing resources along with a reduction in the costs of using and managing these resources. The goal of utility computing is to increase the utilization of resources, minimize costs, and improve flexibility in the use of resources.

The idea of providing resources on demand and payment depending upon usage matches the resource use concept in Cloud computing. Cloud computing can also allocate computing resources, storage, networks, and other basic resources according to user demand. When compared with utility computing, Cloud computing already has many practical applications, the technology involved is feasible, and its architecture is stronger. Cloud computing is concerned with how to develop, operate, and manage different services with its own platform in the Internet age. Cloud computing will not only focus on the provision of basic resources, but also on service delivery. In the Cloud computing environment, in addition to the hardware and other IT infrastructure resources provided in the form of services, application development, operations, and management are also provided in the form of service. Also, the application itself can be provided in the form of operations and the management of different services. Therefore, compared to utility computing, cloud computing covers a broader range of technology and concepts.

1.2.4   Ubiquitous computing

In 1988, Mark Weiser presented the ubiquitous computing idea and predicted that this method of computing would become pervasive. In the late 1990s, the concept of pervasive computing got extensive attention and people began gradually warming to the idea. In 1999, IBM formally proposed the concept of ubiquitous computing. In the same year, IBM held the first session of its UbiComp conference. In 2000, the first Pervasive Computing International Conference was held. In 2002, the *IEEE Pervasive Computing* journal was founded.

The promoters of ubiquitous computing hope the computing embedded into the environment or everyday tools can enable people to interact with computers more naturally. One of the significant goals of ubiquitous computing is to allow computer equipment to sense changes in the surrounding environment and to alter behaviors according to those changes.

Pervasive computing uses radio network technology to enable people to access information without the constraints of time and place. While general mobile computing has no context-specific features, pervasive computing technology can provide the most effective environment by sensing the location of individuals, environmental information, personal situations, and tasks.

1.2.5 Software as a service

SaaS is a web-based software application that provides a software services model. SaaS is a software distribution model: the application is specifically designed for network delivery. SaaS applications are often priced as a "package" cost (a monthly rental fee), which includes the application software license fees, software maintenance, and technical support costs. For the majority of small and medium companies, SaaS is one of the best ways to use advanced technologies.

By 2008, Internet data centers (IDCs) divided SaaS into two categories: hosted application management (hosted AM)—formerly known as an application service provider—and "on-demand software," which is a synonym for SaaS. From 2009, hosted AM has been one part of the IDC outsourcing program, and on-demand and SaaS are treated as the same software delivery model.

Currently, SaaS has become an important force in the software industry. As long as the quality and credibility of SaaS continue to be confirmed, its attraction will not subside.

1.2.6 Virtualization technology

Virtualization is a broad term and, in terms of computers, it usually means that the computing components run in a virtual environment rather than in a real one. Virtualization technology can expand the capacity of the hardware and simplify the software reconfiguration process. CPU virtualization technology can simulate parallel multi-CPUs with a single CPU, can allow a platform to run multiple operating systems and applications, and can run systems in independent space without affecting each other, which significantly improves the efficiency of the computer.

Virtualization technology first appeared in IBM mainframe systems in the 1960s and became popular in the System 370 series in the 1970s. These machines generate many virtual systems that can run independent operating systems on hardware through the Virtual Machine Monitor program. With the widespread deployment of multi-core systems, clusters, grids, and even Cloud computing, the advantages of virtualization technology in commercial applications were gradually realized. It not only reduces IT costs, but also enhances system security and reliability. The concept of virtualization gradually penetrated into people's daily work and life.

Virtualization is a broad term and may mean different things to different people. In computer science, virtualization represents an abstraction of computing resources, not just a virtual machine. For example, the abstraction of physical memory, resulting in virtual memory technology, makes the application think that it has continuously available address space. In fact, the application code and data may be separated into many pages or fragments, or may even be swapped out to a disk, flash memory, and/or other external memories. Even if there is not enough physical memory, the application can be implemented smoothly.

Hyper-threading virtualization and multitasking virtualization are completely different. Multitasking refers to an operating system that runs multiple programs in parallel, and with virtualization technology, it can run multiple operating systems

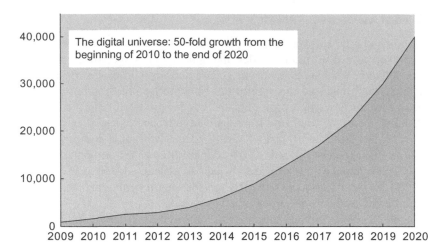

Figure 1.4 The evolution of Cloud computing [6].

simultaneously. Each operating system runs multiple programs and each operating system runs in a virtual CPU or virtual host. On the other hand, hyper-threading technology refers to a single CPU simulating two CPUs to balance program performance, and the two simulated CPUs are not separated, but work together.

1.3 The driving forces of Cloud computing

Cloud computing is the inevitable result of massive information processing requirements led by the development of the Internet and an information society. Its business model is accepted and used more widely by global companies and customers than previous models such as grid computing. In sum, it's the product of technological development and social needs. Cloud computing integrates previous advanced technologies of the computer industry, including large-scale data centers, virtualization, and SaaS.

The Internet-based information explosion is the main factor driving Cloud computing. Figure 1.4 shows the growth (in EB) of the digital universe [6]. In 2006, the whole world generated 161 EB (1 EB equals 1 billion G bytes) data: the thickness of it as a printed book would be 10 times the distance from the Earth to the Sun. In 2009, the whole world generated 988 EB, or about 158G per person; compare this with the only 5 EB data of written records from the previous 5000 years of human history.

1.4 The development status and trends of Cloud computing

Figure 1.5 provides a search volume index comparing Grid computing and Cloud computing from Google trends. In around 2005, IBM, Intel, and other companies

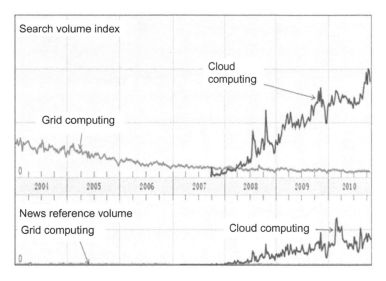

Figure 1.5 Trends of Cloud computing.

and universities in the United States launched a Cloud computing virtual laboratory project. This project first started with experiments at North Carolina State University near IBM headquarters. IBM and Google jointly launched Cloud computing in 2007—known as a new network computing model to challenge the traditional Intel and Microsoft computing model—and it immediately attracted attention from a large number of research institutions.

World-renowned investment bank Merrill Lynch predicts the global Cloud computing market is expected to increase to $160 billion in 2011 and commercial and office software from the Cloud computing market will reach $95 billion. International Data Corporation (IDC) predicts that in the next four years, the China Cloud computing market will be 1.1 trillion RMB Yuan. A huge number of network users—especially small businesses—provide a good user base for the development of Cloud computing in China. Cloud computing will greatly enhance electronic levels of domestic small and medium enterprises (SMEs), and ultimately will enhance the competitiveness of enterprises. This huge market opportunity is very attractive for many companies and research institutions. Cloud computing is considered to be a new generation of high-speed network computing and services platform that will lead to revolutionary changes in the computer field. In fact, many companies and research institutions have already begun research or planning, preparing to get the competitive advantage of this next round of technology. From the perspective of virtualization, computers, networks, storage, databases, and scientific computing devices can be potential Cloud computing resources, according to certain rules and service agreements. IT industry leaders (e.g., IBM [1,7], Google, Amazon [7], Microsoft [8], VMware [9]) have launched "Cloud computing" plans; other well-known companies like Baidu, Alibaba, and Lenovo are also carrying out

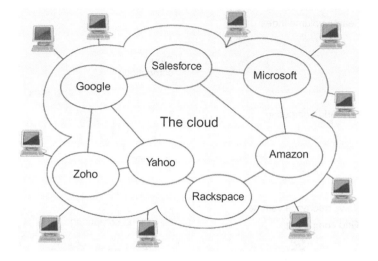

Figure 1.6 Cloud service providers.

related research; as are universities and research institutions around the world. After establishing a Cloud computing platform, an important and key issue is the effective allocation and management of the virtual share resources according to user needs and to improve resource usage efficiency (Figure 1.6).

1.5   The classification of Cloud computing applications

Clouds in nature have very different shapes and slightly different physical processes involved in their formation, but they still have some common characteristics. Based on their similarities, combined with a need for observation and weather forecasting, meteorologists divide the clouds into three levels based on elevation: low, medium, and high.

Drawing similar classifications to those for clouds in nature, there are broad categories that apply in the Cloud computing industry.

1.5.1   Classification by service type

The industry generally believes that Cloud computing can be divided into the following bottom-up categories, depending on the type of service:

1. Infrastructure as a Service (IaaS) in the Cloud: provides infrastructure, including physical and virtual servers, storage, and network bandwidth services directly to users. Users design and implement applications based on their practical requirements, like Amazon EC2 (Amazon Elastic Cloud Computing).

Table 1.1 **Service type classification of Cloud computing**

Classification	Service type	Flexibility/ Generality	Difficulty level	Scale and example
IaaS	Basic computing, storage, network resources	High	Difficult	Large, Amazon EC2
PaaS	Application hosting environment	Middle	Middle	Middle, Google App Engine
SaaS	Application with specific function	Low	Easy	Small, Salesforce CRM

2. Platform as a Service (PaaS) in the Cloud: provides a hosting Cloud platform in which users can put their applications onto the Cloud platform. Development and deployment of the applications must comply with the specific rules and restrictions of the platform, such as the use of certain programming languages, programming frameworks, and data storage models. For example, Google App Engine provides an operating environment for Web applications; once the applications are deployed, other involved management activities—like dynamic resource management—will be the responsibility of the platform.

3. Application as a Service in the Cloud: provides software that can be used directly, most of which is browser-based and specific for a particular function. For example, Salesforce provides the customer relationship management system (CRM). The application is easy to use in the Cloud, but its flexibility is low and it is generally only used for a specific application (Table 1.1).

1.5.2 Classification by deployment method

As an innovative computing model, Cloud computing has many advantages that previous models do not have, but it also brings a series of challenges, related to the business model and techniques. The first is security: customer information is the most valuable asset for enterprises that require a high security level, such as banking, insurance, trade, and the military. Once the information is stolen or damaged, the consequences can be disastrous. The second challenge relates to reliability. For example, banks require their transactions to be completed quickly and accurately, because accurate data records and reliable information transmission is a necessary condition for customer satisfaction. Another problem relates to regulatory issues. Some companies want their IT departments to be completely controlled by the company, free from outside interference and control. Although Cloud computing can provide users with guaranteed data security through system isolation and security measures and can provide users with reliable service through service quality management, it still might not meet all the needs of users.

To solve this series of problems, the industry divides the Cloud into three categories according to the relationship between Cloud computing providers and users,

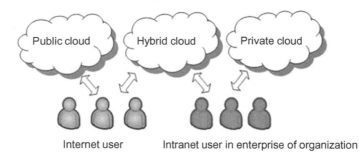

Figure 1.7 Cloud computing service model.

namely, public, private, and hybrid Clouds, as shown in Figure 1.7. Users can choose their own Cloud computing model according to their needs.

1. Public Cloud: The Cloud environment is shared by some businesses and users. In the public Cloud, the service is provided by independent, third-party Cloud providers. The Cloud provider also serves other users; these users share the resources owned by the Cloud provider.
2. Private Cloud: The Cloud environment is built and used by a company independently. The private Cloud is owned by an enterprise or organization. In a private Cloud, users are members of the enterprise or organization, and those members share the resources of the Cloud computing environment. Users outside of the enterprise or organization cannot access the services provided by the Cloud computing environment.
3. Hybrid Cloud: Refers to the mixture of a public and a private Cloud.

1.6   The different roles in the Cloud computing industry chain

Cloud providers: Cloud providers stay in a high position of the Cloud computing industry chain and provide hardware and software equipment and solutions for Cloud users. They need to have a wealth of software, hardware, and industry experience. They provide services for other roles.

Cloud service providers: Cloud service providers use the platform provided by Cloud providers to provide computing services. They need to work closely with the Cloud providers (they can also build their own Cloud environment).

Enterprise users: A huge number of small and medium enterprises are users in the Cloud computing industrial chain. Enterprises can rent Cloud platforms from Cloud providers and service providers according to actual development needs, or they can build a small, private Cloud.

Individual users: Individual users will use services mainly through thin clients, mobile handsets, and other devices. Users no longer need to buy expensive high-performance computers to run software; they also don't need to install, maintain, or upgrade software, so client systems' costs and security vulnerabilities can be reduced.

In addition to the commercial Cloud, open-source Cloud platforms have been widely applied in the industry, such as that in Hadoop [10,11], Eucalyptus [12].

1.7 The main features and technical challenges of Cloud computing

1.7.1 The main features of Cloud computing

1. Virtualization

    Cloud computing platforms and applications are built based mostly on resource virtualization technology. Virtualization plays an important role in improving resource effi ciency and increasing service reliability and security. The authors in [1] describe the practice and principle of virtualization technology in detail.

2. Dynamic (flexibility)

    Cloud resources platforms can dynamically expand or reduce in size depending on user needs, which reduces the investment risk for the user and meets the needs of different users. Cloud computing gives people the sense that there are infinite computing resources that can be used.

3. On-demand service

    Cloud platforms and services can be provided and billed for according to the actual needs of users. Cloud computing eliminates the risk of the one-time large investment, and it allows users to use only the necessary amount of resources depending on their needs. Therefore, services must be based on prices in the short term (e.g., by the hour), so users can free up resources when they are no longer needed.

4. Economies of scale

    Because Cloud computing is built based on large-scale resources (Google, IBM, Microsoft, Amazon), the use of large-scale effects can reduce the rental or use fees and thus can attract more users.

5. High reliability

    Cloud computing platforms need to ensure that customer data is secure and the application platform is reliable. Generally, multiple data and platform backups are used to increase reliability. At the same time, Cloud computing platforms use dynamic network management systems to monitor the status and efficiency of each resource node, to dynamically migrate nodes that have low efficiency or failure, and to ensure that overall system performance is not affected.

6. Dynamic Customization

    Cloud rental resources must be highly customizable. Infrastructure as a service allows users to deploy specialized and virtual appliances. Other services (PaaS and SaaS) provide low flexibility and don't apply to general purpose computing, but are still expected to provide a degree of customization.

Figure 1.8 shows the main features of Cloud computing.

1.7.2 Challenging issues

Security: For companies requiring a high level of data security (such as those in banking, insurance, trade, or the military), customer information security level requirements are extremely high. The ability of Cloud computing to ensure data security is a general concern for these industries. Currently, researchers and service providers have proposed many solutions. In the new application environment, there are still many security issues to be resolved.

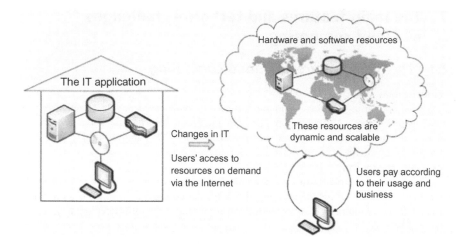

Figure 1.8 Features of Cloud computing.

In general, companies or organizations requiring high security, reliability, and IT that can be monitored—such as that required by financial institutions, government agencies, and large enterprises—are potential users of a private Cloud. Because they already have large-scale IT infrastructures, they only need to invest a small amount to upgrade their IT systems, they can have the flexibility and efficiency brought by Cloud computing, and they can effectively avoid the negative impact of using a public Cloud. In addition, they can also choose the hybrid Cloud and deploy applications demanding low security and reliability—such as human resources management—on the public Cloud to lessen the burden on their IT infrastructures. Most small and medium enterprises and start-up companies will choose a public Cloud, while financial institutions, government agencies, and large enterprises are more inclined to choose a private or hybrid Cloud.

Reliability issues: A Cloud computing platform needs to ensure the reliability of customer data and application platforms. In a large-scale system, a good solution is required to ensure high reliability. A dynamic network management system also monitors the status and efficiency of resource nodes and migrates failed or inefficient nodes dynamically, so the overall system performance will not be affected.

Dynamically allocate on-demand: The dynamic expansion and reduction of resources depending on the needs of users brings new challenges for Cloud platforms and management systems.

Management issues: The management of Cloud computing platform is very complex, including how to efficiently monitor system resources, how to dynamically schedule and deploy resources, and how to manage clients. All are great challenges. Cloud data center resource scheduling technology is at the core of Cloud computing, and is the key technology that allows Cloud computing to be used widely and system performance to be improved, and it also takes into account energy savings. Advanced dynamic resource scheduling algorithms are of great significance for improving computing resource efficiency of schools, government, research institutions, and enterprises; saving energy; improving the sharing of resources; and reducing operating costs. These algorithms deserve further systematic study and research.

Standardization: Cloud computing has only been developed in recent years, and first began to be used and promoted in large companies. Each company's main business is different (such as searching, mass information processing, flexible Cloud computing, resource virtualization), so the methods of implementing technology and service delivery are different. In March 2009, hundreds of IT companies led by IBM, Cisco, SAP, EMC, RedHat, AMD, AT&T, and VMware jointly issued the "Open Cloud Manifesto," which promoted the declaration of cloud computing relevant standards. Other standards for different layers of cloud computers are under development.

Summary

This chapter describes the background of Cloud computing, the driving force behind Cloud computing, the development status and trends of Cloud computing, a preliminary classification of Cloud computing, the main features of Cloud computing, and the challenges Cloud computing has faced. These introductions lay the foundation for this book. The subsequent chapter will focus on the Cloud data center.

References

[1] IBM. Virtualization and Cloud computing (in Chinese), 2009.
[2] Wiki, <http://en.wikipedia.org/wiki/Wiki>, March 15, 2014.
[3] Armbrust M. Above the Clouds: a Berkeley view of Cloud computing. Technical report, 2009.
[4] Foster I, Zhao Y, Raicu I, Lu S. Cloud computing and grid computing 360-degree compared, 2008.
[5] HP Cloud research, <http://www.hpl.hp.com/research/cloud.html>, March 10, 2014.
[6] IDC's digital universe study (sponsored by EMC), December 2012.
[7] Amazon Elastic Compute Cloud. <http://aws.amazon.com/ec2/>, March 12, 2014.
[8] Microsoft, Azure. <http://www.microsoft.com/windowsazure/>, March 10, 2014.
[9] VMware Cloud Computing. <http://www.vmware.com/solutions/cloud-computing/>, March 10, 2014.
[10] Reilly O. Hadoop. The Definitive Guide, 2009.
[11] The Hadoop Project. <http://hadoop.apache.org>, March 10, 2014.
[12] Eucalyptus Public Cloud. <http://open.eucalyptus.com/wiki/Documentation>, March 12, 2014.

Big Data Technologies and Cloud Computing

Main Contents of this Chapter

- The background and definition of big data
- Big data problems
- The dialectical relationship between Cloud computing and big data
- Big data technologies

2.1 The background and definition of big data

Nowadays, information technology opens the door through which humans step into a smart society and leads to the development of modern services such as: Internet e-commerce, modern logistics, and e-finance. It also promotes the development of emerging industries, such as Telematics, Smart Grid, New Energy, Intelligent Transportation, Smart City, and High-End Equipment Manufacturing. Modern information technology is becoming the engine of the operation and development of all walks of life. But this engine is facing the huge challenge of big data [1]. Various types of business data are growing by exponential orders of magnitude [2]. Problems such as data collection, storage, retrieval, analysis, and the application of data can no longer be solved by traditional information processing technologies. These issues have become great obstacles to the realization of a digital society, network society, and intelligent society. The New York Stock Exchange produces 1 terabyte (TB) of trading data every day; Twitter generates more than 7 TB of data every day; Facebook produces more than 10 TB of data every day; the Large Hadron Collider located at CERN produces about 15 PB of data every year. According to a study conducted by the well-known consulting firm International Data Corporation (IDC), the total global information volume of 2007 was about 165 exabytes (EB) of data. Even in 2009 when the global financial crisis happened, the global information volume reached 800 EB, which was an increase of 62% over the previous year. In the future, the data volume of the whole world will be doubled every 18 months. The number will reach 35 (zettabytes) ZB in 2020, about 230 times the number in 2007, yet the written record of 5000 years of human history amounts to only 5 EB data. These statistics indicate the eras of TB, PB, and EB are all in the past; global data storage is formally entering the "Zetta era."

Beginning in 2009, "big data" has become a buzzword of the Internet information technology industry. Most applications of big data in the beginning were in the Internet industry: the data on the Internet is increasing by 50% per year, doubling every 2 years. Most global Internet companies are aware of the advent of the "big data" era and the great significance of data. In May 2011, McKinsey Global Institute published a report titled "Big data: The next frontier for innovation, competition, and productivity" [3], and since the report was released, "big data" has become a hot topic within the computer industry. The Obama administration in the United States launched the "Big Data Research and Development Initiative" [4] and allocated $200 million specifically for big data in April 2012, which set off a wave of big data all over the world. According to the big data report released by Wikibon in 2011 [5], the big data market is on the eve of a growth spurt: the global market value of big data will reach $50 billion in the next five years. At the beginning of 2012, the total income of large data—related software, hardware, and services was around $5 billion. As companies gradually realize that big data and its related analysis will form a new differentiation and competitive advantage and will improve operational efficiency, big data—related technologies and services will see considerable development, and big data will gradually touch the ground and big data market will maintain a 58% compound annual growth rate over the next five years. Greg McDowell, an analyst with JMP Securities, said that the market of big data tools is expected to grow from $9 billion to $86 billion in 10 years. By 2020, investment in big data tools will account for 11% of overall corporate IT spending.

At present the industry does not have a unified definition of big data; big data has been defined in differing ways as follows by various parties:

> Big Data refers to datasets whose size is beyond the capability of typical database software tools to capture, store, manage, and analyze.
>
> —McKinsey.

> Big Data usually includes datasets with sizes beyond the capability of commonly used software tools to capture, curate, manage, and process the data within a tolerable elapsed time.
>
> —Wikipedia.

> Big Data is high volume, high velocity, and/or high variety information assets that require new forms of processing to enable enhanced decision making, insight discovery, and process optimization.
>
> —Gartner.

Big data has four main characteristics: Volume, Velocity, Variety, and Value [6] (referred to as "4V," referencing the huge amount of data volume, fast processing speed, various data types, and low-value density). Following are brief descriptions for each of these characteristics.

Volume: refers to the large amount of data involved with big data. The scale of datasets keeps increasing from gigabytes (GB) to TB, then to the petabyte (PB) level; some even are measured with exabytes (EB) and zettabytes (ZB). For instance, the video surveillance cameras of a medium-sized city in China can produce tens of TB data every day.

Variety: indicates that the types of big data are complex. In the past, the data types that were generated or processed were simpler, and most of the data was structured. But now, with the emerging of new channels and technologies, such as social networking, the Internet of Things, mobile computing, and online advertising, much semi-structured or unstructured data is produced, in the form of text, XML, emails, blogs, and instant messages—as just a few examples—resulting in a surge of new data types. Companies now need to integrate and analyze data from complex traditional and nontraditional sources of information, including the companies' internal and external data. With the explosive growth of sensors, smart devices, and social collaborative technologies, the types of data are uncountable, including text, microblogs, sensor data, audio, video, click streams, log files, and so on.

Velocity: The velocity of data generation, processing, and analysis continues to accelerate. There are three reasons: the real-time nature of data creation, the demands from combining streaming data with business processes, and decision-making processes. The velocity of data processing needs to be high, and processing capacity shifts from batch processing to stream processing. There is a "one-second rule" in the industry referring to a standard for the processing of big data, which shows the capability of big data processing and the essential difference between it and traditional data mining.

Value: Because of the enlarging scale, big data's value density per unit of data is constantly reducing, however, the overall value of the data is increasing. Big data is even compared to gold and oil, indicating big data contains unlimited commercial value. According to a prediction from IDC research reports, the big data technology and services market will rise from $3.2 billion in 2010 to $16.9 billion in 2015, will achieve an annual growth rate of 40%, and will be seven times the growth rate of the entire IT and communication industry. By processing big data and discovering its potential commercial value, enormous commercial profits can be made. In specific applications, big data processing technologies can provide technical and platform support for pillar industries of the nation by analyzing, processing, and mining data for enterprises; extracting important information and knowledge; and then transforming it into useful models and applying them to the processes of research, production, operations, and sales. Meanwhile, many countries are strongly advocating the development of the "smart city" in the context of urbanization and information integration, focusing on improving people's livelihoods, enhancing the competitiveness of enterprises, and promoting the sustainable development of cities. For developing into a "smart city," a city would need to utilize the Internet of Things, Cloud computing, and other information technology tools comprehensively; integrate the city's existing information bases; integrate advanced service concepts from urban operations; establish a widely deployed and deeply linked information network; comprehensively perceive many factors, such as resources, environment, infrastructures, and industries of the city; build a synergistic and shared urban information platform; process and utilize information intelligently, so as to provide intelligent response and control for city operation and resource allocation; provide the intelligent basis and methods for the decision making in social management and public services; and offer intelligent information resources and open information platforms to enterprises and individuals.

Data is undoubtedly the cornerstone of the new IT services and scientific research, and big data processing technologies have undoubtedly become the hot spot of today's information technology development. The flourishing of big data processing technologies also heralds the arrival of another round of the IT revolution. On the other hand—with the deepening of national economic restructuring and industrial upgrading—the role of information processing technologies will become increasingly prominent, and big data processing technologies will become the best breakthrough point for achieving advances in core technology, progress chasing, application innovation, and reducing lock-in in the informatization of the pillar industries of a nation's economy [7].

2.2   Big data problems

Big data is becoming an invisible "gold mine" for the potential value it contains. With the accumulation and growth of production, operations, management, monitoring, sales, customer services, and other types of data, as well as the increase of user numbers, analyzing the correlation patterns and trends from the large amount of data makes it possible to achieve efficient management, precision marketing. This can be a key to opening this "gold mine." However, traditional IT infrastructure and methods for data management and analysis cannot adapt to the rapid growth of big data. We summarize the problems of big data into seven categories in Table 2.1.

2.2.1   The problem of speed

Traditional relational database management systems (RDBMS) generally use centralized storage and processing methods instead of a distributed architecture. In many large enterprises, configurations are often based on IOE (IBM Server, Oracle Database, EMC storage). In the typical configuration, a single server's configuration is usually very high, there can be dozens of CPU cores, and memory can reach the hundreds of GB. Databases are stored in high-speed and large-capacity disk arrays and storage space can be up to the TB level. The configuration can meet the demands of traditional Management Information Systems, but when facing evergrowing data volume and dynamic data usage scenarios, this centralized approach is becoming a bottleneck, especially for its limited speed of response. Because of its dependence on centralized data storage and indexing for tasks such as importing and exporting large amounts of data, statistical analysis, retrieval, and queries, its performance declines sharply as data volume grows, in addition to the statistics and query scenarios that require real-time responses. For instance, in the Internet of Things, the data from sensors can be up to billions of items; this data needs real-time storage, queries, and analysis; traditional RDBMS is no longer suitable for such application requirements.

Table 2.1 **Problems of big data**

Classification of big data problems	Description
Speed	Import and export problems
	Statistical analysis problems
	Query and retrieval problems
	Real-time response problems
Types and structures	Multisource problems
	Heterogeneity problems
	The original system's infrastructure problems
Volume and flexibility	Linear scaling problems
	Dynamic scheduling problems
Cost	Cost difference between mainframe and PC servers
	Cost control of the original system's adaptation
Value mining	Data analysis and mining
	Actual benefit from data mining
Security and privacy	Structured and nonstructured
	Data security
	Privacy
Connectivity and data sharing	Data standards and interfaces
	Protocols for sharing
	Access control

2.2.2 *The type and architecture problem*

RDMBS has developed very mature models for the storage, queries, statistics, and processing of data that are structured and have fixed patterns. With the rapid development of the Internet of Things and Internet and mobile communication networks, the formats and types of data are constantly changing and developing. In the field of Intelligent Transportation, the data involved may contain text, logs, pictures, videos, vector maps, and various other kinds of data from different monitoring sources. The formats of this data are usually not fixed; it will be difficult to respond to changing needs if we adopt structured storage models. So we need to use various modes of data processing and storage and to integrate structured and unstructured data storage to process this data, whose types, sources, and structures are different. The overall data management model and architecture also require new types of distributed file systems and distributed NoSQL database architecture to adapt to large amounts of data and changing structures.

2.2.3 *Volume and flexibility problems*

As noted earlier—due to huge volume and centralized storage—there are problems with big data's speed and response. When the amount of data increases and the amount of concurrent read and write becomes larger and larger, a centralized file system or single database will become the deadly performance bottleneck. After all, a single machine can only withstand limited pressure. We can distribute the pressure to many machines up to a point at which they can withstand by adopting frameworks and methods with linear scalability, so the number of files or database servers can dynamically increase or decrease according to the amount of data and concurrence, to achieve linear scalability.

In terms of data storage, a distributed and scalable architecture needs to be adopted, such as the well-known Hadoop file system [8] and HBase database [9]. Meanwhile, in respect to data processing, a distributed architecture also needs to be adopted, assigning the data processing tasks to many computing nodes, in which we the correlation between the data storage nodes and the computing nodes needs to be considered. In the computing field, the allocation of resources and tasks is actually a task scheduling problem. Its main task is to make the best match between resources and tasks or among tasks, based on resource usage status (e.g., including the CPU, memory, storage, and network resources) of each individual node in the cluster and the Quality of Service (QoS) requirement of each user task. Due to the diversity of users' QoS requirements and the changing status of resources, finding the appropriate resources for distributed data processing is a dynamic scheduling problem.

2.2.4 The cost problem

For centralized data storage and processing, when choosing hardware and software, a basic approach is to use very high-end mainframe or midrange servers and high-speed, high-reliability disk arrays to guarantee data processing performance. These hardware devices are very expensive and frequently cost up to several million dollars. For software, the products from large software vendors—such as Oracle, IBM, SAP, and Microsoft—are often chosen. The maintenance of servers and databases also requires professional technical personnel, and the investment and operation costs are high. In the face of the challenges of massive data processing, these companies have also introduced an "All-In-One" solution in the shape of a monster machine—such as Oracle's Exadata or SAP's Hana—by stacking multi-server, massive memory, flash memory, high-speed networks, and other hardware together to relieve the pressure of data. However, the hardware costs in such approaches are significantly higher than an ordinary-sized enterprise can afford.

The new distributed storage architecture and distributed databases—such as HDFS, HBase, Cassandra [10], MongoDB [11]—don't have the bottleneck of centralized data processing and aggregation as they use a decentralized and massive parallel processing (MPP) architecture. Along with linear scalability, they can deal with the problems of storage and processing of big data effectively. For software architecture, they also have some automanagement and autohealing mechanisms to handle occasional failure in massive nodes and to guarantee the robustness of the overall system, so the hardware configuration of each node does not need to be high. An ordinary PC can even be used as a server, so the cost of servers can be greatly reduced; in terms of software, open-source software also gives a very large price advantage.

Of course, we cannot make a simple comparison between the costs of hardware and software when we talk about cost problems. If we want to migrate systems and applications to the new distributed architecture, we must make many adjustments from the platforms in the bottom to the upper applications. Especially for database schema and application programming interfaces, there is a big difference between NoSQL databases and the original RDBMS; enterprises need to assess the cost, cycle, and risk of migration and development. Additionally, they also need to consider the cost from service, training, operation, and maintenance aspects. But in general the trend is for these new data architectures and products to become better developed and more sophisticated, as well as for some commercial operating companies to provide professional database development and consulting services based on open source. The new distributed, scalable database schema is, therefore, bound to win in the big data wave, defeating the traditional centralized mainframe model in every respect: from cost to performance.

2.2.5 The value mining problem

Due to huge and growing volumes, the value density per data unit is constantly shrinking, while the overall value of big data is steadily increasing. Big data is analogous to oil and gold, so we can mine its huge business value [12]. If we want to extract the hidden patterns from large amount of data, we need deep data mining and analysis. Big data mining is also quite different from traditional data mining models. Traditional data mining generally focuses on moderate data size and its algorithm is relatively complex and convergence is slow, while in big data the quantity of data is massive and the processes of data storage, data cleaning, and ETL (extraction, transformation, loading) deal with the requirements and challenges of massive volume, which generally suggests the use of distributed and parallel processing models. For example, in the case of Google and Microsoft's search engines, hundreds or even thousands of servers working synchronously are needed to perform the archive storage of users' search logs generated from search behaviors of billions of worldwide users. Similarly, when mining the data, we also need to restructure traditional data mining algorithms and their underlying processing architectures, adopting the distributed and parallel processing mechanism to achieve fast computing and analysis over massive amounts of data. For instance, Apache's Mahout [13] project provides a series of parallel implementations of data mining algorithms. In many application scenarios, the mining results even need to be returned in real time, which poses significant challenges to the system: data mining algorithms usually take a long time, especially when the amount of data is huge. In this case, maybe only a combination of real-time computation and large quantities of offline processing can meet the demand.

The actual gain from data mining is an issue to be carefully assessed before mining big data's value, as well as the awareness that not all of the data mining programs will lead to the desired results. Firstly, we need to guarantee the authenticity and completeness of the data. For example, if the collection of information intro-duces big noise itself, or some key data is not included, the value that is dug out will be undermined. Second, we also need to consider the cost and benefit of the mining. If the investments of manpower and hardware and software platforms are costly and the project cycle is long, but the information extracted is not very valu-able for an enterprise's production decisions or cost-effectiveness, then the data mining is impractical and not worth the effort.

2.2.6 The security and privacy problem

From the perspective of storage and safety reliability, big data's diverse formats and huge volume have also brought a lot of challenges. For structured data, RDBMSs have already formed a set of comprehensive mechanisms for storage, access, security, and backup control after decades of development. The huge vol-ume of big data has impacted traditional RDBMS: centralized data storage and pro-cessing are shifting to distributed parallel processing, as already mentioned. In most cases, big data is unstructured data, thus a lot of distributed file storage systems and distributed NoSQL databases are derived to deal with this kind of data. But such emerging systems need to be further developed, especially in areas such as user management, data access privileges, backup mechanisms, and security controls. Security, in short, first is the prevention of data loss, which requires reasonable backup and redundancy mechanisms for the massive volume of structured and unstructured data, so data will never be lost under any circumstances. Second, secu-rity refers to protecting the data from unauthorized access. Only the users with the right privileges and permissions can see and access the data. Since large amounts of unstructured data may require different storage and access mechanisms, a unified security access control mechanism for multisource and multitype data has yet to be constructed and become available. Because big data means more sensitive data is put together, it's more attractive to potential hackers: a hacker will be able to get more information if he manages a successful attack—the "cost performance ratio" is higher. All of these issues make it easier for big data to become the target of attack. In 2012, LinkedIn was accused of leaking 6.5 million user account pass-words; Yahoo! faced network attacks, resulting in 450,000 user ID leaks. In December 2011, Chinese Software Developer Network's security system was hacked, and 6,000,000 user login names, passwords, and email addresses were leaked.

Privacy problems are also closely associated with big data. Due to the rapid development of Internet technology and the Internet of Things, all kinds of informa-tion related to our lives and jobs have been collected and stored. We are always exposed to the "third eye." No matter when we are surfing the Internet, making a phone call, writing microblogs, using Wechat, shopping, or traveling, our actions are always being monitored and analyzed. The in-depth analysis and modeling of user behaviors can serve customers better and make precision marketing possible. However, if the information is leaked or abused, it is a direct violation to the user's privacy, bringing adverse effects to users, and even causing life and property loss.

In 2006, the US DVD rental company Netflix organized an algorithm contest. The company released a million renting records from about 500,000 users, and publicly offered a reward of one million dollars, organizing a software design contest to improve the accuracy of their movie recommendation system; with the condition of victory was an improvement in their recommendation engine's accuracy by 10%. Although the data was carefully anonymized by the company, a user was still identified and disclosed by the data; a closeted lesbian mother, going by the name "Anonymous" sued Netflix. She came from the conservative Midwest. On Twitter. com, a popular site in the United States, many users are accustomed to publishing their locations and activities at any time. There are a few sites, such as "PleaseRobMe.com" and "WeKnowYourHouse.com," that can speculate the times that the users are not at home, get the user's exact home address, and even find photos of the house, just based on the information the users published. Such Web sites are designed to warn us that we are always exposed to the public eye; if we don't develop an awareness of safety and privacy, we will bring disaster upon ourselves. Nowadays, many countries around the world—including China—are improving laws related to data use and privacy to protect privacy information from being abused.

2.2.7 Interoperability and data sharing issues

In the process of enterprise information development in China, fragmentation and information-silos are common phenomena. Systems and data between different industries have almost no overlap, while within an industry—such as within the transportation and social security systems—they are divided and constructed by administrative regions such that information exchange and collaboration across regions are very difficult. More seriously, even within the same unit—such as in the development of information systems within a district hospital—subsystems for data such as medical record management, bed information, and drug management are developed discretely, and there is no information sharing and no interoperability. "Smart City" is one of the key components in China's Twelfth Five-Year Plan for information development. The fundamental goals of "Smart City" are: to achieve interoperability and the sharing of information, so as to realize intelligent e-government, social management, and improvement in people's lives. Thus, in addition to creating a Digital City where information and data are digitized, we also need to establish interconnection—to open access to the data interfaces of all disciplines, so as to achieve interoperability—and then to develop intelligence. For example, in the emergency management of urban areas, we need data and assistance from many departments and industries, such as: transportation, census, public security, fire, and health care. At present the data sharing platform developed by the US federal government, www.data.gov, and the data resource Network of Beijing Municipal Government, www.bjdata.gov.cn, are great moves toward open access to data and data sharing.

To achieve cross-industry data integration, we need to make uniform data standards and exchange interfaces as well as sharing protocols, so we can access, exchange, and share data from different industries, different departments, and different formats on a uniform basis. For data access, we also need to have detailed access control to regulate which users can access which type of data under what circumstances. In the big data and Cloud computing era, data from different industries and enterprises may be stored on a single platform and data center, and we need to protect sensitive information—such as data related to corporate trade secrets and transaction information. Although their processing relies on the platform, we should require that—other than authorized personnel from the enterprises—platform administrators and other companies cannot gain access to such data.

2.3   The dialectical relationship between Cloud computing and big data

Cloud computing has development greatly since 2007. Cloud computing's core model is large-scale distributed computing, providing computing, storage, networking, and other resources to many users in service mode, and users can use them whenever they need them [14]. Cloud computing offers enterprises and users high scalability, high availability, and high reliability. It can improve resource utilization efficiency and can reduce the cost of business information construction, investment, and maintenance. As the public Cloud services from Amazon, Google, and Microsoft become more sophisticated and better developed, more and more companies are migrating toward the Cloud computing platform.

Because of the strategic planning needs of the country as well as positive guidance from the government, Cloud computing and its technologies have made great progress in recent years in China. China has set up models in several cities, including Beijing, Shanghai, Shenzhen, Hangzhou, and Wuxi. Beijing's "Lucky Cloud" plan, Shanghai's "CloudSea" plan, Shenzhen's "International Joint Laboratory of Cloud Computing," Wuxi's "Cloud Computing Project," and Hangzhou's "West Lake Cloud Computing Platform for Public Service" have been launched. Other cities, such as Tianjin, Guangzhou, Wuhan, Xi'an, Chongqing, and Chengdu, have also introduced corresponding Cloud computing development plans or have set up Cloud computing alliances to carry out research, development, and trials of Cloud computing. But the popularity of Cloud computing in China is still largely limited by infrastructure and a lack of large-scale industrial applications, so Cloud computing has not yet gained its footing. The popularity of the Internet of Things and Cloud computing technology relate to the idea that they are humanity's great vision, so that it can achieve large-scale, ubiquitous, and collaborative information collection, processing, and application. However, it is based on the premise that most industries and enterprises have good foundations and experience in informatization and have the urgent need to transform the existing system architecture and to improve the efficiency of the system. The reality is that most of China's Small and Medium Enterprises have only just begun in the area of informatization, and only a few large companies and national ministries have the necessary foundation in information development.

The outbreak of big data is a thorny problem encountered in social and informatization development. Because of the growth of data traffic and data volume, data formats are now multisource and heterogeneous, and they require real-time and accurate data processing. Big data can help us discover the potential value of large amounts of data. Traditional IT architecture is incapable of handling the big data problem, as there are many bottlenecks, such as: poor scalability; poor fault tolerance; low performance; difficulty in installation, deployment, and maintenance; and so on. Because of the rapid development of the Internet of Things, the Internet, and mobile communication network technology in recent years, the frequency and speed of data transmission has greatly accelerated. This gives rise to the big data problem, and the derivative development and deep recycling use of data make the big data problem even more prominent.

Cloud computing and big data are complementary, forming a dialectical relationship. Cloud computing and the Internet of Things' widespread application is people's ultimate vision, and the rapid increase in big data is a thorny problem that is encountered during development. The former is a dream of humanity's pursuit of civilization, the latter is the bottleneck to be solved in social development. Cloud computing is a trend in technology development, while big data is an inevitable phenomenon of the rapid development of a modern information society. To solve big data problems, we need modern means and Cloud computing technologies. The breakthrough of big data technologies can not only solve the practical problems, but can also make Cloud computing and the Internet of Things' technologies land on the ground and be promoted and applied in in-depth ways.

From the development of IT technologies, we can summarize a few patterns:

1. The competition between Mainframe and personal PCs ended in the PC's triumph. The battle between Apple's iOS and the Android, and the open Android platform has taken over more than 2/3 of market share in only a couple of years. Nokia's Symbian operating system is on the brink of oblivion because it is not open. All of these situations indicate that modern IT technologies need to adopt the concept of openness and crowdsourcing to achieve rapid development.
2. The collision of existing conventional technologies with Cloud computing technology is similar to the aforementioned situations; the advantage of Cloud computing technology is its utilization of the crowdsourcing theory and open-source architecture. Its construction is based on a distributed architecture of open platform and novel open-source technologies, which allow it to solve problems that the existing centralized approach is difficult to solve or cannot solve. TaoBao, Tencent, and other large Internet companies once also relied on proprietary solutions provided by big companies such as Sun, Oracle, and EMC. Then they abandoned those platforms because of the cost and adopted open-source technologies. Their products have also, in turn, ultimately contributed to the open-source community, reflecting the trend in information technology development.
3. The traditional industry giants are shifting toward open-source architecture; this is a historic opportunity for others to compete. Traditional industry giants and large state enterprises—such as the National Grid, telecommunications, banking, and civil aviation—rely too heavily on sophisticated proprietary solutions provided by foreign companies for historical reasons, resulting in a pattern that lacks innovation and has been hijacked by foreign products. Analyzing from the perspective of the path and the plan to solve the big

data problem, we must abandon the traditional IT architecture gradually, and must begin to utilize the new generation of information technology represented by Cloud technology. Despite the fact that advanced Cloud computing technology originated mainly in the United States, because of open-source technology, the gap between Chinese technology and the advanced technology is not large. The urgent big data problem of applying Cloud computing technologies to large-scale industry is also China's historic opportunity to achieve breakthrough innovations, defeat monopolies, and catch up with international advanced technologies.

2.4   Big data technologies

Big data brings not only opportunities but also challenges. Traditional data processing has been unable to meet the massive real-time demand of big data; we need the new generation of information technology to deal with the outbreak of big data. Table 2.2 classifies big data technologies into five categories.

Infrastructure support: mainly includes infrastructure-level data center management, Cloud computing platforms, Cloud storage equipment and technology, network technology, and resource monitoring technology. Big data processing needs the support from Cloud data centers that have large-scale physical resources and

Table 2.2 Classification of big data technologies

Classification of big data technologies	Big data technologies and tools
Infrastructure support	Cloud Computing Platform
	Cloud Storage
	Virtualization Technology
	Network Technology
	Resource Monitoring Technology
Data acquisition	Data Bus
	ETL Tools
Data storage	Distributed File System
	Relational Database
	NoSQL Technology
	Integration of Relational Databases and Non-Relational Databases
	In-Memory Database
Data computing	Data Queries, Statistics, and Analysis
	Data Mining and Prediction
	Graph Analysis
	BI (Business Intelligence)
Display and interaction	Graphics and Reports
	Visualization Tools
	Augmented Reality Technology

Cloud computing platforms that have efficient scheduling and management functionalities.

Data acquisition: data acquisition technology is a prerequisite for data processing; first we need the means of data acquisition for collecting the information and then we can apply top-layer data processing technologies to them. Besides the various types of sensors and other hardware and software equipment, data acquisition involves the ETL (extraction, transformation, loading) processing of data, which is actually preprocessing, which includes cleaning, filtering, checking and conversion, and converting the valid data into suitable formats and types. Meanwhile, to support multisource and heterogeneous data acquisition and storage access, a enterprise data bus is needed to facilitate the data exchange and sharing between the various enterprise applications and services.

Data storage: after collection and conversion, data needs to be stored and archived. Facing the large amounts of data, distributed file storage systems and distributed databases are generally used to distribute the data to multiple storage nodes, and are also needed to provide mechanisms such as backup, security, access interfaces, and protocols.

Data computing: data queries, statistics, analysis, forecasting, mining, graph analysis, business intelligence (BI), and other relevant technologies are collectively referred to as data computing technologies. Data computing technologies cover all aspects of data processing and utilize the core techniques of big data technology.

Display and interaction: display of data and interaction with data are also essential in big data technologies, since data will eventually be utilized by people to provide decision making support for production, operation, and planning. Choosing an appropriate, vivid, and visual display can give a better understanding of the data, as well as its connotations and associated relationships, and can also help with the interpretation and effective use of the data, to fully exploit its value. For the means of display, in addition to traditional reporting forms and graphics, modern visualization tools and human−computer interaction mechanisms—or even Augmented Reality (AR) technology, such as Google Glasses—can be used to create a seamless interface between data and reality.

2.4.1 Infrastructure support

Big data processing needs the support of cloud data centers that have large-scale physical resources and Cloud computing platforms that have efficient resource scheduling and management. Cloud computing management platforms can: provide flexible and efficient deployment, operation, and management environments for large data centers and enterprises; support heterogeneous underlying hardware and operating systems with virtualization technology; provide applications with cloud resource management solutions that are secure, high performance, highly extensible, highly reliable, and highly scalable; reduce the costs of application development, deployment, operation, and maintenance; and improve the efficiency of resource utilization.

As a new computing model, Cloud computing has gained great momentum in both academia and industry. Governments, research institutions, and industry leaders are actively trying to solve the growing computing and storage problems in the Internet age using Cloud computing. In addition to Amazon Web Services (AWS), Google's App Engine, and Microsoft's Windows Azure Services—along with other commercial cloud platforms—there are also many open-source Cloud computing platforms, such as: OpenNebula [15,16], Eucalyptus [17], Nimbus [18], and OpenStack [19]. Each platform has its own significant features and constantly evolving community.

AWS is the most popular Cloud computing platform; in the first half of 2013, its platform and Cloud computing services have earned $1.7 billion, with year-on-year growth of 60%. The most distinct features of its system architecture are open data, functioning via Web Service interfaces, and the achievement of loose-coupling via Service Oriented Architecture (SOA). The web service stack AWS provides can be divided into four layers:

1. The Access Layer: provides management console, API, and various command-line tools.
2. The Common Service Layer: includes authentication, monitoring, deployment, and automation.
3. The PaaS Layer: includes parallel processing, content delivery, and messaging services.
4. The IaaS Layer: includes Cloud computing platform EC2, Cloud storage services S3/EBS, network services VPC/ELB, and database services.

Eucalyptus is an open-source Cloud computing platform that attempts to clone AWS. It has realized functionalities similar to Amazon EC2, achieving flexible and practical Cloud computing with computing clusters and workstation clusters; it provides compatibility interfaces for EC2 and S3 systems. The applications that use these interfaces can interact directly with Eucalyptus, and it supports Xen [20] and KVM [21] virtualization technology, as well as Cloud management tools for system management and user account settlements. Eucalyptus consists of five major components, namely, cloud controller CLC, cloud storage service Walrus, cluster controller CC, storage controller SC, and node controller NC. Eucalyptus manages computing resources by way of "Agents": components that can collaborate together to provide the required Cloud services.

OpenNebula is an open-source implementation of the virtualization management of virtual infrastructure and Cloud computing initiative by the European Research Institute in 2005. It's an open-source tool used to create IaaS private Clouds, public Clouds, and hybrid Clouds, and is also a modular system that can create different Cloud architectures and interact with a variety of data center services. OpenNebula has integrated storage, network, virtualization, monitoring, and security technologies. It can deploy multilayered services in a distributed infrastructure in the form of virtual machines according to allocation policies. OpenNebula can be divided into three layers: the interface layer, the core layer, and the driver layer.

1. The interface layer provides native XML-RPC interfaces and implements various APIs, such as: EC2, Open Cloud Computing Interface, and OpenNebula Cloud API, giving users a variety of access options.

2. The core layer provides core functionalities such as unified plug-in management, request management, VM lifecycle management, hypervisor management, network resources management, and storage resource management in addition to others.

3. The final layer is the driver layer. OpenNebula has a set of pluggable modules to interact with specific middleware (e.g. virtualization hypervisor, cloud services, file transfer mechanisms or information services), these adaptors are called Drivers.

OpenStack is an open-source Cloud computing virtualization infrastructure with which users can build and run their Cloud computing and storage infrastructure. APIs compatible with Amazon EC2/S3 allows users to interact with Cloud services provided by OpenStack, and it also allows client tools written for AWS to work with OpenStack. OpenStack is among the best as far as the implementation of SOA and the decoupling of service-oriented components. The overall architecture of OpenStack is also divided into three layers. The first layer is the access layer for applications, management portals (Horizon), and APIs; the core layer comprises computing services (Nova), storage services (including the object storage service Swift and block storage service Cinder), and network services (Quantum); layer 3 is for shared services, which now includes identity management service (keystone) and image service (Glance).

Nimbus System is an open-source system, providing interfaces that are compatible with Amazon EC2. It can create a virtual machine cluster promptly and easily so that a cluster scheduling system can be used to schedule tasks, just like in an ordinary cluster. Nimbus also supports different virtualization technologies (XEN and KVM). It is mainly used in scientific computing.

2.4.2 Data acquisition

Sufficient scale of data is the basis of big data strategic development for enterprises, so data acquisition has become the first step of big data analysis. Data acquisition is an important part of the value mining of big data, and the subsequent analysis and data mining rely on it. The significance of big data is not in grasping the sheer scale of the data, but rather in the intelligent processing of the data—the analysis and mining of valuable information from it—but the premise is to have a large amount of data. Most enterprises have difficulty judging which data will become data assets in the future and the method for refining the data into real revenue. For this, even big data service vendors cannot give a definitive answer. But one thing is for sure: in the era of big data, one who has enough data is likely to rule the future: the acquisition of big data now is the accumulation of assets for the future.

Data acquisition can be accomplished via sensors in the Internet of Things and also can be derived from network information. For example, in Intelligent Transportation, data acquisition may include information collection based on GPS positioning, image collection based on traffic crossroads, and coil signal collection based on intersections. Data acquisition on the Internet, in contrast, collects a variety of page and user visit information from various network media, such as: search engines, news sites, forums, microblogs, blogs, and e-commerce sites, and the contents are mainly text, URL, access logs, dates, and pictures. Preprocessing, such as: cleaning, filtering, and duplicate removal, is then needed, followed by categorization, summarization, and archiving.

ETL tools are responsible for extracting the different types and structures of data from distributed, heterogeneous data sources, such as: text data, relational data, pictures, video, and other unstructured data, to a temporary middle layer to clean, convert, classify, integrate, and finally load them into the corresponding data storage systems. These systems include data warehouses and data marts, which serve as the basis for online analytical processing and data mining. ETL tools for big data are different from the traditional ETL process: on the one hand the volume of big data is huge, on the other hand the data's production speed is very fast. For example, video cameras and smart meters in a city generate large amounts of data every second, thus preprocessing of data has to be real time and fast. When choosing ETL architecture and tools, a company also adopts modern information technology, such as: distributed memory databases, real-time stream processing systems.

There are various applications and various data formats and storage requirements for modern enterprises, but between enterprises and within enterprises, there exists the problems of fragmentation and information islands. Enterprises cannot always easily achieve controlled data exchange and sharing, and the limitations of development technologies and environments also set up barriers to enterprise data sharing. This can hinder data exchange and sharing between applications and the enterprise's ability to control, manage, and secure data. To achieve cross-industry and cross-departmental data integration—especially in the development of a Smart City—we need to develop unified data standards as well as exchange interfaces and sharing protocols, so data from different industries and different departments with different formats can be accessed, exchanged, and shared based in a unified way. With enterprise data bus (EDS), we can provide data access functions to all kinds of data and can separate the enterprise's data access integration from the enterprise's functional integration.

EDS creates an abstraction layer for data access, so corporate business functions can avoid the details of data access. Business components only need to contain service function components (used to implement services) and data access components (by the use of EDS). By means of EDS, we can provide a unified data conversion interface between the data models for enterprise management and application systems, and can effectively reduce coupling between the various application services. In big data scenarios, there are a large number of synchronized data access requests in EDS. The performance degradation of any module in the bus will greatly affect the functionality of the bus, so EDS needs to be implemented in a large-scale, concurrent, and highly scalable way as well.

2.4.3 Data storage

Big data is accumulating large amounts of information each year. Combined with existing historical data information, it has brought great opportunities and challenges to the data storage and data processing industry. In order to meet the fast-growing storage demand, Cloud storage requires high scalability, high reliability, high availability, low cost, automatic fault tolerance, and decentralization. Common forms of Cloud storage can be divided into distributed file systems and distributed databases. Distributed file systems use large-scale distributed storage nodes to meet the needs of storing large amounts of files, and distributed NoSQL databases support the processing and analysis of massive amounts of unstructured data.

Early on when Google was facing the problems of storage and analysis of large numbers of Web pages, it developed Google File System (GFS) [22] and the MapReduce distributed computing and analysis model [23–25] based on GFS. Since some applications need to deal with a large amount of formatted and semi-formatted data, Google also built a large-scale database system called BigTable [26], which supports weak consistency and is capable of indexing, querying, and analyzing massive amounts of data. This series of Google products has opened the door to massive data storage, querying, and processing in the Cloud computing era, and has become the de facto standard in this field, with Google remaining a technology leader.

Google's technology was not open source, so Yahoo and open-source communities developed Hadoop system collaboratively, which is an open-source implementation of MapReduce and GFS. The design principles of its underlying file system HDFS is completely consistent with GFS, and an open-source implementation of BigTable is also provided, which is a distributed database system named HBase. Since their launch, Hadoop and HBase have been widely applied all over the world. They are now managed by the Apache Foundation. Yahoo's own search system runs on Hadoop clusters of hundreds of thousands of servers.

GFS has fully considered the harsh environment it faces in running a distributed file system in a large-scale data cluster:

1. A large number of nodes may encounter failure so fault tolerance and automatic recovery functions may need to be integrated into the system.
2. Construct special file system parameters: files are usually measured in GB, and there may be a large number of small files.
3. Consider the characteristics of applications, support file append operations, optimize sequential read and write speeds.
4. Some specific operations of the file system are no longer transparent and need the assistance of application programs.

Figure 2.1 depicts the architecture of the GFS: a GFS cluster contains a primary server (GFS Master) and several chunkservers, which are accessed by multiple clients (GFS Client). Large files are split into chunks with fixed sizes; a chunk server stores the blocks on local hard drives as Linux files and reads and writes chunk data according to specified chunk handles and byte ranges. In order to guarantee reliability, each chunk has three replicas by default. The Master server manages all of the metadata of the file system, including namespaces, access control, mapping of files to chunks, physical locations of chunks, and other relevant information. By joint design of the server side and client side, GFS provides applications with optimal performance and availability support. GFS was designed for Google applications themselves; there are many deployments of GFS clusters in Google. Some clusters have

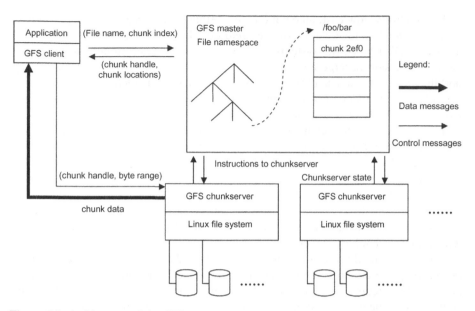

Figure 2.1 Architecture of the GFS.

more than a thousand storage nodes, storage space over PB, and are visited by thousands of clients continuously and frequently from different machines.

In order to deal with massive data challenges, some commercial database systems attempt to combine traditional RDBMS technologies with distributed, parallel computing technologies to meet the requirements of big data. Many systems also try to accelerate data processing on the hardware level. Typical systems include IBM's Netezza, Oracle's Exadata, EMC's Greenplum, HP's Vertica, and Teradata. From a functionality perspective, these systems can continue supporting the operational semantics and analysis patterns of traditional databases and data warehouses. In terms of scalability, they can also use massive cluster resources to process data concurrently, dramatically reducing the time for loading, indexing, and query processing of data.

Exadata and Netezza have both adopted data warehouse AIO solutions. By combining software and hardware together, they have a seamlessly integrated database management system (DBMS), servers, storage, and networks. For users, an AIO machine can be installed quickly and easily, and can satisfy users' needs via standard interfaces and simple operations. These AIO solutions have many shortcomings, too, though, including expensive hardware, large energy consumption, expensive system service fees, and the required purchase of a whole system when upgrade is needed. The biggest problem of Oracle's Exadata is the Shared-Everything architecture, resulting in limited IO processing capacity and scalability. The storage layers in Exadata cannot communicate with each other, so any results of intermediate computing have to be delivered from the storage layer to the RAC node, then delivered to the corresponding storage layer node by the RAC node, and before it can be computed. The large number of data movements results in unnecessary IO and network resource consumption. Exadata's query performance is not stable; its performance tuning also requires experience and in-depth knowledge.

NoSQL databases by definition break the paradigm constraints of traditional relational databases. From a data storage perspective, many NoSQL databases are not relational databases, but are hash databases that have key-value data format. Because of the abandonment of the powerful SQL query language, transactional consistency, and normal form constraints of relational databases, NoSQL databases can solve challenges faced by traditional relational databases to a great extent. In terms of design, they are concerned with high concurrent reading and writing of data and massive amounts of data storage. Compared with relational databases, they have a great advantage in scalability, concurrency, and fault tolerance. Mainstream NoSQL databases include Google's BigTable, an open-source implementation similar to BigTable named HBase, and Facebook's Cassandra.

As some Google applications need to process a large number of formatted and semi-formatted data, Google built a large-scale database system with weak consistency named BigTable. BigTable applications include search logs, maps, an Orkut online community, an RSS reader, and so on.

Figure 2.2 describes the data model of BigTable. The data model includes rows, columns, and corresponding timestamps, with all of the data stored in the cells. BigTable contents are divided by rows, and many rows form a tablet, which is saved to a server node.

Similar to the aforementioned systems, BigTable is also a joint design of client and server, making performance meet the needs of applications. The BigTable system relies on the underlying structure of a cluster system, a distributed cluster task scheduler, and the GFS, as well as a distributed lock service Chubby. Chubby is a very robust coarse-grained lock, which BigTable uses to store the bootstrap location of BigTable data, thus users can obtain the location from Chubby first, and then access the data. BigTable uses one server as the primary server to store and manipulate metadata. Besides metadata management, the primary server

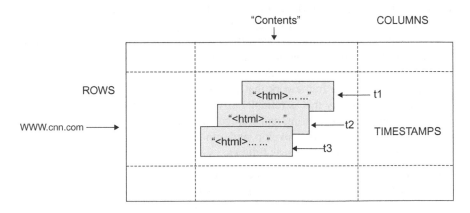

Figure 2.2 Data model in BigTable.

is also responsible for remote management and load deployment of the tablet server (the general sense of the data server). Client uses the programming interfaces for metadata communication with the main server and data communication with tablet servers.

As for large-scale distributed databases, mainstream NoSQL databases—such as HBase and Cassandra—mainly provide high scalability support and make some sacrifices in consistency and availability, as well as lacking traditional RDBMS ACID semantics and transaction support. Google Megastore [27], however, strives to integrate NoSQL with a traditional relational database and to provide a strong guarantee for consistency and high availability. Megastore uses synchronous replication to achieve high availability and consistent view of the data. In short, MegaStore provides complete serialized ACID semantics for "low-latency data replicas in different regions" to support interactive online services. Megastore combines the advantages of NoSQL and RDBMS, and can support high scalability, high fault tolerance, and low latency while maintaining consistency, providing services for hundreds of production applications in Google.

2.4.4 Data computing

Data queries, statistics, analysis, mining, and other requirements for big data processing have motivated different computing models of big data, and we divide big data computing into three categories: offline batch computing, real-time interactive computing, and stream computing.

2.4.4.1 Offline batch computing

With the widespread application and development of Cloud computing technologies, analysis systems based on open-source Hadoop distributed storage system and MapReduce data processing mode have also been widely used. Hadoop can support PB levels of distributed data storage through data partitioning and an auto-recovery mechanism, and can analyze and process this data based on MapReduce's distributed processing model. The MapReduce programming model can easily make many general data batch processing tasks and operations parallel on a large-scale cluster and can have automated failover capability. Led by open-source software such as Hadoop, the MapReduce programming model has been widely adopted and is applied to Web search, fraud detection, and a variety of other practical applications.

Hadoop is a software framework that can achieve distributed processing of large amounts of data in a way that is reliable, efficient, and scalable, relying on horizontal scaling to improve computing and storage capacity by adding low-cost commodity servers. Users can easily develop and run applications for massive data. We summarize Hadoop's advantages as follows:

1. **High reliability:** data storage and processing is worthy of trust.
2. **High scalability:** data allocation and computing task completion occurs in available computer clusters, and these clusters can be expanded to the scale of thousands of nodes easily.

3. High efficiency: data can be dynamically moved between nodes and the dynamic balance of each node is ensured, thus the processing speed is very fast.
4. High fault-tolerance: multiple copies of data can be saved automatically and failed tasks are reassigned automatically.

Big data processing platform technologies [28] utilizing the Hadoop platform include MapReduce, HDFS, HBase, Hive, Zookeeper, Avro [29], and Pig, which has formed a Hadoop ecosystem, as shown in Figure 2.3.

1. The MapReduce programming model is the heart of Hadoop and is used for the parallel computation of massive datasets. It is this programming model that has achieved massive scalability across hundreds or thousands of servers within a Hadoop cluster.
2. Distributed File System HDFS provides mass data storage based on the Hadoop processing platform. NameNode provides metadata services, and DataNode is used to store the file blocks of the file system.
3. HBase is built on HDFS and is used to provide a database system that has high reliability, high performance, column storage, scalability, and real-time read and write. It can store unstructured and semi-structured sparse data.
4. Hive [30] is a large data warehouse based on Hadoop that can be used for data extraction, transformation, and loading (ETL); storage; querying; and analysis of large-scale data stored in Hadoop.
5. Pig [31] is a large-scale data analysis platform based on Hadoop that can transform SQL-like data analysis requests into a series of optimized MapReduce operations and can provide a simple operation and programming interface for complex massive data parallel computing.
6. Zookeeper [32] is an efficient and reliable collaborative system; it is used to coordinate a variety of services on distributed applications. Zookeeper can be used to build a coordination service that can prevent single-point failures and can deal with load balancing effectively.
7. As high performance, binary communication middleware, Avro provides data serialization capabilities and RPC services between Hadoop platforms.

The Hadoop platform is mainly for offline batch applications and is typically used to schedule batch tasks on static data. The computing process is relatively

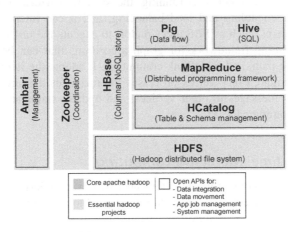

Figure 2.3 The Hadoop ecosystem.

slow. To get results, some queries may take hours or even longer, so it is impotent when faced with applications and services with real-time requirements. MapReduce is a good cluster parallel programming model and can meet the needs of a majority of applications. Although MapReduce is a good abstract of distributed/parallel computing, it is not necessarily suitable for solving any computing problem. For example, for those applications that require results in real time, such as advertisement placement based on the pay-per-click traffic model, social recommendations based on real-time data analysis of users' behavior, or anti-fraud statistics based on Web search and clickstream, MapReduce cannot provide efficient processing for these real-time applications because the processing of the application logic requires multiple rounds of tasks—or the splitting of the input data into a fine grain. The MapReduce model has the following limitations:

1. The intermediate data transfer is difficult to be fully optimized.
2. The restart of individual tasks is costly.
3. The storage cost for intermediate data is high.
4. The master node can easily become a bottleneck.
5. Support is limited to a unified file chunk size, which makes it difficult to deal with a complex collection of documents that have a variety of sizes.
6. Structured data is difficult to store and access directly.

In addition to the MapReduce computing model, workflow computing models represented by Swift [33,34] and graph computing models represented by Pregel [35] can handle application processes and graph algorithms that contain large-scale computing tasks. As a bridge between scientific workflow and parallel computing, the Swift system is a parallel programming tool for fast and reliable specification, execution, and management of large-scale science and engineering workflows. Swift uses a structured approach to manage workflow definition, scheduling, and execution. It uses the simple scripting language SwiftScript. SwiftScript can concisely describe complex parallel computing [36] based on dataset types and iterations. Meanwhile, it can dynamically map datasets for large-scale data with different data formats. When it is running, the system provides an efficient workflow engine for scheduling and load balancing, and it can interact with resource management systems, such as PBS and Condor, to execute the tasks. Pregel is a distributed programming framework for graph algorithms that can be used in graph traversal, shortest path, and PageRank computing. It adopts the iterative computing model: In each round, every vertex processes the messages that are received in the last round, sends messages to other vertices, and updates status and topology (outgoing edges, incoming edges).

2.4.4.2   Real-time interactive computing

Nowadays, real-time computing generally needs to process large amounts of data, in addition to meeting some of the requirements of non-real-time computing (e.g., accurate results). The most important requirement of real-time computing is the response to computing results in real time—generally at the millisecond level.

Real-time computing can generally be categorized into the following two application scenarios:

1. The amount of data is huge and the results cannot be computed in advance, while user response has to be in real time.

   It is mainly used for specific data analysis and processing. When the amount of data is large and it is impossible to list all query combinations for possible conditions or the exhaustive condition combinations do not help, then real-time computing can play a role in postponing the computing process until the query phase, though it needs to provide users with real-time responses. In this case, it can process part of the data in advance and combine it with the real-time computing results to improve processing efficiency.

2. The data source is real-time and continuous and requires user response to be real time.

   When the data source is real time and continuous, it is called streaming data. So-called streaming data means the data is viewed as a data stream. A data stream is a collection of a series of data records that are unbounded in time distribution and number. A data record is the smallest unit of data streams. For example, the data generated by sensors of the Internet of Things may be continuous. We will introduce stream processing systems in the next section separately. Real-time data computing and analysis can analyze and count data dynamically and in real time, this has important practical significance on system monitoring, scheduling, and management.

The real-time computing process of massive data can be divided into the following three phases: real-time data collection, real-time data analysis and processing, and real-time query services, as shown in Figure 2.4.

Real-time data collection: It must ensure collection of all of the data and must provide real-time data for real-time applications. Response time must be real time and low latency. Configuration should be simple and deployment should be easy. The system needs to be stable and reliable. Currently, big data acquisition tools from Internet companies include Facebook's open-source Scribe [37], LinkedIn's open-source Kafka [38], Cloudera's open-source Flume [39], Taobao's open-source TimeTunnel [40], and Hadoop's Chukwa [41], which can all meet the acquisition and transmission requirements for log data, which is hundreds of megabytes (MB) per second.

Real-time data computing: Traditional data operations usually include collecting data and storing it in a DBMS first, then interacting with DBMS via queries to get the answers users want. Throughout the entire process the users are active, while the DBMS system is passive. However, for real-time big data, which requires real-timeliness, huge data volume, and diverse data formats, traditional relational database architecture is not suitable. The new real-time computing architectures generally adopt the distributed architecture of MPP, and data storage and processing are then assigned to large-scale nodes to meet the real-time requirements. For data

Figure 2.4 Process of real-time calculation.

storage they use large-scale distributed file systems, such as Hadoop's HDFS file system or the new NoSQL distributed databases.

Real-time query service: Its implementation can be categorized in three ways: (1) Full Memory, which provides data read services directly, and dumps to disks or databases for backup regularly. (2) Semi-Memory, which uses Redis, Memcache, MongoDB, BerkeleyDB, and other databases to provide real-time querying services and leaves backup operations to these systems. (3) Full Disk, which uses NoSQL databases such as HBase that are based on distributed file system (HDFS). As for key-value engines, it is vital to design the distribution of the key.

Among real-time and interactive computing technologies, Google's Dremel [36] system is the most prominent. Dremel is Google's "interactive" data analysis system. It can build clusters of scale of thousands and can process PB-level data. As the initiator of MapReduce, Google has developed the Dremel system to shorten the processing time to the second level, as a strong complement to MapReduce. As a report engine for Google BigQuery, Dremel is very successful. Like MapReduce, Dremel also needs to run together with data and to move computing to data. It requires file systems such as GFS as the storage layer. Dremel supports a nested data model, similar to Javascript Object Notation (JSON). The traditional relational model inevitably has a large number of join operations in it: is often powerless when dealing with large-scale data. Dremel also uses column storage, so it only needs to scan the part of the data that is needed to reduce access to CPU and disks. Meanwhile, column storage is compression friendly; using compression can reduce storage space and achieve maximum efficiency.

Spark [42] is a real-time data analysis system developed by the AMP Lab at the University of California, Berkeley; it adopts an open-source cluster computing environment similar to Hadoop, but Spark is superior in the design and performance of task scheduling and workload optimization. Spark uses in-memory distributed datasets, in addition to providing interactive queries, and it can also optimize the workload of iterations [43]. Spark is implemented in Scala and uses it as the application programming framework, which can be tightly integrated. Scala can easily operate on distributed datasets as it does on local collection objects. Spark supports iterative operations on distributed datasets and is an effective complement to Hadoop, supporting fast data statistics analysis. It can also run concurrently on the Hadoop file system, supported by a third-party cluster framework named Mesos. Spark can be used to build large-scale, low-latency data analysis applications.

Impala [44], released by Cloudera recently, is similar to Google's Dremel system. It is an effective tool for big data real-time queries. Impala can offer fast, interactive SQL queries on HDFS or HBase; besides a unified storage platform, it also uses Metastore and SQL syntax—the same as those used by Hive. It provides a unified platform for batch and real-time queries.

2.4.4.3 Streaming computing

In many real-time application scenarios, such as real-time trading systems, real-time fraud analysis, real-time ad delivery [45], real-time monitoring, or real-time analysis of social networks, the data volume is large, the requirement for real-time response is high, and the data sources are continuous. New arrival data must be processed immediately or the subsequent data will pile up and the processing will never end. We often need a sub second or even sub millisecond response time, which requires a highly scalable streaming computing solution.

Stream Computing [46,47] is designed for real-time and continuous data, analyzing the movement process in real-time while the stream data is changing; capturing the information that may be useful to the users; and sending the result out. In the process, the data analysis and processing system is active, and the users are in a passive state of reception, as shown in Figure 2.5.

Traditional stream computing systems are generally based on an event mechanism, and the amount of data processed by them is small. The new stream processing technologies, such as Yahoo's S4 [46,47], are mainly used to solve stream processing issues that have a high data rate and a large amount of data.

S4 is a general-purpose, distributed, scalable, partially fault-tolerant, pluggable platform. Developers can easily develop applications for unbounded, uninterrupted stream data processing on it. Data events are routed to processing elements (PEs); PEs consume these events and handle them as follows:

1. send out one or more events that may be processed by other PEs;
2. publish results.

S4's design is primarily driven by data acquisitions and machine learning in a production environment on a large scale. Its main features include:

1. A simple programming interface to handle data streaming.
2. A high-availability cluster that is scalable on commodity hardware.
3. Use of local memory on every processing node to avoid disk I/O bottlenecks and to minimize latency.
4. Use of a decentralized, peer-to-peer architecture; all nodes provide the same functions and responsibilities with no central node to take special responsibility. This greatly simplifies deployment and maintenance.
5. Use of a pluggable architecture to keep the design as generic and customizable as possible.
6. A user-friendly design concept—that is, one that is easy to program and is flexible.

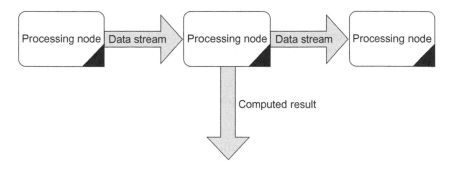

Figure 2.5 Process of stream computing.

There are many shared characteristics between S4's design and IBM's stream processing core SPC middleware [48]. Both systems are designed for large amounts of data. Both have the ability to use user-defined operations to collect information in continuous data streams. The main difference is in the structural design: SPC's design is derived from the Publish/Subscribe mode, whereas S4's design comes from a combination of the MapReduce and Actor models. Yahoo! believes that because of its P2P structure, S4's design has achieved a very high degree of simplicity. All nodes in the cluster are identical; there is no central control.

SPC is a distributed stream processing middleware to support applications that extract information from large-scale data streams. SPC contains programming models and development environments to implement distributed, dynamic, scalable applications. Its programming models include APIs for declaring and creating processing units (PE), as well as a toolset for assembling, testing, debugging, and deploying applications. Unlike other stream processing middleware, in addition to supporting relational operators, it also supports nonrelational operators and user-defined functions.

Storm [49] is a real-time data processing framework similar to Hadoop and open sourced by Twitter. This kind of stream computing solution with high scalability and the capability of processing high-frequency and large-scale data can be applied to real-time searches, high-frequency trading, and social networks. Storm has three acting scopes:

1. Stream Processing
   Storm can be used to process new data in real time and to update a database; it has both fault tolerance and scalability.
2. Continuous Computation
   For this use, Storm is set up as a distributed function that waits for invocation messages. When it receives an invocation, it computes the query and sends back the results.
3. Distributed RPC
   Storm is also set up as a distributed function that waits for invocation messages. When it receives an invocation, it computes the query and sends back the results.

2.4.5   Data presentation and interaction

Computing results need to be presented in a simple and intuitive way, so users can understand and use them to form effective statistics, analyses, predictions, and decision-making processes to be applied to production practices and business operations. For this reason the display technology of big data, as well as technology for interacting with data, plays an important role in the big data picture.

Excel spreadsheets and graphics are data display methods that people have known and used for a long time; they are very convenient for everyday simple data applications. Many Wall Street traders still rely on Excel and years of accumulated and summarized formulae to carry out large stock trades. Microsoft and a number of entrepreneurs have seen the market potential and are developing big data processing platforms that use Excel for presentation and interaction, and that integrate Hadoop and other technology.

The perception and processing speed of graphics by the human brain is far greater than that of texts. Therefore, presenting data by means of visualization can expose latent or complex patterns and relationships in data at a deeper level. With the rise of big data, there have emerged many novel means of data presentation and interaction, as well as start-up companies that focus on this area. These novel methods include interactive charts, which can be displayed on Web pages and support interactions, and which can operate and control icons, animations, and demos. Additionally, interactive map applications—such as Google Maps—can create dynamic markers, generate routes, and superimpose panoramic aerial maps. Due to its open API interfaces, it can be combined with many user maps and location-based service applications, for which it has gained extensive application. Google Chart Tools also offer a variety of flexible approaches to Web site data visualization. From simple line graphs, to geographic maps, to gauges (measuring instruments), to complex tree graphs, Google Chart Tools provide a large number of well-designed charting tools.

Tableau [50], a big data start-up company from Stanford, is becoming one of the most outstanding data analysis tools. Tableau combines data computing and aesthetic charts perfectly, as shown in Figure 2.6. Its program is easy to use: users can

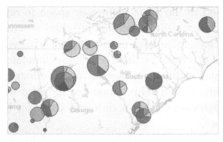

Daily sales dashboard

Track customers and sales over time. Drill into region or customer segment and search for individual customers.

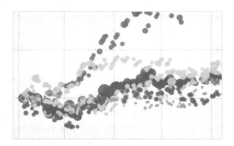

Public technology equities

Find market trends and inspect the daily trading details of publicly traded technology stocks.

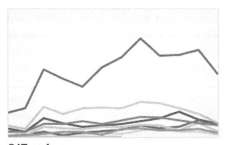

SAT performance

Explore students' SAT performance across year, gender, and college.

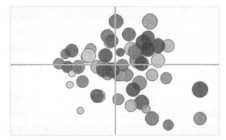

Sports comparison

This comparison tool's simplicity allows you to get an overview of the sweet 16, Elite 8, and final four.

Figure 2.6 Visualization examples of Tableau.

drag and drop large amounts of data onto a digital "canvas" and can create a variety of charts promptly. Tableau's design and implementation philosophy is: the easier the manipulation of the data is on the page, the more thoroughly companies can understand whether their business decisions are right or wrong. Fast processing and easy sharing are other features of Tableau. In only a few seconds, a Tableau Server can publish an interactive control panel on the Internet. A user only needs a browser to filter and select data easily and to get a response to her questions, which will increase the user's enthusiasm for using the data.

Another big data visualization start-up company—Visual.ly [51]—is known for its abundant infographics resources. It is a creation and sharing platform of infographics combined with social network. We live in an era of data acquisition and content creation. Visual.ly is the product of the data age: a brand-new visual infographics platform. Many users are willing to upload infographics to a Web site and then share it with others. Infographics will greatly stimulate visual expression performance and will promote mutual learning and discussion between users. It is not complicated to use Visual. ly to make infographics. It is an automated tool that makes the insertion of different types of data quick and easy, and it expresses the data with graphics.

In addition, 3D digital rendering technology has been applied widely in many areas, such as in digital cities, digital parks, modeling and simulations, and design and manufacturing, with highly intuitive operability. Modern AR technology applies virtual information to the real world via computer technologies: real environment and virtual objects are superimposed in the same picture or space in real time. Combining virtual 3D digital models and real-life scenarios provides a better sense of presence and interaction. With AR technology, users can interact with virtual objects, such as trying on virtual glasses or virtual clothes, or driving simulated aircrafts. In Germany, when engineering and technical personnel are conducting mechanical installation, maintenance, or tuning with a helmet-mounted monitor, the internal structures of the machine and its associated information and data can be fully presented, which was not possible before.

Modern motion-sensing technologies, such as Microsoft's Kinect and Leap's Leap Motion somatosensory controller, are capable of detecting and perceiving body movement and gestures, and then converting the actions into computer and system controls, freeing people from the constraints of keyboard, mouse, remote control, and other traditional interactive devices, and making users interact with computers and data directly with their bodies and gestures. This can create the super-cool action in the movie "Minority Report," in which Tom Cruise moves data in the air. Even more advanced technology can give us experiences close to those in the movie "Avatar."

Today's hottest wearable technologies, such as Google glass, have combined big data technology, AR, and somatosensory technology organically. With the improvement of data and technologies, we can perceive the realities around us in real time. Through big data searching and computing, we can achieve real-time identification and data capture of the surrounding buildings, businesses, people, and objects, and can project them onto our retinas, which can help us in real time to work, shop, and relax at great convenience. Of course, the drawbacks of this new device and technology are obvious. We are able to be monitored constantly: with privacy being encroached upon and violated at all times. In the future we may have to wear a mask before we go out.

2.4.6 Related work

The scale of big data brings great challenges to data storage management and data analysis, and data management mechanisms are evolving. Meng and other scholars [52] have analyzed the basic concepts of big data and have compared it with major applications of big data. They have also explained and analyzed the basic framework of big data processing and the affect of Cloud computing technology on data management and have summarized new challenges we face in the era of big data. Tao et al. [53] have described and analyzed related concepts and features of big data, and domestic and overseas development of big data technology, especially from the data mining perspective, and the challenges we face in the era of big data. Meanwhile, some scholars have pointed out that the real time and validity needs of data processing requires a technological change of conventional data processing techniques, starting with big data characteristics for developing technologies for big data collection, storage, management, processing, analysis, sharing, and visualization [54]. This work pays more attention to the analysis of big data characteristics and development trends, and as opposed to problems related to big data—discussed more thoroughly in the present text.

Compared with traditional data warehousing applications, big data analysis has large volumes of data, and complex queries and analysis. From the perspective of big data analysis and data warehouse architectural design, literature [55] has first listed several important features that a big data analysis platform needs. It then goes on to analyze and summarize current mainstream implementation platforms, such as parallel databases, MapReduce, and hybrid architectures of both, and points out their strengths and weaknesses. HadoopDB [56,57] is an attempt to combine the two architectures. Other scholars [58,59] discuss the competition and symbiotic relationship of RDBMS and MapReduce and analyze the challenges they encountered during development. They also point out that relational data management technology and nonrelational data management technology complement each other—in constant competition—and will find the right position within the new big data analysis ecosystem. In the study of NoSQL systems, researchers like Shen Derong [60] summarize the related research of NoSQL systems systematically, including architecture, data model, access method, index technique, transaction characteristics, system flexibility, dynamic load balancing, replication policy, data consistency policy, multilevel caching mechanisms based on flash, data processing policies based on MapReduce, and the new generation of data management systems. The papers aforementioned tend to introduce data storage for big data, analyze different storage policies, and detail their advantages and disadvantages, but they stop short of comprehensively presenting big data technologies, and do not address the synergy between different big data technologies. They also don't consider the relationship between big data technology and Cloud computing.

Modern science in the twenty-first century brings tremendous challenges to scientific researchers. The scientific community is facing the "data deluge" problem [2] that comes from experimental data, analog data, sensor data, and satellite data. Data size and the complexity of scientific analysis and processing are growing exponentially. The Scientific Workflow Management System provides some necessary supports for scientific computing, such as data management, task dependencies, job scheduling and execution, and resource tracking. Workflow systems, such as Taverna [61], Kepler [62], Vistrails [63], Pegasus [64], Swift [39], and VIEW [65], have a wide range of applications in many fields, such as physics, astronomy, bioinformatics, neuroscience, earth science, and social science. Meanwhile, the development of scientific equipment and network computing has challenged the reliable workflow systems in terms of data size and application complexity. We have combined scientific workflow systems with Cloud platforms as a service [66] of Cloud computing, to deal with the growing amount of data and analysis complexity. A Cloud computing system with a large-scale data center resource pool and an on-demand resource allocation function can provide scientific workflow systems better services than the environments already mentioned, which enables the workflow systems to handle scientific questions at the PB level.

Summary

Big Data is the hot frontier of today's information technology development. The Internet of Things, the Internet, and the rapid development of mobile communication networks have spawned big data problems and have created problems of speed, structure, volume, cost, value, security privacy, and interoperability. Traditional IT processing methods are impotent when faced with big data problems, because of their lack of scalability and efficiency. Big Data problems need to be solved by Cloud computing technology, while big data can also promote the practical use and implementation of Cloud computing technology. There is a complementary relationship between them. We focus on infrastructure support, data acquisition, data storage, data computing, data display, and interaction to describe several types of technology developed for big data, and then describe the challenges and opportunities of big data technology from a different angle from the scholars in the related fields. Big data technology is constantly growing with the surge of data volume and processing requirements, and it is affecting our daily habits and lifestyles.

Acknowledgments

We would like to express our gratitude to the colleagues that have given support and advice on this article, especially the faculty and students in the Extreme Scale Network Computing and Service Laboratory at the School of Computer Science and Engineering, University of Electronic and Science Technology of China.

References

[1] Zikopoulos PC, Eaton C, DeRoos D, Deutsch T, Lapis G. Understanding big data. New York, NY: McGraw-Hill; 2012.
[2] Bell G, Hey T, Szalay A. Beyond the data deluge. Science 2009;323(5919):1297−8.
[3] Manyika J, Chui M, Brown B, Bughin J, Dobbs R, Roxburgh C, et al. Big data: the next frontier for innovation, competition, and productivity. MacKinsey Global Institute; 2011.
[4] Big Data Research and Development Initiative, <http://www.whitehouse.gov/sites/default/files/microsites/ostp/big_data_press_release_final_2.pdf>.
[5] Available from: http://wikibon.org/wiki/v/Big_Data_Market_Size_and_Vendor_RevenuesBig_Data_Market_Size_and_Vendor_Revenues.
[6] Gupta R, Gupta H, Mohania M. Cloud computing and big data analytics: what is new from databases perspective? Big data analytics. Berlin, Heidelberg: Springer; 2012. p. 42−61.
[7] Li GJ, Cheng XQ. Research status and scientific thinking of big data. Bull Chin Acad Sci 2012;27(6):647−57 (In Chinese).
[8] Apache Hadoop. <http://hadoop.apache.org/>.
[9] Khetrapal A, Ganesh V. HBase and hypertable for large scale distributed storage systems. Department of Computer Science, Purdue University; 2006.
[10] Available from: http://cassandra.apache.org/.
[11] Available from: http://www.mongodb.org/.
[12] Labrinidis A, Jagadish HV. Challenges and opportunities with big data. Proc VLDB Endowment 2012;5(12):2032−3.
[13] Available from: http://mahout.apache.org/.
[14] Foster I, Zhao Y, Raicu I, Shiyong L. Cloud computing and grid computing 360-degree compared. Grid computing environments workshop, IEEE, 2008. p. 1−10.
[15] OpenNebula. <http://www.opennebula.org>.
[16] OpenNebulaArchitecture. <http://www.opennebula.org/documentation:archives:rel2.2:architecture>.
[17] Nurmi D, Wolski R, Grzegorczyk C, Obertelli G, Soman S, Youseff L, et al. The eucalyptus open-source cloud-computing system. Ninth IEEE/ACM international symposium on cluster computing and the grid, 2009. p. 124−31.
[18] Keahey K, Freeman T. Contextualization: providing one-click virtual clusters. IEEE fourth international conference on eScience, 2008. p. 301−08.
[19] Openstack. <http://www.openstack.org>.
[20] Barham P, Dragovic B, Fraser K, Hand S, Harris T, Ho A, et al. Xen and the art of virtualization. ACM SIGOPS Oper Syst Rev 2003;37(5):164−77.
[21] KVM (Kernel Based Virtual Machine). <http://www.linux-kvm.org/page/Main>.
[22] Ghemawat S, Gobioff H, Leung ST. The Google file system. Proceedings of the 19th ACM symposium on operating systems principles. New York, NY: ACM Press; 2003. p. 29−43.
[23] Zheng QL, Fang M, Wang S, Wang XQ, Wu XW, Wang H. Scientific parallel computing based on MapReduce model. Micro Electron Comput 2009;26(8):13−7 (In Chinese).
[24] Dean J, Ghemawat S. MapReduce: simplified data processing on large clusters. Commun ACM 2008;51(1):107−13.
[25] Li YL, Dong J. Study and improvement of MapReduce based on Hadoop. Comput Eng Des 2012;33(8):3110−6 (In Chinese).

[26] Chang F, Dean J, Ghemawat S, Hsieh WC, Wallach DA, Burrows M, et al. BigTable: a distributed storage system for structured data. Proceedings of the seventh USENIX symposium on operating systems design and implementation. Berkeley: USENIX Association; 2006. p. 205—18.

[27] Baker J, Bond C, Corbett JC, Furman JJ, Khorlin A, Larson J, et al. Megastore: providing scalable, highly available storage for interactive services. CIDR 2011, 11: p. 223—34.

[28] Taylor RC. An overview of the Hadoop/MapReduce/HBase framework and its current applications in bioinformatics. BMC Bioinformatics 2010;11(Suppl. 12):S1.

[29] Avro. <http://avro.apache.org/>.

[30] Thusoo A, Sarma JS, Jain N, Shao Z, Chakka P, Anthony S, et al. Hive: a warehousing solution over a map-reduce framework. Proc VLDB Endowment 2009;2(2):1626—9.

[31] Olston C, Reed B, Srivastava U, Kumar R, Tomkins A. Pig latin: a not-so-foreign language for data processing. Proceedings of the 2008 ACM SIGMOD international conference on management of data. ACM; 2008. p. 1099—110.

[32] Gopalakrishna K, Hu G, Seth P. Communication layer using ZooKeeper. Yahoo! Inc., Tech. Rep.; 2009.

[33] Swift Workflow System. <http://www.ci.uchicago.edu/Swift/main/>.

[34] Zhao Y, Hategan M, Clifford B, Foster I, von Laszewski G, Nefedova V, et al. Swift: fast, reliable, loosely coupled parallel computation. IEEE congress on Services, 2007. p. 199—206.

[35] Malewicz G, Austern MH, Bik AJC, Dehnert JC, Horn I, Leiser N, et al. Pregel: a system for large-scale graph processing. Proceedings of the 2010 ACM SIGMOD international conference on management of data. ACM; 2010. p. 135—46.

[36] Melnik S, Gubarev A, Long JJ, Romer G, Shivakumar S, Tolton M, et al. Dremel: interactive analysis of web-scale datasets. Proc VLDB Endowment 2010;3 (1—2):330—9.

[37] Scribe. <https://github.com/facebook/scribe>.

[38] Kafka. <http://kafka.apache.org/>.

[39] Flume. <https://github.com/cloudera/flume>.

[40] TimeTunnel. <http://code.taobao.org/p/TimeTunnel/src/>.

[41] Rabkin A, Katz R. Chukwa: a system for reliable large-scale log collection. Proceedings of the 24th international conference on large installation system administration. USENIX Association; 2010. p. 1—15.

[42] Zaharia M, Chowdhury M, Franklin MJ, Shenker S, Stoica I. Spark: cluster computing with working sets. Proceedings of the second USENIX conference on hot topics in cloud computing. 2010. p. 10—10.

[43] Zaharia M, Chowdhury M, Das T, Dave A, Ma J, McCauley M, et al. Resilient distributed datasets: a fault-tolerant abstraction for in-memory cluster computing. Proceedings of the 9th USENIX conference on Networked Systems Design and Implementation. USENIX Association; 2012. p. 2—2.

[44] Kornacker M, Erickson J. Cloudera Impala: real-time queries in Apache Hadoop, for real. 2012. <http://blog.cloudera.com/blog/2012/10/cloudera-impala-real-time-queries-in-apache-hadoop-for-real/>.

[45] Schroedl S, Kesari A, Neumeyer L. Personalized ad placement in web search. Proceedings of the fourth annual international workshop on data mining and audience intelligence for online advertising (AdKDD), Washington, DC. 2010.

[46] Malkin J, Schroedl S, Nair A, Neumeyer L. Tuning hyperparameters on live traffic with S4. In TechPulse 2010: Internal Yahoo! Conference, 2010.

[47] Neumeyer L, Robbins B, Nair A, Kesari A. S4: distributed stream computing platform. IEEE international conference on data mining workshops (ICDMW). 2010. p. 170−7.

[48] Amini L, Andrade H, Bhagwan R, Eskesen F, King R, Selo P, et al. SPC: a distributed, scalable platform for data mining. Proceedings of the fourth international workshop on data mining standards, services and platforms. ACM; 2006. p. 27−37.

[49] Storm. Distributed and fault-tolerant real-time computation, <http://storm-project.net/>.

[50] Tableau. <http://www.tableausoftware.com/>.

[51] Visual.ly. <http://visuanl.ly/>.

[52] Meng XF, Ci X. Big data management. concept, techniques and challenges. J Comput Res Dev 2013;50(1):146−69 (In Chinese).

[53] Tao XJ, Hu XF, Liu Y. Overview of big data research. J Syst Simul 2013;25S:142−6 (In Chinese).

[54] Yan XF, Zhang DX. Big data research. Comput Technol Dev 2013;23(4):168−72 (In Chinese).

[55] Wang S, Wang HJ, Qin XP, Zhou X. Architecting big data: challenges, studies and forecasts. Chin J Comput 2011;34(10):1741−52 (In Chinese).

[56] Abouzeid A, Bajda-Pawlikowski K, Abadi D, Silberschatz A, Rasin A. HadoopDB: an architectural hybrid of MapReduce and DBMS technologies for analytical workloads. Proc VLDB Endowment 2009;2(1):922−33.

[57] Abouzied A, Bajda-Pawlikowski K, Huang JW, Abadi DJ, Silberschatz A. HadoopDB in action: building real world applications. In: Elmagarmid AK, Agrawal D, editors. Proceedings of the SIGMOD. Indianapolis, IN: ACM Press; 2010. p. 1111−4. Available from: http://dx.doi.org/10.1145/1807167.1807294.

[58] Qin XP, Wang HJ, Du XY, Wang S. Big data analysis—competition and symbiosis of RDBMS and MapReduce. J Softw 2012;23(1):32−45 (In Chinese).

[59] Qin XP, Wang HJ, Li FR, Li CP, Chen H, Zhou X, et al. New landscape of data management technologies. J Softw 2013;24(2):175−97 (In Chinese).

[60] Shen DR, Yu G, Wang XT, Nie TZ, Kou Y. Survey on NoSQL for management of big data. J. Softw 2013;24(8):1786−803 (In Chinese).

[61] Hull D, Wolstencroft K, Stevens R, Goble C, Pocock MR, Li P, et al. Taverna: a tool for building and running workflows of services. Nucleic Acids Res 2006;34(Suppl. 2): W729−32.

[62] Ludäscher B, Altintas I, Berkley C, Higgins D, Jaeger E, Jones M, et al. Scientific workflow management and the Kepler system. Concurrency Comput: Pract Exp 2006;18(10):1039−65.

[63] Freire J, Silva CT, Callahan SP, Santos E, Scheidegger CE, Vo HT. Managing rapidly-evolving scientific workflows. Provenance and annotation of data. Berlin, Heidelberg: Springer; 2006. p. 10−18.

[64] Deelman E, Singh G, Su MH, Blythe J, Gil Y, Kesselman C, et al. Pegasus: a framework for mapping complex scientific workflows onto distributed systems. Sci Programming 2005;13(3):219−37.

[65] Lin C, Lu S, Lai Z, Chebotko A, Fei X, Hua J, et al. Service-oriented architecture for VIEW: a visual scientific workflow management system. IEEE international conference on Services computing, 2008, 1: p. 335−42.

[66] Zhao Y, Li Y, Tian W, Xue R. Scientific-workflow-management-as-a-service in the Cloud. Second international conference on cloud and green computing (CGC). 2012. p. 97−104.

Resource Modeling and Definitions for Cloud Data Centers

3

Main Contents of this Chapter

- Cloud data center resource models
- Cloud data center resources
- Properties of Cloud resources
- Classification of Cloud resources
- Operations of Cloud resources

3.1 Resource models in Cloud data centers

Figure 3.1 shows the architecture of Cloud data centers. The following is a brief description of the major processes [1]:

1. **User requests:** the user initiates the request through the Internet (such as via login to Cloud service provider's Web portal).
2. **Scheduling management:** the scheduling center makes decisions based on the user's identity (e.g., geographic location) and the operational characteristics of the request (e.g., quantity and quality requirements); the request is submitted to the appropriate data center, then the data center management program submits it to a scheduling domain; the scheduling domain allocates the request via implementation of a scheduling algorithm.
3. **Feedback:** the scheduling algorithm provides available resources to the user.
4. **Scheduling execution:** the scheduling results (such as deploying steps) are sent to the next stage.
5. **Updating and optimization:** the scheduler updates resource information and optimizes resources among different data centers according to the objective functions.

The following are detailed descriptions of major Cloud data center resources.

3.2 Data center resources

Figure 3.2 is the proposed model of data center resources, reflecting the relative hierarchy of the resources, considering resource definitions mainly from the perspective of service providers in a bottom-up way, including physical server (cluster) → virtual server (cluster) → security group → middleware/application services → scheduling domain → data center. Figure 3.3 provides a UML diagram of the resource model to demonstrate the relationship between all of the entities and their resources.

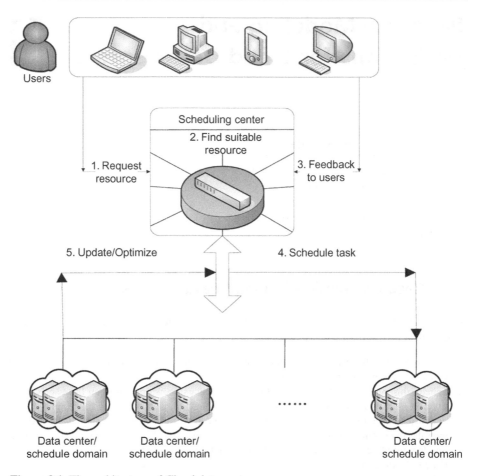

Figure 3.1 The architecture of Cloud data centers.

Resource entity: refers to all the independent and available resources for Cloud providers in the data center.

Physical server: physical computing devices that form the data center; each physical server can provide multiple virtual servers; each physical server can be composed of multiple CPUs, memories, hard drives, and network cards.

Physical cluster: consists of a number of physical servers, the necessary network, and storage infrastructure.

Virtual server: virtual computing platform on the physical server created with virtualization software, consisting of a number of virtual CPUs, hard drives, and network cards.

Virtual cluster: a virtual server group consisting of a number of virtual servers and the necessary network and storage infrastructure.

Shared storage: provides large-capacity storage for data center computing resources and can be shared by all devices and applications.

Middleware: Software as a Service (SaaS) built on a single or on multiple physical (or virtual) servers.

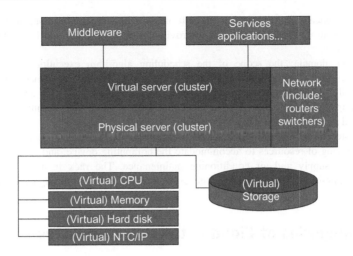

Figure 3.2 Data center resources model.

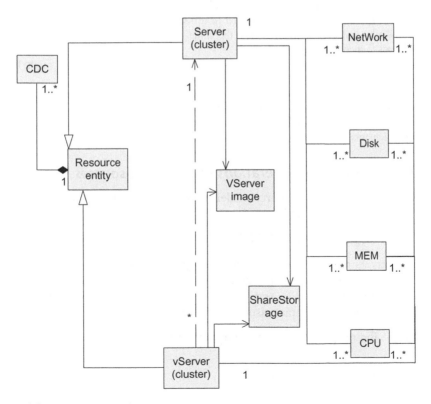

Figure 3.3 UML diagram of resources.

Service (application): a form of SaaS, built on a single or on multiple physical (or virtual) server(s) or in multiple data centers to provide software services and integrated applications to users.

Scheduling domain: the scope of the scheduling algorithm execution. The scheduling algorithms—such as maximum utilization, load balancing, and performance optimization—are usually implemented within a region (domain). Multiple domains applying different scheduling algorithms do not interfere with each other. Also, a scheduling domain can be expanded and shrunk automatically.

Data center: It may be distributed across multiple systems in different geographic locations, is the pooling of resources to accommodate the computing device, and is also responsible for energy supply and air conditioning maintenance. The rack in a data center hosts different physical servers, network switches/routers, and air conditioning equipment.

3.3   Categories of Cloud data center resources

Cloud data center resources can be described and defined in the following three categories:

1. From the service provider point of view: the user can directly use the hardware and software components (including computing, storage, and networking), middleware, and application services, which can be distributed in different geographic locations. Providers can dynamically configure all data centers the same or can create multiple data center infrastructures to meet user needs.
2. From the user point of view: the user can select the configuration, though it might be preconfigured. The location of specific resources is transparent to the user.
3. From the perspective of elements constituting a data center: hardware computing resources (e.g., physical facilities and networks), power supply, cooling, software (and copyright), management (human) resources, and so forth constitute the total cost of data center elements.

3.3.1 Properties and operations of various resources

Following the data center resource model in Figures 3.2 and 3.3, the following will introduce their properties and operations.

3.3.1.1 Physical servers (PMs)

Physical servers refer to server resources and provide computer software for users. They are usually divided into file servers, database servers, and application servers. Compared to an ordinary PC, servers demand a higher level of stability, security, performance, and other characteristics [2] (Figure 3.4).

3.3.1.1.1 The main properties of a physical server
Static:

ServerID (long): Server number
Location (long): position in the index

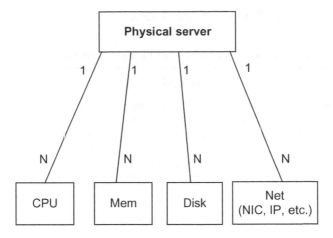

Figure 3.4 Components of a physical server.

ServerType (boolean): whether the physical machine is running a virtual machine (VM)
pOS: operating system
CPUNum (int): CPU number
CPUKernel (int): the number of cores
CPU (String): CPU frequency
ComputingPower: server computing capability (obtained through benchmarking)
VCPUAllocate (int): number of virtual CPUs
Mem (int): memory size (G)
MemSpeed (float): memory transfer rate (Mb/s)
MemDelay (long): memory latency (ms)
Disk ([long] [float]): hard numbers, hard disk size, (the same type of server's hard drive)
DiskCleanTime (Date): the last time, disk defragmentation
NIC ([][][]): three-dimensional array, including the card number, MAC address of network card, network card bandwidth information
IP: IP address

News:

CPUtilization: occupancy rate of physical server CPU (taking into account multi-Core)
MemUtilization: physical server footprint
PowerConsumption: physical server power consumption data
Schedule_Domain_ID: schedule domain ID

3.3.1.1.2 Physical server states

Running: physical servers running
Closing: the physical server is down
Error: physical server error
InScheduling: is scheduling or performing maintenance

3.3.1.1.3 Main operations of a physical server

Table 3.1 Summary of physical server operations

Operation	Description
pServer.PowerOn(serverID)	Start specify physical
pServer. PowerOff (serverID)	Shutdown specify physical
pServer.GetAttributes(serverID)	Specify ID attributes of the physical servers, including CPU, memory, hard drives, and other information
pServer.Allocate(userAccount)	Physical server resource allocation

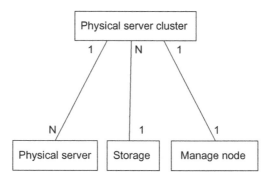

Figure 3.5 A physical server cluster.

3.3.1.1.4 Server operation error
ERROR_NOSUCHSERVER: cannot find servers
ERROR_SERVERISRUNNING: server already running
ERROR_SERVERISCLOSED: server is down

3.3.1.2 Physical server cluster

Multiple physical servers form a group of computer systems through networking. A cluster system is often referred to as a single computer node, typically through a LAN connection, but there are other possible connections. A computer cluster can be used to improve the calculation of a single computer speed, reliability, and load balancing [3] (Figure 3.5).

3.3.1.2.1 Main properties of a physical server cluster
ClusterID (long): cluster number
ClusterDescriptor (Sting): cluster description
ServerIDs (long []): physical machine that it contains
NumsOfServers (int): the number of physical machines
SharedDisk (DiskID): common data storage
ManagementNode (IP): a management node IP for a cluster

ClusterNet: network (external bandwidth is more than any external connection to the server's external bandwidth and the bandwidth of each server)
Schedule_Domain_ID: domain ID

3.3.1.2.2   States of a physical server cluster

Active: physical servers in the cluster are working (e.g., cluster computing tasks are being completed)
InActive: physical server cluster is not working
InScheduling: is scheduling or performing maintenance

3.3.1.2.3   Operations of a physical server cluster

Table 3.2 Physical server cluster operating summary

Operation	Description
Cluster.Create	Create a cluster
Cluster.Delete(ClusterID)	Remove a cluster
Cluster. GetAttributes (ClusterID)	Get the specified ID attribute of the physical server clusters
Cluster.AddServer (ClusterID,ServerID)	Add specifies the physical machine to be added to the specified cluster
Cluster.DelServer (ClusterID,ServerID)	Delete specifies the physical machine to be deleted from the specified cluster

3.3.1.2.4   Physical server errors

ERROR_NOSUCHCLUSTER: cannot find the number of clusters
ERROR_CLUSTERNOTEXIST: specifies the number of clusters does not exist
ERROR_CLUSTERCREATE: failed to create cluster
ERROR_CLUSTERDELETE: failed to delete cluster
ERROR_CLUSTEROPERATION: cluster deletions failed

3.3.1.3   *Virtual machines*

A virtual server is created from a physical server with virtualization software. It has complete hardware system functions, and runs in a completely isolated environment of complete computer systems. One physical server can create multiple VMs. Different VMs depend on the selection of the different VM images; a VM image is an image file of an operating system that is already installed, so a VM can be configured fairly quickly [4] (Figure 3.6).

3.3.1.3.1   Properties of VMs

Static:

VMImageID: corresponding to VM images (including memory, OS, CPU)
ServerID: corresponding to the physical server
VMID: the primary key of the VM
ComputingPower: server computing capability (obtained through benchmarking)

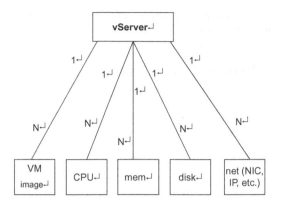

Figure 3.6 Virtual machines.

VMemInitialization: the initial size of memory
VMemIncrement: incremental memory for each increase or decrease in the size of memory
VMemType: type of memory (corresponding to different performance)
VDiskID: corresponding storage device (different ID for different types)
VDiskType: storage type
DiskInitialization: the initial size of the hard disk
DiskIncrement: hard disk the size of each increase or decrease
IP: IP of the VM

News:

CPUUtilization: CPU utilization
VMemUtilization: memory usage
Bandwidth: bandwidth size
PerformanceID: selects logo, to ensure efficiency or guarantee performance (e.g., load balancing) optional
SecureGroupID: belongs to security group
UserID: user ID

3.3.1.3.2   Operations of VMs

Table 3.3 **Main operations of VMs**

Operation	Description
VServer.Run	Run virtual server
VServer.Close	Close virtual server
VServer.Reboot	Restart virtual server
VServer.Move	Move VMs from one physical server to another
VServer.AddDisk	Increase hard drive size
VServer.DelDisk	Reduce hard drive size
VServer.AddMem	Increase memory size
Vserver.DelMem	Reduce memory size
VServer.Snapshot	Create virtual server snapshot

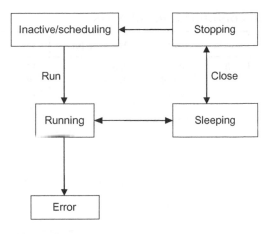

Figure 3.7 State transitions of VMs.

3.3.1.3.3 States of VMs
Inactive: the VM has been created, but it has not yet started
Running: the VM has started; the status of running
Stopping: stop the VM
Sleeping: sleep
Error: the state of VM error
InScheduling: scheduling or maintenance (Figure 3.7)

3.3.1.3.4 Typical configurations of VMs
Table 3.4 gives typical configurations of VMs, which can be created as templates (plus operating systems) for the user.

3.3.1.4 Virtual clusters

A virtual cluster can be formed with many VMs through networking (Figure 3.8).

3.3.1.4.1 Main properties of a virtual cluster
VClusterID (long): virtual cluster number
VClusterDescript (Sting): description of the virtual cluster
VServerIDs (long []): contains the VM number

3.3.1.4.2 States of a virtual cluster
Active: virtual server cluster working
InActive: virtual server cluster not working
InSchedule: virtual server cluster preparation

Table 3.4 Typical configurations of VMs

Type	#vCPU	vRAM	vDisk	Machine bits	vNIC	Cost
Basic	1	2 GB	80 GB	32/64	1 IP	¥ 0.8/h
Small	1	4 GB	100 GB	32/64	1 IP	¥ 1.0/h
Middle	2	8 GB	400 GB	32/64	1 IP	¥ 2.0/h
Large	4	16 GB	800 GB	32/64	2 IP	¥ 4.0/h
Huge	8	32 GB	1000 GB	32/64	4 IP	¥ 8.0/h

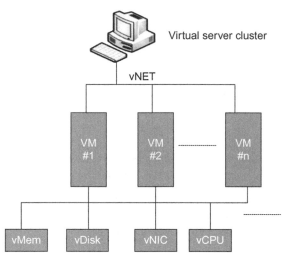

Figure 3.8 A virtual cluster.

3.3.1.4.3   Operations of a virtual cluster

Table 3.5 Operations of virtual server cluster

Operation	Description
VCluster.Create	Create a Virtual Cluster
VCluster.Delete(VClusterID)	Delete a Virtual Cluster by VClusterID
VCluster.Start(VClusterID)	Start a Virtual Cluster by VClusterID
VCluster.Stop(VClusterID)	Stop a Virtual Cluster by VClusterID
VCluster.GetProperties(VClusterID)	Get the Properties of one Virtual Cluster by VClusterID
VCluster.AddServer(VClusterID,VServerID)	Add the VM with number of VServerID to the Virtual Cluster with number of VClusterID
VCluster.DelServer (VClusterID,VServerID)	Remove the VM of VServerID from the Virtual Cluster of VClusterID
VCluster.ListvServer (VClusterID)	List the information of all the VMs on the Virtual VCluster of VClusterID
VCluster.listVNET (VClusterID)	List the information of all the Virtual Net on the Virtual VCluster of VClusterID
VCluster.createVNET (VClusterID)	Create a Virtual Net for the Virtual CLulster of VClusterID

3.3.1.4.4   Operational errors on VMs

ERROR_NOSUCHVCLUSTER: can't find the number of this virtual cluster
ERROR_VCLUSTERNOTEXIST: can't find the virtual cluster of such a number
ERROR_VCLUSTERCREATE: failed to create virtual cluster
ERROR_VCLUSTERDELETE: failed to delete virtual cluster
ERROR_VCLUSTEROPERATION: virtual cluster operation failed

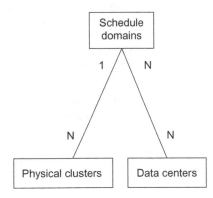

Figure 3.9 Schedule domains.

3.3.1.5   Schedule domains

A schedule domain may consist of one or more physical clusters. A schedule domain can only execute one scheduling algorithm (such as load balance or maximum utilization) in a period of time. Schedule domains belong to a data center at the system level, but there is a special case in which one data center has only one schedule domain (Figure 3.9).

3.3.1.5.1   Properties of schedule domains

ScheduleDomain_PM_Set: physical machines in this schedule domain
ScheduleDomain_ID: schedule domain's ID
LocationID: information of location in data center
IPSection: IP sections in schedule domain
ScheduleDomain_PM_CountOfOverLoad: the number of overloaded physical machines in this schedule domain
ScheduleDomain_Status: schedule domain's status
ScheduleDomain_Strategy: strategy of this schedule domain

3.3.1.5.2   Operations of schedule domains

Table 3.6 Operations of schedule domains

Operation	Description
Create_Schedule_D () Delete_Schedule_D() Expand_Schedule_D() Reduce_Schedule_D() Apply_Schedule_Strategy() Query_Schedule_Strategy() Optimize_Schedule_D()	Create a new Schedule Domain Eliminate this Schedule Expand a Schedule Domain Reduce a Schedule Domain Execute the Schedule Domain's Schedule Strategy Ask for the Schedule Domain's Strategy Do optimizing in this Schedule Domain

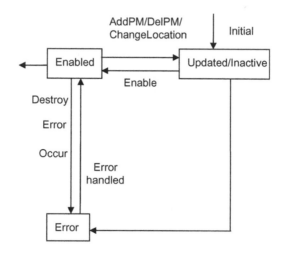

Figure 3.10 States of schedule domains.

3.3.1.5.3   States of schedule domains

Inactive: schedule domain is created, but has not started
Enabled: schedule domain has started
Error: schedule domain is in error
Updating: schedule domain is in the status of updating or reconfiguration (Figure 3.10)

3.3.1.6   Storage

Most data centers adopt the independent storage area network (SAN) and network-area storage (NAS) (or block and file) storage systems. SAN architecture allows the server to connect any disk array or tape library, so that the server can directly access the required data regardless of the data's location. The SAN can be used in a Cloud data center, and hundreds or even thousands of storage devices can be

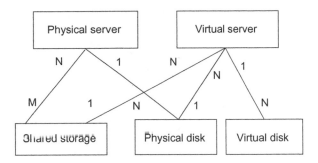

Figure 3.11 Shared storage.

connected together to form a low-cost, manageable SAN with a fast fiber-optic network. A SAN can not only reduce system pressure caused by data transference on certain networks, which accordingly reduces the cost of storage, but it can also easily monitor and adjust storage devices by centralizing them to achieve flexible management [5] (Figure 3.11).

3.3.1.6.1   Properties of shared storage

Static:

> StorageID: ID of storage device
> StorageNodeID: ID of a node in this storage device
> TotalCapacity: amount of storage capacity in this device
> Distribution: distribution of block storage resources' capacity
> Storage Location: location of storage
> Storage Media: kind of storage media
> Organization: organization
> Method: block storage, object storage

Dynamic:

> Utilization: the distribution of the utilization of block storage resources
> Performance Distribution: the distribution of the performance of block storage resources
> WRSpeed: current write/read speed

Table 3.7 Storage operations

Operation	Description
Storage.Increase	Increases the capacity of storage
Storage.Decrease	Decreases the capacity of storage
Storage.Backup	Data backup: actively backs up VM
Storage.Move	Data transfer: automatically executes when the physical machine fails
Storage.Allocate	Assigns storage for VM; returns results
Storage.QueryAlloc	Queries VM allocation, whose virtual storage is allocated from this physical storage

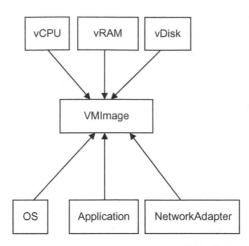

Figure 3.12 Composition of a VM image.

3.3.1.6.2   Storage operations

3.3.1.6.3   States of storage
Running: status of normal and enabled storage
Error: status of unusable storage
Updated: capacity or firmware is reconfiguring

3.3.1.7   VM image

A VM image is an executable image file from a VM; this image file is in a special storage format. We can create a new VM by uploading the image file to the physical machine. Usually some software, like mysql or ms office, is installed on these new VMs beforehand. Users can choose different VM images to install [5] (Figure 3.12).

3.3.1.7.1   Properties of a VM image
VMImageID: ID of a VM image
Size(float): the size of VM image (in GB)
VCPUType(String): type of CPU
VCPUNum(int): amount of CPU
VCPUKernel(int): number of CPU kernels per CPU
VCPU(String): CPU frequency
VMem(int): capacity of memory
VDisk(int): capacity of storage
OS(String): type of operation system
Application(String): users can choose a suit of software that can fit their needs depending on their purpose (e.g., deploying websites, computing, or storage)
NetworkAdapter(String): Network (e.g., Bridged, NAT, or Custom)

3.3.1.7.2 VM image operations

Table 3.8 VM image operations

Operation	Description
VMImage.Select	Select an appropriate physical machine
VMImage.Upload	Transfer the image file to a physical machine
VMImage.Save	Save the used VM as an image file
VMImage.Delete	Delete a VM image file

3.3.1.7.3 States of VMs

InUsing: Some VM is using this VM image.
NotUsing: This VM image is not in use.

3.3.1.8 Network resources

A network resource is defined as part of the infrastructure of a data center, including switches, routers, VLAN, DNS, and IP addresses. Figure 3.13 shows the main network resources, including VNET, which is a virtual network used by a VM (cluster), and PNET, which is a physical network used by a physical machine (cluster). The system defines a series of IP/MAC address pairs; when the VM is created

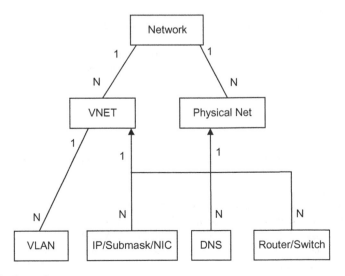

Figure 3.13 Network resources.

and activated, the management system for this VM allocates MAC/IP address pairs and ensures that each VM will be given a unique IP address. When the user opens an instance of the VM, the user can define a private network VLAN so that the VNET can be independent of the physical network [2].

3.3.1.8.1 Network resource properties

VNET Properties

    VNET may include one or more clusters and VLAN, which includes the switches, routers, and other resources

    VExBandWidth (int) VNET external bandwidth

    VInBandWidth (int) VNET internal bandwidth

    VIPValue (string) IP Address resources; allocates to VMs

    VSubmask (string) Subnet mask that allocates to VM

    VNIC (string) Virtual network card, which is an interface used to associate with a VM; when the VM or virtual cluster is created, VNIC is established at the same time.

    VMAC (string) MAC address allocates to VM VNIC

    VDNSValue (string) Domain name for VNET

PNET(PhysicalNet) Properties

    PNET can include resources including several physical machines, switches, and routers.

    ExBandWidth (int) PNET external bandwidth

    InBandWidth (int) PNET internal bandwidth

    IPValue (string) IP address resources; allocates to physical machines

    Submask (string) Subnet mask;is used to allocate to physical machines

    NIC (string) MAC address allocates to physical machine

    DNS Value (string) Domain name for PNET

Switch Properties

    Description: (string) Description of type of performance

    PortNum: (int) Number of ports

    Bandwidth: (int) Bandwidth of switch's port (static data)

    BandwidthUtilization: (int) dynamic utilization ratio of a switch's port bandwidth

Router Properties

    Description: (string) Description of type of performance

    PortNum: (int) Number of ports

    Bandwidth: (int) Bandwidth of router's port (static data)

    BandwidthUtilization: (int) Router's port bandwidth utilization ratio (dynamic)

VLAN Properties

    A VLAN corresponds to one or more SecureGroups

    VLANIPValue: (string) IP section allocates to this VLAN

    VLANSubmask: (string) Subnet mask allocates to this VLAN

    BandWidthMatrix: (2D array) Measures bandwidth between different VM servers (or switches/routers) (Table 3.9)

Table 3.9 **Network operations**

Operation	Description
VNET.AllocIP	Reallocates IP for a VM in VNET
VNET.RetrieveIP	Retrieves the IP address of a VM in VNET
VNET.AllocSubMask	Reallocates subnet mask for VNET
VNET.RetrieveSubMask	Retrieves the subnet mask of a VNET
VNET.SetMAC	Reallocates MAC address for a VM in VNET
VNET. RetrieveMAC	Retrieves MAC address from VM in VNET
VNET.GetDNS	Gets possible domain name of VNET
PNET. AllocIP	Allocates IP address for this PNET
PNET.RetrieveIP	Retrieves IP address from this PNET
PNET. AllocSubMask	Allocates subnet mask for this PNET
PNET.RetrieveSubMask	Retrieves subnet mask from this PNET
VNET.AllocVLAN	Allocates a VLAN for users on this VNET
VLAN. AllocIP	Allocates IP address for this VLAN
VLAN.RetrieveIP	Retrieves IP address from this VLAN
VLAN. AllocSubMask	Allocates subnet mask for this VLAN
VLAN.RetrieveSubMask	Retrieves subnet mask from this VLAN
VLAN.AllocGateway	Allocates gateway for this VLAN

3.3.1.9 Data centers

As shown in Figure 3.1, Cloud data centers are entities (including physical servers, virtual servers, operating systems, applications, middleware, and application services) that can be virtual or physical. They may have the highest level of resources that a Cloud service provider can offer.

3.3.1.9.1 Properties of data centers

Data centers' properties include (but are not limited to):

Location: describes the characteristics of physical location of data centers
ID: for recognizing different data centers in various locations
Size: can be the physical form of the number of servers in data centers or can be related to determining the physical setting
pClusters: information from data center physical clusters
pServers: information from data center physical machines
Schedule_Domain_ID: information from data center scheduling domain

3.3.1.9.2 Data center states

Ready: data center has been customized or deployed and is awaiting start
Starting: data center begins to be used
Busy: busy or in use
Free: to be in idle

3.3.1.9.3   Data center operations

Table 3.10 **Data center operations**

Operation	Description
vCenter.Create	Create a virtual data center and start all virtual servers
vCenter.List	List all virtual data center resources (e.g., virtual clusters, virtual servers)
vDisk.List	Display virtual disk information
vDisk.Create	Create disk file for virtual center that can be deployed with virtual server
publicIP.List	List public IPs of data center
publicIP.Allocate	Allocate public IPs for virtual data center
DiskImage.List	Display disk image information from data center
DiskImage. Register	Register disk image for virtual data center

3.3.1.10   Machine room resources

Building space, electricity, and air conditioning facilities of a data center are key elements of the total cost of data centers.

3.3.1.10.1   Space

With the increasing number of data centers and computing facilities, the space a data center occupies is one of the major factors of the cost of a data center.

Properties:

TotalSpace: capacity of data centers (sq.m)
ActiveSpace: actual volume occupied by computing facilities (sq.m)
LeasedSpace: occupied capacity of computing facilities leased to users
PricePerSquareMeter: price per sq.m

3.3.1.10.2   Power supply

Electricity supplies power to computing facilities in a data center, battery backup, onsite power generation, and power supply and generator for redundant backup. From a cost perspective, we need to consider power supply, depreciation, and maintenance costs.

Properties:

TotalPowerSupply: power required when the data center is operating at full capacity (unit: kW MW)
UtilizedCapacity: actual power consumed by data center (unit: kW MW)
PriceOfPerWatt: price per watt of power
AveragePowerDensity: power consumption per square meter in data center
DepreciationCost: depreciation (depreciation costs consider per month per watt)
MaintenanceCost: maintenance costs (depreciation costs consider per month per watt)

3.3.1.10.3 Air conditioning

Air conditioning is a key element in maintaining the temperature of the machine room of a data center and in keeping all of the physical servers within a certain temperature range (not too hot or too cold). Along with air circulation, it is a major factor in the cost of the data center.

Properties:

CoolingFactor: relationship between air conditioning and requirements of computing facilities (as CPU optimization) as it relates to power consumption;
CostOfCoolingPerMonth: direct cost of air conditioning per month;
Maintenance: depreciation of air conditioning maintenance costs (depreciation costs need to be considered per month per watt) as it relates to CostOfCoolingPerMonth; can be measured as a coefficient;
CoolingForTemperature: air conditioning costs needed for maintaining servers in data center within a certain temperature range.

3.4 Constraints and dependencies among resources

We will introduce several possible constraints and dependencies among resources.

The actual industry standards used to achieve processing rules and constraints can be expressed in business process execution Language for Web Services (WS-BPEL). WS-BPEL is an XML-based language that defines the logical process stream for several services used in forming the business process. It measures constraints and dependencies throughout the network and can be selected by users.

3.4.1 Software/hardware based relations

There are different combinations of relevance among physical servers, virtual server hardware platforms, and operating systems (and even some applications). So actually we always deploy an application platform beforehand and provide it to users as a kind of service [6].

3.4.2 Associated hardware and software platforms and network

Similarly, the network bandwidth in a data center's physical servers, virtual servers, and their applications is constrained by the total bandwidth of the data center and the method of networking utilized. It's almost always predetermined or within a range (dynamic characteristics of network bandwidth usage) [6].

3.4.3 Reliability constraints

Consider the relationship of resources for improving overall system reliability. Major equipment and backup should not be located in the same physical machine. For the primary computing device, storage, network equipment, power supply, and air conditioning facilities, different redundant backup can be adopted to improve overall reliability [7].

3.4.4   Time constraints

If a specific combination of hardware, software platforms, and network resources is assigned to a user at a certain time, other users cannot use it during the same period of time (but can wait for an idle period occurs) [7].

3.4.5   Relationship among performance, system capacity (storage), and bandwidth

With an increase in the number of physical servers and storage capacity in a data center, each server's read and write operations may take up a great deal of bandwidth (the quantitative relationship can be obtained through experimentation. The delay of read and write operations may increase (this quantitative relationship can also be obtained through experimentation) [7].

3.4.6   Scheduling domain constraints on the scope of algorithm execution

The most important purpose of defining a schedule domain is to restrain the range of schedule executions. Usually the maximum optimization, load balancing, and performance optimization scheduling algorithms are implemented in one schedule domain. Multiple domains do not interfere with each other by performing different scheduling algorithms. Moreover, schedule domains can be used to expand or reduce size by hand [7].

3.5   Data modeling of resources in a Cloud data center

3.5.1   Relationship of resources

The UML relationship of resources is shown in Figure 3.14, which is appended at the end of the paper.

3.5.2   Data management of main resource

3.5.2.1   Data center

Figure 3.14 shows an example of two data centers; properties of Cloud data centers are displayed. Figure 3.15 shows an example of two schedule domains: one applies a heat balance algorithm, the other applies a load balance algorithm.

3.5.2.2 Schedule domains

ID	Location	Size	ScheduleDomain_ID	DCServerIP
1	Region#1	4000	2	129.46.163.13
2	Region#2	1000	2	129.46.163.12

Figure 3.14 Cloud data center information.

S..	Sc...	Lo...	IPS...	Sc...	Sche...	ScheduleD...	SDServerIP
1	11-20	2	192....	0	OK	HeatBalance	192.168.2.1
2	1-10	1	192....	0	OK	LoadBalance	192.168.1.100

Figure 3.15 Schedule domains.

P...	Location	V...	OS	CU	CPUType	CPUN...	CPUK...	CPUUt...
1	domain#1	1	windows server ...	10	intel core E5300	4	4	0.34
2	domain#1	2	windows server ...	10	intel core E5300	4	4	0.38
3	domain#1	3	Ubuntu server 9...	10	intel core E5300	4	4	0.23
4	domain#1	4	Ubuntu server 9...	10	intel core E5300	4	4	0.34
5	domain#1	5	windows server ...	10	intel core E5300	4	4	0.76
6	domain#1	6	RedHatE5	10	intel core E5300	4	4	0.44
7	domain#1	7	Ubuntu server 9...	10	intel core E5300	4	4	0.34
8	domain#1	8	windows server ...	10	intel core E5300	4	4	0.55
9	domain#1	9	windows server ...	10	intel core E5300	4	4	0.16

Figure 3.16 Physical machine [8].

MemUtilization	MemMaxUtilizat...	MemDelay	DiskType
0.7	0.9	500	kuyu
0.1	0.9	500	kuyu
0.7	0.9	500	kuyu
0.4	0.9	500	kuyu
0.7	0.9	500	kuyu
0.4	0.9	500	kuyu
0.6	0.9	500	kuyu
0.1	0.9	500	kuyu
0.5	0.9	500	kuyu

Figure 3.17 Physical machine [3].

3.5.3 Physical machine queries

SQL: Select * from [PM] where Location = 'domain#1'

An example of PM query results in domain #1 are shown in Figures 3.16−3.18. Major information defined for PMs is displayed. This information can be used for monitoring, scheduling, and deploying Cloud resources.

3.5.4 Add physical machine

string
a = System.DateTime.Now.ToString("yyyy/MM/dd") + System.DateTime.Now
.ToLongTimeString();
SQL: Insert   Into   [PM]   Values('10','domain#1','10','RedHatE5,windows   server
2003','10','intel   core   E5300','4','4','0.44','0.8','3.2','2','6','0','0.5','0.9','500','kuyu',
'"' + a + '"','100','1000','0.77','100','0.71','192.168.1.101','','1','40')

Figure 3.19 shows an example of adding a new PM to a schedule domain (#1); Figure 3.20 relates to deleting a PM.

BandWidthUtilization	IP	ScheduleDomain_ID	Temperature
0.64	192.1...	1	39
0.63	192.1...	1	41
0.34	192.1...	1	40
0.23	192.1...	1	38
0.11	192.1...	1	38
0.23	192.1...	1	40
0.64	192.1...	1	42
0.54	192.1...	1	41
0.77	192.1...	1	40

Figure 3.18 Physical machine [2].

8	domain#1	8	windows server ...	10	intel core E5300
9	domain#1	9	windows server ...	10	intel core E5300
10	domain#1	10	RedHatE5,windo...	10	intel core E5300
N...	NULL	N...	NULL	NULL	NULL

Figure 3.19 Add physical machine No. 10.

PMID	Location	VMNum	OS	CU	CPUType
1	domain#1	1	windows server ...	10	intel core E5300
2	domain#1	2	windows server ...	10	intel core E5300
3	domain#1	3	Ubuntu server 9...	10	intel core E5300
4	domain#1	4	Ubuntu server 9...	10	intel core E5300
5	domain#1	5	windows server ...	10	intel core E5300
6	domain#1	6	RedHatE5	10	intel core E5300
7	domain#1	7	Ubuntu server 9...	10	intel core E5300
8	domain#1	8	windows server ...	10	intel core E5300
10	domain#1	10	RedHatE5,windo...	10	intel core E5300

Figure 3.20 Delete physical machine No. 9.

PMID	Location	VMNum	OS	CU	CPUType
1	domain#1	1	windows server ...	10	intel core E5300
2	domain#1	2	windows server ...	10	intel core E5300
3	domain#1	3	Ubuntu server 9...	10	intel core E5300
4	domain#1	4	Ubuntu server 9...	10	intel core E5300
5	domain#1	5	windows server ...	10	intel core E5300
6	domain#1	6	RedHatE5	10	intel core E5300
7	domain#2	7	Ubuntu server 9...	10	intel core E5300
8	domain#2	8	windows server ...	10	intel core E5300
10	domain#2	10	RedHatE5,windo...	10	intel core E5300

Figure 3.21 Update physical machine location.

3.5.5 Delete physical machine

SQL: Delete from [PM] Where PMID = '9'

3.5.6 Update physical machine information

SQL: update PM set Location = 'domain#2' where PMID > 6

Figure 3.21 shows the updating of PM schedule domain information. This operation allows some properties of PMs and VMs to be changed.

3.5.7 Query VM

SQL: Select * from [VM] where VM < 17

An example of VM query results are shown in Figures 3.22 and 3.23. Major VM information as defined in previous sections is displayed. This information can be used for monitoring, scheduling, and deploying VMs in a Cloud.

VMID	VMImageID	VMImageDiskID	ServerID	Vmem	VMemUtilization
1	1	1	1	1.5	0.48
2	2	2	2	1.5	0.36
3	3	3	3	1.5	0.33
4	4	4	4	1.5	0.21
5	1	5	5	1.5	0.19
6	4	6	6	1.5	0.66
7	3	7	7	1.5	0.48
8	3	8	8	1.5	0.53
9	2	9	9	1.5	0.48
10	2	10	10	1.5	0.11
11	3	11	11	1.5	0.74
12	1	12	12	1.5	0.49
13	1	13	13	1.5	0.42
14	4	14	14	1.5	0.14
15	4	15	15	1.5	0.47
16	4	16	16	1.5	0.48

Figure 3.22 Query VM [8].

StartTime	EndTime	PreStartTime	PreEn...	ScheduleDomain_ID	PMID	ChangedPMTemperatur
2010-9-...	2010-10...	2010-9-26 ...	2010-1...	1	1	7.5
2010-9-...	2010-10...	2010-9-27 ...	2010-1...	1	1	8.7
2010-9-...	2010-10...	2010-9-27 ...	2010-1...	1	3	7.3
2010-9-...	2010-10...	2010-9-27 ...	2010-1...	1	3	6.3
2010-9-...	2010-10...	2010-9-28 ...	2010-1...	1	3	5.5
2010-9-...	2010-10...	2010-9-28 ...	2010-1...	1	3	8.8
2010-9-...	2010-10...	2010-9-26 ...	2010-1...	1	8	7.7
2010-9-...	2010-10...	2010-9-26 ...	2010-1...	1	8	8.4
2010-9-...	2010-10...	2010-9-28 ...	2010-1...	1	7	7.6
2010-9-...	2010-10...	2010-9-28 ...	2010-1...	1	7	7.7
2010-9-...	2010-10...	2010-9-28 ...	2010-1...	1	4	7.5
2010-9-...	2010-10...	2010-9-28 ...	2010-1...	1	2	5.9
2010-9-...	2010-10...	2010-9-27 ...	2010-1...	1	2	8.5
2010-9-...	2010-10...	2010-9-26 ...	2010-1...	1	6	6.6
2010-9-...	2010-10...	2010-9-26 ...	2010-1...	1	1	7.4
2010-9-...	2010-10...	2010-9-26 ...	2010-1...	1	1	7.5

Figure 3.23 Query VM [3].

3.5.8 Add VM

```
string
a = System.DateTime.Now.ToString("yyyy/MM/dd              ") + System.DateTime.Now
.ToLongTimeString();
string
b = System.DateTime.Now.ToString("yyyy/MM/dd              ") + System.DateTime.Now
.AddHours [12].ToLongTimeString();
SQL: Insert Into [VM] Values('17','2','17','17','1.5','0.54','1.5','1','kingston','xijie','in-
telcore E5300','2','2','2.6','0.3','260','1','1','192.168.1.101','100','1','1','1','1',
' 17','0','"' + a + '"','"' + b + '"','"' + a + '"','"' + b + '"','1','4','7.6') (Figure 3.24)
```

13	1	13	13	1.5	0.42
14	4	14	14	1.5	0.14
15	4	15	15	1.5	0.47
16	4	16	16	1.5	0.48
17	5	17	17	1.5	0.24

Figure 3.24 Add VM No. 17.

11	3	11	11	1.5	0.74
12	1	12	12	1.5	0.49
13	1	13	13	1.5	0.42
15	4	15	15	1.5	0.47
16	4	16	16	1.5	0.48

Figure 3.25 Delete VM No. 14.

VMID	VMImageID	VMImageDiskID	ServerID	Vmem	VMemUtilization	VMemInitialization
1	1	1	1	1.5	0.48	1.5
2	2	2	2	1.5	0.36	1.5
3	3	3	3	1.5	0.33	1.5
4	4	4	4	1.5	0.21	1.5
5	1	5	5	1.5	0.19	1.5
6	4	6	6	1.5	0.66	1.5
7	3	7	7	1.5	0.48	1.5
8	3	8	8	1.5	0.53	1.5
9	2	9	9	1.5	0.48	1.5
10	2	10	10	1.5	0.11	1.5
11	3	11	11	1.5	0.74	2
12	1	12	12	1.5	0.49	2
13	1	13	13	1.5	0.42	2
15	4	15	15	1.5	0.47	2
16	4	16	16	1.5	0.48	2
17	5	17	17	1.5	0.24	2

Figure 3.26 Update VM memory.

3.5.9   Delete VM

SQL: Delete from [VM] Where PMID = '14' (Figure 3.25)

3.5.10   Update VM information

SQL: update VM set VMemInitialization = '2.0' where VMID > 10 (Figure 3.26)

3.6   Conclusion

In this chapter, we introduce the way to model resources in Infrastructure as a Service. The definitions and models defined in this chapter are aimed to be general enough to describe a variety of Cloud providers. The chapter provides definitions, properties, and operations, as well as data modeling, for Cloud data center resources; both modeling and operational methods are introduced in detail. This can help developers better understand how to build information systems and manage resources in Cloud data centers.

Appendix 1: The UML Relationship of Resources

VmInfo			
IP	⟨pi, fi⟩	Text	⟨M⟩
vmName		Text	⟨M⟩
vmSpecs		Integer	⟨M⟩
vmStatus		Text	⟨M⟩
pmIP		Text	⟨M⟩
username		Text	⟨M⟩
password		Text	⟨M⟩
stuPassword		Text	⟨M⟩
stuUsername		Text	⟨M⟩
vmOperatePlatform		Text	⟨M⟩
Identifier_1 ⟨pi⟩			

PmInfo			
IP	⟨pi⟩	Text	⟨M⟩
CPU		Float	⟨M⟩
Mem		Float	⟨M⟩
Bandwidth		Float	⟨M⟩
pmUsername		Text	⟨M⟩
pmPassword		Text	⟨M⟩
Identifier_1 ⟨pi⟩			

Relationship_1

Relationship_2

DomainInfo			
domainId	⟨pi⟩	Integer	⟨M⟩
balanceLevel		Float	⟨M⟩
delay		Integer	⟨M⟩
DomainType		Text	⟨M⟩
DomainAlgorithm		Text	⟨M⟩
Identifier_1 ⟨pi⟩			

VmSpecs			
vmSpecsNo	⟨pi⟩	Integer	⟨M⟩
vmSpecsContext		Text	⟨M⟩
CPU		Float	⟨M⟩
Mem		Float	⟨M⟩
Bandwidth		Float	⟨M⟩
vmType		Integer	⟨M⟩
cost		Long float	⟨M⟩
isEnable		Integer	⟨M⟩
scheduleDomainId		Integer	⟨M⟩
Identifier_1 ⟨pi⟩			

VmRequest			
vmID	⟨pi⟩	Serial	⟨M⟩
vmType		Integer	⟨M⟩
taskType		Text	⟨M⟩
scheduleDomainType		Text	⟨M⟩
startTime		Timestamp	⟨M⟩
endTime		Timestamp	⟨M⟩
Identifier_1 ⟨pi⟩			

ClusterInfo			
IP	⟨pi⟩	Text	⟨M⟩
clusterName		Text	⟨M⟩
clusterConfig		Text	⟨M⟩
clusterStatus		Text	⟨M⟩
lastUseTime		Timestamp	⟨M⟩
userName		Text	⟨M⟩
Identifier_1 ⟨pi⟩			

References

[1] Fujistu, API design for IaaS Cloud computing service, 2010.

[2] IBM IaaS Resource Model & REST APIs Document Version 1.0, July 02, 2010.

[3] DMTF 2009-11-11, White paper, Interoperable Clouds: Distributed Management Task Force, Inc. (DMTF).

[4] Amazon, Amazon Elastic Compute Cloud, <http://aws.amazon.com/ec2/>, last access, March 26, 2014.

[5] IBM: IBM Cloud Computing, <http://www.ibm.com/ibm/cloud/>, last access, April 2, 2014.

[6] VMWare: Vmware Cloud computing, <http://www.vmware.com/solutions/cloud-computing/>, last access, March 25, 2014.

[7] Hyser C, et al. Autonomic virtual machine placement in the data center, HP Laboratories, February 26, 2008.

[8] Google: Barroso L, et al. The datacenter as a computer: an introduction to the design of warehouse-scale machines, 2009.

Cloud Resource Scheduling Strategies

Main Contents of this Chapter

- Key technologies of resource scheduling
- Current Cloud data center scheduling strategies
- Classification and constraining conditions of scheduling strategies

4.1 Key technologies of resource scheduling

Cloud computing is based on computer science's long-term technical accumulation, which includes key technology such as SaaS, PaaS, virtualization, and mass data centers, among others. Data centers (probably distributed in different geographical multiple systems) are the places that accommodate computing equipment and are responsible for providing energy and air conditioning maintenance for the computing devices. A data center could be a single construction or it could be located within several buildings. Dynamic distribution manages virtual and shared resources in the new application environment—Cloud computing data centers face new challenges. Because Cloud computing application platform resources may be distributed widely and in manifold ways with many different user requirements, real-time dynamic change can be difficult to accurately predict. Such factors as system performance and cost also need to be considered, making the problem very complicated. Efficient scheduling strategies and algorithms must be designed to adapt to different business requirements and to satisfy different business goals. The current major data center scheduling strategies include: first come, first service; load balance; and maximizing efficiency, among others. Improving system performance and service quality is a key technology goal of data centers. However—with the constant expansion of data center scale—energy consumption is increasingly becoming a serious problem of particular note because energy consumption greatly affects cost and environment.

Key technologies of resource scheduling include:

- Scheduling strategies: It is the top level of resource scheduling management, which needs to be defined by data center owners and managers. It mainly determines the resource scheduling goals and makes sure to satisfy all immediately required handling strategies when resources are insufficient.
- Optimization goals: Scheduling center needs to identify different objective functions to determine the pros and cons of different types of scheduling. Now there are optimal objective functions, such as minimum costs, maximum profits, and maximum resource utilization.

- Scheduling algorithms: Good scheduling algorithms need to produce optimal results according to objective functions in a very short time without consuming too many resources. In a general way, the problems scheduling algorithms need to solve are basically NP-hard problems, which need a great amount of calculation and are not commonly used. The industry generally uses approximate optimal scheduling algorithms and uses different scheduling algorithms for different applications.
- Scheduling system architecture: It is closely related to the basic infrastructure of data centers. Nowadays the multistage distributed system structure as shown in Figure 2.3 is mainly utilized.
- Data center resource demarcation and mutual restrictive relationships: Clear analysis of resources and their mutual restrictive relationships help scheduling algorithms to synthesize and balance various factors.
- Data center business flow characteristic analysis: Mastering business flow characteristics helps to optimize scheduling algorithms.

4.2   Comparative analysis of scheduling strategies

4.2.1   Amazon

Amazon's Cloud computing scheduling strategy combines strategies for cost first, then satisfies different user requirements such as load balancing or high reliability:

1. Differential costs: It uses a charge scheduling allocation strategy that involves different regions having different costs among which customers can choose.
2. Accelerating response speed: Preconfigures typical virtual machine applications.
3. Business classification: Users can be classified immediately by type of business using client, reservations, and other information. Fees differ and booking client fees are a little lower than immediate user client fees.
4. General charge standard: Long-term usage fees in unit time are lower than short-term usage fees.
5. Load balance: Round Robin is one of the scheduling strategy technologies. It only requires an IP address list circular function, as opposed to traditional single IP addresses provided for DNS usage. The server responds to requests, provides the first IP address to the first request, the second IP address to the next request, and repeats the process until the final IP is distributed. Then the server repeats this process. Round Robin is very suitable for servers in different areas or for servers with contents in several data centers or servers (Table 4.1).

4.2.2   IBM

4.2.2.1   Performance related: satisfying user requirements

IBM belongs to large enterprise, and its internal business (with subsidiaries and its research institute, for example) has big demands for computing resources. The IBM Cloud computing platform [11] is based on a virtual computing experiment project [1−3] experience that has been developed together with North Carolina State University (NCSU) for many years.

Table 4.1 Virtual application types currently provided by Amazon EC2

Application type		Memory (GB)	CPU (ECU)	Storage (GB)
Standard instance (for most ordinary applications)	Small instance	1.7	1	160
	Big instance	7.5	4	850
	Oversized instance	15	8	1690
High storage instance (high-throughput applications, such as e-commerce, etc.)	High memory oversized instance	17.1	6.5	420
	High memory double oversized instance	34.2	13	850
	High memory fourth oversized instance	68.4	26	1690
High CPU instance (compute-intensive applications)	High CPU medium instance	1.7	5	350
	High CPU oversized instance	7	20	1690

Note: EC2 computing unit (ECU, EC2 Compute Unit): an EC2 computing unit (ECU) provides the CPU capacity as 1.0−1.2 GHz, 1.0 Opteron1, 1.0−1.2 GHz, or Xeon processors in 2007.

IBM resource scheduling management adopts the following measures:

- Preconfigures virtual machines or provides optional models, letting users choose the virtual resources' hardware platform, CPU, memory, and operating systems online, indicating such information as start time and end time), and submitting booking or immediate-use request.
- Dynamic monitoring resource status. Monitoring is executed by IBM® Tivoli® Monitoring; users can monitor detailed information via the Tivoli Enterprise portal and can fully combine this information with Cloud portals.
- Automatic resource deployment and dynamic updates. After users make the choice, the system begins a process—which includes Web service, Tivoli Provisioning Manager, optional IBM Tivoli Security Compliance Manager, BPEL, and IBM Enterprise Workload Manager Remote Deployment Manager/Cluster Systems Managements/Network Installation Manager —to construct a server whose process is completely automatic and only takes about an hour.
- Immediate use and booking. Immediate use is for users to request resource upon arrival while booking is for users to reserve resources in advance.
- Users who receive resources can request extensions of time in advance when using resources, and—of course—the user can also terminate in advance.

Meanwhile, various scheduling strategies that consider different users, user priorities and groups are also introduced in [2, 3].

4.2.3 HP

4.2.3.1 Cost based: cost model

HP began data center research work very early [3−6]. An HP data center document [5] systematically introduces HP data center cost model's detailed scheme and technical methods, which becomes an important reference for the cost model. Equation 4.1 describes each element a data center considers with respect to cost: including building space occupation, power supply, refrigeration, and maintenance.

$$\text{Total Cost} = \text{SpaceCost} + \text{PowerCost} + \text{CoolingCost} + \text{OperationCost} \qquad (4.1)$$

Among these elements, SpaceCost includes building/space costs; PowerCost considers data center power supply costs; CoolingCost refers to data center air conditioning expenses; OperationCost includes fees such as manager, software, and hardware depreciation and maintenance.

HP's cost model is very comprehensive and provides examples for data centers to consider related costs.

4.2.3.2   Load balance: automatically assesses virtual machine burden and carries out dynamic migration

Patel et al. [6] mainly considers load balance strategy for making CPU, storage, and network resource utilization close to an average value. Through real-time monitoring of a virtual machine's CPU, storage, and network resource utilization, the machine can accomplish automatic configuration and dynamic migration so as to achieve a balanced load (Figure 4.1).

4.2.4   VMWare

At present, the VMWare company focuses on resource virtualization, disaster recovery, and dynamic migration [7,8].

4.2.4.1   Improve resource utilization

The main consideration of the VMWare company data centers is improving resource utilization, dynamic virtual machine migration, and disaster recovery through virtualization. Managing virtual machines (increasing, deleting, and updating) is mostly carried out manually, and scheduling generally uses timing arrangements.

4.2.4.2   Improve reliability

Improving reliability mainly occurs through preset dynamic migration or automatic transfer, backup, and restoration.

By establishing a remote server group, VMWare can double a center's virtualized IT structure. Using vReplicator service between the operating end and the remote end, a real-time application copy can be created from the virtual machine at the operating end to ESX host storage in the remote end. This can allow for disaster recovery in different places. VReplicator operates with virtual machines, monitors virtual machine disk file data changes, and—after a full disk data copy operation is completed, every other 5 minutes—automatically copies different

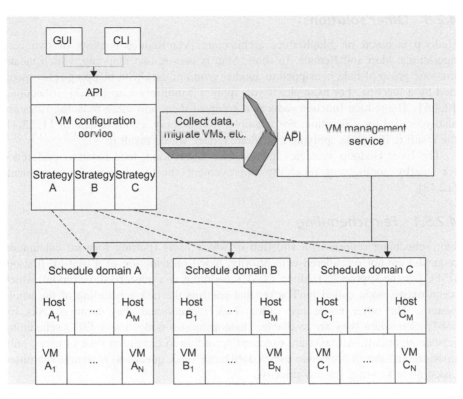

Figure 4.1 HP automatic management virtual machine (dynamic migration) system structure [6].

data between the disk data and the disaster recovery end. When the operating server has a service disruption, vReplicator automatically performs a failover operation for virtual machine backup, whose disaster recovery end is on standby status. Backup machine data and settings exactly match the virtual machine source, so after starting, the application can be immediately taken over and restarted, providing service for final users.

4.2.4.3 Load balance: Distributed Resource Scheduling

At present, this product mainly realizes load balance through distributed scheduling. Dynamic resource scheduling performs three crucial resource-related operations: (1) It calculates the demand of resources that each VM should request based on the reservation and shares settings and constraints for VMs, as well as resource pool nodes; (2) it does initial placement of VMs on to hosts automatically; and (3) it suggests and performs live VM migrations to do load balancing across hosts in a dynamic environment when the VM's resource demands vary during a period of time.

4.2.5   Other solutions

Hadoop is based on MapReduce architecture. MapReduce consists of two core operations: Map and Reduce. In short, Map is one-on-one mapping, which means that one group of data is mapped to another group of data with mapping rules specified by a function. For example, if you apply a 2 multiply map {1,2,3}, it becomes {2,4,6}. The reduce function reduces a group of data, and these reducing rules are also specified by a function. For example, if you apply a sum reduce to {1,2,3,4}, the result is 10, while applying a quadrate reduce would result in 30.

The basic Hadoop strategies include: fair distribution, load balance, preference for nearby nodes, and reliability improvement (backup + dynamic adjustment) [12,13].

4.2.5.1   Fair scheduling

Fair scheduling represents a situation in which users (putting forward calculation requests) are not considered with priority, based on adoption of a first-in, first-out (FIFO) queue approach. Hadoop's task scheduling is a master−slave model, which has a master node called JobTracker that controls the task scheduling of the whole system. The other nodes are called TaskTrackers and they arrange tasks for JobTracker when they are available. Hadoop master nodes use a FIFO scheduling service algorithm. All tasks are executed according to execution time of users' submission, and the master node uses a JobQueue (task queue) to maintain submitted tasks: no tasks are given any priority.

4.2.5.2   Load balance

The master node dynamically allocates tasks through slave nodes to achieve balanced loads. After load balance information is collected from slaves, dynamic configuration can be triggered. Dynamic configuration is just an operation in which data is migrated from one slave node to another. Migration just means the data is copied from the slave with the higher load to another slave with a lower load, and that the data is deleted from the original, higher load slave.

4.2.5.3   Delayed scheduling for locality in Hadoop

Hadoop slave nodes use a greedy algorithm: the default scheduling algorithm is always trying to find the slave node that is nearest to the customer so large data does not need to be transmitted throughout the network. If the closest slave node is busy, then the task can be allocated to another available node.

4.2.5.4   Reliability improvement

Generally when making block backup for data, backup data is distributed in several (such as three or more) nodes. The main control program pings each live node regularly, and if a particular work node does not return correlative information within a specified time—indicating node failure, the main control program defines that node as invalid, all Map tasks and Reduce tasks assigned to that node will be reset into the initial free state, and other working nodes can handle those tasks.

4.3 Classification of main scheduling strategies

4.3.1 Performance related

4.3.1.1 First come, first served

To fully satisfy a virtual machine's resource requirement, a first come, first served strategy is generally used, combined with user priority. Early IBM virtual computing was set up in this way and was mostly used in companies or schools. There may not be specific scheduling optimization goal functions, but it still needs to define administrator resource allocation. The server can be divided into categories such as ordinary, high throughput, or extensive computing for users to choose.

4.3.1.2 Load balance

The goal of load balance is to create a balanced average resource utilization of the physical machines. Typical load balance strategies are used by VMWare and SUN plan [14,15].

Optimization goal: the utilization of resources = the average utilization of all physical servers (CPU, memory utilization, and network bandwidth).

When there is a resource assigned, the system must immediately calculate and monitor each resource utilization (or directly use a load balance allocation algorithm) and then allocate users' requests to the resource with the lowest utilization.

Load balancing can be realized through software or through hardware. Hardware can utilize special load balance devices, such as multilayer switches, which can dispense packets in a cluster. Normally, implementation, configuration, and maintenance solutions from hardware require time and capital investment. As for software, scheduling algorithms—such as Round Robin—can be used.

4.3.1.3 Improve reliability

Optimization objectives: make each resource's reliability to the specified requirement (such as Amazon's 99.9% business guarantee [10]). Reliability and the server itself (average breakdown time, average maintenance time) are related, and breakdown, power outages, and dynamic migration produce business disruption that will influence reliability.

If a physical server's reliability is 90% and user required business reliability is 99.99%, scheduling should provide for at least a double-machine backup. If dynamic migration decreases business reliability by 0.1%, scheduling strategy must reduce (or avoid) dynamic migration.

Under certain premises, a system should reduce the average number of virtual machine migrations (average migration numbers, total migration numbers, or maximum migration numbers for a single virtual machine). A system also needs statistics on the quantitative influence on virtual machine migration on reliability.

Ways to improve reliability: backup redundancy should not place master machine and backup machine in the same physical machine or frame. Specific indicators can be proposed by users (as a demand option for users to choose).

4.3.2 Cost based

4.3.2.1 Improve overall utilization

Optimization objective: the highest resource utility = the highest utility that all resources in the data center can reach (or with the least number of physical machines satisfying the user's requests).

Input: resource distribution in the data center and user requests for specific virtual machine.

Output: physical machine's ID allocation for user requests.

The CPU utilization of a physical (virtual) server = number of CPUs that have been allocated/the number of CPUs that the physical machine can provide. This parameter can represent the service condition of the current physical server and can sort the physical server's utility from high to low. The price of every virtual machine in unit time = the cost of a virtual machine in unit time $\times (1 + a)$, where a is the profit margin, which can be provided by the provider. The cost of a virtual machine in unit time can be estimated by the resources it occupies.

4.3.2.2 Maximum profit

Optimization objective: Maximum profit = Max (the income of all kinds of resources; the cost of all kinds of resources).

Main factors to be considered:

1. Cost in unit time for unit resource (may be different in each physical machine) = Fixed Cost (depreciation and labor included) + Variable Cost (including power consumption).
2. Virtual machine power consumption ratio = Total Cost when virtual machine is at full load/total CPU capacity of virtual machine.
3. Cost of every physical machine = Boot Cost (every time a new physical machine starts) + Cost in unit time with unit resource $\times$ time $\times$ resource amount.
4. Income of every user's request equals the unit time cost of the virtual machine user selected, total income of resources equals the total income from all users.
5. After user finishes request, migration validation should be done to check whether the condition is satisfied. If it is, then migration occurs, which can reduce the number of booted physical machines to save costs.

4.3.2.3 Minimum operation costs

Reducing operation costs as much as possible includes cutting down on air conditioning, electricity, and space costs.

Optimization goal: Minimum Cost = Min (all resource cost)

The main factors to be considered:

1. Cost in unit time per unit resource (may be different for each physical machine) = Fixed Cost (depreciation and labor included) + Variable Cost (including power consumption).
2. Virtual machine power consumption ratio = Total Cost when virtual machine has full load/total CPU capacity of virtual machine.
3. Cost of every physical machine = Boot Cost (every time a new physical machine starts) + Cost in unit time with unit resource × time × resource amount.
4. Income of every user request equals the unit time cost of the virtual machine user selected, total income of resources equals the total income from all users.

References [16] and [17] both introduce the scheduling strategy and algorithm related to heat-sensitivity, Refs. [18] and [19] propose strategy and algorithm for managing and reducing power consumption, Ref. [20] introduces strategy and algorithm to improve sharing and utility to reduce cost, Ref. [21] provides comparison of 22 data centers' power consumption indices, Ref. [22] proposes temperature-sensitivity scheduling strategy and algorithms, which can be used in a data center to allocate loads.

Since air conditioning power cost is the main cost in a data center, the industry generally measures energy efficiency for a data center. Industry usually adopts a power consumption index in a data center to measure power utilization. A data center power consumption index is the total power consumption (including that by computing equipment, heat, ventilation, air conditioning, light, and other power consumption) divided by the power consumption of the computing equipment. In a power consumption index, the higher the better; in practice the value would be between 0.8 and 0.9 (Table 4.2).

4.3.2.4 Combining scheduling strategies

Above all, selecting different strategies should consider both service requirements and business goals in practice. In Table 4.3, compatibility of every basic scheduling strategy is collected. If internal service of a company is the first requirement, then minimum cost, utility, and load balance should be considered. If business application is the main requirement, maximum profit should be considered. For instance, the maximum profit strategy should be selected and configured with the appropriate load balance and reliability strategies as constraints.

Since combined strategy can result in many new scheduling strategies, the 7 essential scheduling strategies may create 128 combined strategies. A recommended method would be setting a basic scheduling strategy as the main strategy and then setting other strategies as constraints to generate new strategies. Here the maximum utilization compatibility with high reliability is used as an example:

Maximum utilization means utilization of all working physical servers reaches the maximum level (there is an upper limit to ensure service performance), so some

Table 4.2 Comparison analysis of main scheduling strategies [9]

Type	Strategy	Optimization goal	Complexity	Strength	Weakness
Performance first	Load balance	Makes the utilization of a resource reach the average value	Low	Supports basic resource performance (performance can be configured—good performance utility domain)	Mainly ensures performance while other characteristics may not be reached easily
	High reliability	Makes reliability of all resources reach predefined requirement (like ensuring service, this strategy can be used 99.95% of the time)	Low	Ensures service reliability	If different requirements exist, a great deal of resources and cost are added
	Maximum user request satisfaction	No explicit goal function	Low	Classifies user level according to priority, safety level, and so on	Can only be qualitatively allocated when not quantitatively allocated
Cost first	Maximum utility	Maximizing resource utilization = all computing resources in data center are at maximum utilization	Higher	Makes resource utilization higher with lower costs	Cannot satisfy other relative performance requirements, like load balance, reliability, and fast service
	Maximum profits	Maximum Profits = Max (Income of all types of resources; Cost of using all types of resources)	High	Fits into the profit requirements of most business providers	Cannot satisfy other relative performance requirements like load balance, reliability, and fast service
	Minimum cost	Minimum Cost = Min (Cost of all resources)	High	Fits into the profit requirements of most providers	Cannot satisfy other relative performance requirements like load balance, reliability, and fast service

Table 4.3 Basic integrated scheduling strategy relationship compatibility (√) or incompatibility (×)

	Maximum user request satisfaction	Load balance	High reliability	Maximum utilization	Maximum profit	Minimum cost	Energy efficiency	Capability optimization
Maximum user request satisfaction		√	√	×	×	×	√	√
Load balance			√	×*	×	×	√	√
High Reliability				×*	√	×	√	√
Maximum utilization					√	√	×	×
Maximum profit						√	×	×
Minimum cost							×	×
Energy efficiency								√
Capability optimization								

Note: The high reliability mentioned in the table mainly refers to the general load. When user requirements are much higher than resources, many scheduling strategies are compatible.

physical servers would be shut down if necessary. If high reliability is also considered (like in the master copy), an additional constraint that might influence the master copy could be added based on other constraints before shutting down the physical servers. If that constraint is triggered, then the shut down operation would not occur. In a similar way, when allocating virtual machines to a physical server to improve resource utilization, satisfying high reliability could also be added as a constraint.

4.4　Some constraints of scheduling strategies

4.4.1　Space: association and anti-association

The association rule represents putting two or more virtual machines on the same server. Anti-association means two or more virtual machines cannot be allocated to the same server.

4.4.2　Scheduling domain: scheduling locality

A domain is constituted of one or more physical servers or clusters. Some automatic schedulers, like load balance or maximum utilization, can only happen in a single scheduling domain within the scheduling system. Scheduling in several domains is possible and is very important, while sometimes manually operation is needed. From a layering view, a scheduling domain can only occur at the system layer or smaller (of course, it may consist of only one scheduling domain in a data center).

4.4.3　Time: limited available time

Tasks allocated to the same resource cannot share the same execution time. If a virtual machine occupies a resource during a period of time, then other users cannot use the same resource at the same time unless they have higher priority within the scheduling domain.

4.4.4　Migration versus nonmigration

Some virtual machines are particularly important and cannot be migrated automatically. If migrations are needed, notify the manager and he will handle it.

4.5　Scheduling task execution time and trigger conditions

When resource costs are taken into consideration, not all scenarios trigger the scheduler to respond instantaneously. For instance, if the monitor notices that the

CPU utilization has surpassed the threshold, this could be just temporary, so an instantaneous schedule would not be reasonable. Common optimization scheduling usually adopts cyclical timing. For uncommon situations—as when a physical machine is broken—the scheduler would be triggered instantaneously.

A scheduling condition may be classified as one of three types:

1. Regular scheduling performance: considers business demand when scheduling execution time is set (i.e., at regular intervals; if business demand is high, it can be set to 1 min. If business demand is small, it can be set to 10 min).
2. Uncommon condition: occurs when physical resources are broken or load balance has surpassed the predefined threshold.
3. Optimization with manual operation: arranges schedule manually.

Summary

This chapter analyzes the scheduling strategies of a data center, compares all of the prominent scheduling strategies from current businesses, and proposes basic scheduling strategy recommendations. In real applications, service requirements need to be taken into consideration to select different strategies. For those companies whose main requirements are business applications, the maximum profit strategy is the best solution. Additionally, we recommend performance and cost should both be considered; for instance, load balance and reliability satisfaction can be set as constraints-when the maximum profits strategy is selected.

Appendix: Some elementary terms

Resource

Resources can be divided into many different types with a variety of division standards. In this chapter, "resource" only refers to those necessary for a scheduler to consider when deciding where a virtual machine should be created or migrated.

Resource provider

Physical machines and clusters are physical resource providers.

Resource user

A virtual machine is a resource user when considered in terms of physical resources or is just a resource from the point of view of the end user.

Resource scheduling

Resource scheduling is a process whereby resource providers allocate resources to users. For a Cloud data center, the types of resources scheduling strategies must consider include physical servers, physical server clusters, shared memories, bandwidths, virtual machine images, and security groups.

When requirements surpass capacity and capacity varies with time, a Cloud data center can adopt resource management to allocate resources dynamically to make resource usage more efficient. For virtual machine scheduling, the following three questions need to be considered carefully:

1. Scheduling strategy and goal: What's the standard for allocating the required virtual machine to a physical machine?
2. Main problem scheduling algorithm must solve: Which physical machine will be allocates the required virtual machine?
3. Deployment and configuration of the required virtual machine: Predefined configuration and dynamic configuration differ. Problems 1 and 2 have a close relationship to the scheduling algorithm.

Resource management

Generally speaking, resource management is a broader concept than resource scheduling, because in addition to scheduling, it also includes resource monitoring, automatic installation and configuration, and the implementation of scheduling tasks.

Scheduling strategy

This is the highest strategy in scheduling management, and must be chosen by the data center owner and managers. The main aim is to fulfill the goals of the scheduled resources and to provide strategies when resources cannot satisfy all real-time requirements. Additionally, unique situations—like hardware failure, high temperature, and resource overload—require migration to be taken into consideration.

References

[1] Amazon Elastic Compute Cloud. <http://aws.amazon.com/ec2/>; 2014.
[2] Vouk M. Cloud Computing—Issues, Research and implementations, 30th international conference on information technology interfaces, 2008.
[3] Vouk M, Averitt S, et al. Using Virtual Computing Laboratory (VCL) technology to power Cloud computing, In: The proceedings of second international conference on the virtual computing initiative, 2008.
[4] HP Cloud Research, <http://www.hpl.hp.com/research/cloud.html>; 2014.
[5] Hpdatacenter, <http://h20195.www2.hp.com/v2/GetPDF.aspx/4AA1-8079ENW.pdf>; 2014.
[6] Patel CD, et al. Cost model for planning, development and operation of a data center, 2005.

[7] Introduction Cloud Computing Architecture White Paper, 2009.

[8] Vmware Cloud Computing, <http://www.vmware.com/solutions/cloud-computing/>; 2014.

[9] Tian W, Jing C, Hu J, Analysis of resource allocation and scheduling policies in Cloud datacenter, accepted for publication. In: IEEE third international conference on networks security wireless communications and trusted computing, 2011.

[10] Barroso L, et al. The datacenter as a computer: an introduction to the design of warehouse-scale machines, 2009.

[11] IBM Cloud Computing, <http.//www.ibm.com/ibm/cloud/>; 2014.

[12] Cisco Cloud computing—Data center strategy, architecture, and solutions point of view, White Paper for U.S. Public Sector, 2009.

[13] The Hadoop Project. Available at: <http://hadoop.apache.org>; 2014.

[14] Hyser C, et al. Autonomic virtual machine placement in the data center, 2008.

[15] Sun Cloud Computing, <http://www.sun.com/solutions/cloudcomputing/>; 2014.

[16] Cloud-Standards, <http://cloud-standards.org/wiki/index.php?title = Main_Page#NIST_Working_Definition_of_Cloud_Computing>; 2014.

[17] Wang L, et al. Towards thermal aware workload data center. In: The proceedings of the tenth international symposium on pervasive systems, algorithms and networks, 2009.

[18] Tang Q, et al. Energy-efficient, thermal-aware task scheduling for homogeneous, high performance computing data centers: a cyber-physical approach, IEEE transactions on parallel and distributed systems, 2008.

[19] Bianchini R, et al. Power and energy management for server systems, Computer, 2004

[20] Wang L. Efficient power management of heterogeneous soft real-time clusters. In: The proceedings of real-time systems symposium, Barcelona, 2008.

[21] Cardosa M, et al. Shares and utilities based power consolidation in virtualized server environments. In: The proceedings of 11th IFIP/IEEE international symposium on integrated network management, IEEE communications society, 2009.

[22] Pacific Northwest National Laboratory, Data center energy efficiency, <http://esdc.pnl.gov/SC07_BOF/SC07BOF_Tschudi.pdf>; 2007.

Load Balance Scheduling for Cloud Data Centers

5

Main Contents of this Chapter

- Related work on resource scheduling for data centers
- Online algorithm model and analysis
- Comparison of several online algorithms

5.1 Introduction

Cloud data centers can be distributed networks in structure, containing many compute nodes (such as servers), storage nodes, and network devices. Each node is formed by a series of resources, such as CPU, memory, and network bandwidth, which are called multidimensional resources. Each has corresponding properties discussed in this paper. The definitions and models defined in this paper are aimed to be general enough to be used by a variety of Cloud providers and to focus on Infrastructure as a Service. In traditional data centers, applications are tied to specific physical servers that are often overworked to deal with heavy workloads. Such configurations make data centers expensive to maintain—with wasted energy and floor space, low resource utilization, and significant management overhead. With virtualization technology, today's Cloud data centers have become more flexible, more secure, and provide better support for on-demand allocation. In a virtualization situation, Cloud data centers have the ability to migrate an application from one set of resources to another in a nondisruptive manner. This ability is essential in modern Cloud computing infrastructure that aims to efficiently have and manage extremely large data centers. One key technology playing an important role in Cloud data centers is resource scheduling. There are quite a few load balance scheduling algorithms. Most of them are for the load balancing of traditional Web servers or server farms. One of the challenging scheduling problems in Cloud data centers is the allocation and migration of reconfigurable virtual machines (VMs) and the integrated features of physical machine (PM) hosting. Unlike traditional load balance scheduling algorithms that consider only one physical server factor— such as CPU—online resource scheduling algorithm (OLRSA) considers CPU, memory, and network bandwidth integrated for PMs and VMs. The major contributions are as follows:

- Providing a modeling approach to VM scheduling problems of capacity sharing by modifying traditional interval scheduling and considering life cycles and multidimensional characteristics of both VMs and PMs.

• Designing and implementing online load balancing scheduling algorithms with computational complexity and competitive analysis.
• Providing performance evaluation of multiple metrics, such as makespan, load efficiency, imbalance value, and makespan capacity, to adjust makespan capacity by simulating different algorithms.

5.2   Related work

A great amount of work has been devoted to scheduling algorithms and it can basically be divided into two types: online load balance algorithms and offlineload balance algorithms. The major difference is that online schedulers only know the current requests and status of all PMs, whereas offline schedulers know all requests and every status of all PMs throughout time. Andre et al. [1] discussed the detailed design of a data center. Armbrust et al. [2] summarized the key issues and solutions in Cloud computing. Foster et al. [3] provided detailed comparison between Cloud computing and Grid computing. Buyya et al. [4] introduced a way to model and simulated Cloud computing environments. Wickremasinghe et al. [5] introduced three general scheduling algorithms for Cloud computing and provided simulation results. Wood et al. [6] introduced techniques for VM migration and proposed some migration algorithms. Zhang [7] compared major load balance scheduling algorithms for traditional Web servers. Singh et al. [8] proposed a novel load balance algorithm called VectorDot that deals with hierarchical and multidimensional resource constraints by considering servers and storage in a Cloud. Arzuaga and Kaeli [9] proposed a quantifying measure of load imbalance on virtualized enterprise servers. Tian [10] provided a comparative study of major existing scheduling strategies and algorithms for Cloud data centers. Sun et al. [11] presented a novel heuristic algorithm to improve integrated utilization considering multidimensional resources. Tian et al. [12] introduced a dynamic load balance scheduling algorithm considering only current allocation periods and multidimensional resources, without considering life cycles of both VMs and PMs. Li et al. [13] proposed a Cloud task scheduling policy based on an ant colony optimization algorithm to balance the entire system and minimize the makespan of a given task set. Galloway in Ref. [14] introduced an online greedy algorithm, in which PMs can be dynamically shut down or started, but the start time and end time (life cycle) are not considered. Hu et al. [15] discussed an algorithm named Genetic, which measures historical data and current states in order to determine allocations. Most of the existing research does not consider the real-time and fixed-interval constraints of VM allocation. We will address this issue in this chapter.

5.3   Problem formulation and description

In this chapter we model VM allocations as Modified Interval Scheduling Problems (MISPs) with fixed processing times. More explanations and analysis

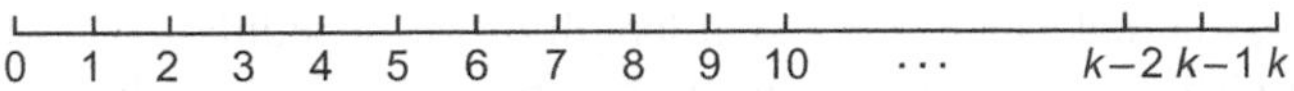

Figure 5.1 Slot formats.

about traditional interval scheduling problems (ISPs) with fixed processing times can be found in Ref. [16] and the references therein. We present a general formulation of a MISP and evaluate its results when compared with well-known existing algorithms. A set of requests $1,2,\ldots,n$ where the ith request corresponds to an interval of time starting at s_i and finishing at f_i is associated with a capacity requirement c_i.

Several assumptions follow:

1. All data are deterministic and—unless otherwise specified—the time is formatted in slotted windows. As shown in Figure 5.1, we partition the total time period $[0, T]$ into slots with equal length (s_0), with the total number of slots $k = T/s_0$. The start time s_i and finish time f_i are integer numbers of one slot. Then the interval of a request can be represented in slot format with (start time, finish time). For example, if $s_0 = 5$ min, an interval $(3, 10)$ means that it has a start time and a finish time at the 3rd slot and 10th slot, respectively. The actual duration of this request is $(10 - 3) \times 5 = 35$ min.
2. All tasks are independent. There are no predetermined constraints other than those implied by the start and finish times.
3. The required capacity of each request is a positive real number between $(0, 1]$. Notice that the capacity of a single PM is normalized to 1.
4. Assume that—when processed—each VM request is assigned to a single PM, thus interrupting a request and resuming it on another machine is not allowed, unless explicitly stated otherwise.
5. Each PM is always available, that is, each machine is continuously available in $[0, \infty)$.

The traditional ISP with fixed processing time: In a set of requests $1, 2,\ldots,n$ where the ith request corresponds to an interval of time starting at s_i and finishing at f_i, each request needs a capacity of 1—occupying the whole capacity of a machine during a fixed processing time.

Interval scheduling with capacity sharing (ISWCS): The only difference from traditional interval scheduling is that a resource (a concrete, PM) can be shared by different requests if the total capacity of all requests allocated to the single resource at any time does not surpass the total capacity that the resource can provide.

Sharing compatible intervals for ISWCS: A subset of intervals with total required capacity not surpassing the total capacity of a PM at any time, therefore the capacity of a PM can be shared.

The formulation of ISWCS can be described as follows. Given a set of m identical machines (PMs) $PM_1, PM_2,\ldots,PM_m$ and a set of n requests (VMs), with a processing time for each request (e.g., consider only CPU processing), the objective of load balance is to assign each request to one of the PMs so the loads placed on all machines are balanced. The online scheduler only has access to the current requests and status of all PMs. In the literature, the makespan is used to measure the load balance, which is simply the maximum total load (processing time) on any machine.

Traditionally, the makespan is the total length of the schedule (e.g., when all of the jobs have finished processing when each job occupies the whole capacity of a machine during processing).

Theorem 5.1 The offline scheduling algorithm allocating minimum makespan in a general case is NP-complete.

Proof We sketch a brief proof as follows, with the detailed proof referred to in Ref. [16]. We show that this scheduling problem (called the Load balance Scheduling Problem) is a polynomial time reducible to a well-known NP-complete problem: the Subset Sum Problem. Thus consider an instance of Subset Sum with numbers $w_1, w_2, \ldots, w_n$, which correspond to the CPU load of n VM requests and have the total CPU load W. To achieve load balance, in an ideal situation, all m machines would share the same amount of the total CPU load, W/m. This requires all allocations on all PMs to be satisfied. Suppose there are j VMs on PM_i; this requires that $L_i = W/m$. It reduces to the Subset Sum Problem, which completes the proof.

Remarks Notice that Theorem 5.1 considers offline load balance scheduling for a single resource CPU on identical machines. When there are multiple resources to be considered in a heterogeneous case (like in this paper), the problem is more difficult, but can still be proven to be NP-complete in a similar way (a detailed proof is provided in Ref. [17] by transforming the problem to a three-dimensional matching problem or a multidimensional vector bin-packing problem). The load balance of ISWCS is different from the load balance of traditional multiprocessor scheduling. First, each request may have different capacity demand in ISWCS, whereas each job occupies the entire capacity of one machine in traditional multiprocessor scheduling. Second, ISWCS has fixed process intervals, whereas in traditional multiprocessor scheduling the job can be delayed without considering start time or end time. Traditional metrics, such as makespan, may not reflect the real load for ISWCS problems. For example, consider when there are $n = 7$ jobs, $m = 3$ machines, and each machine has the capacity $C = 3$. The first six jobs all have start times of zero and end times of 1, with capacity 1. The last job has the start time zero and end time 3, with capacity 1. The traditional List Scheduling (LS) algorithm [18] allocates two jobs of the first six jobs to each machine and the last job to the first machine, and has a makespan of 3. The optimal solution is to allocate three of the first six jobs to the first two machines and the last job to the third machine, which will also have a makespan equal to 3. However, this does not reflect the real load of each machine. Actually, LS would allocate the maximum load of 5 to all machines, while the maximum load is 3 for all machines in the optimal solution. The reason is that both capacities share and the ISWCS problem uses a fixed processing interval constraint.

In view of this issue, we redefine makespan to be capacity makespan.

Capacity makespan: In any allocation of VM requests to PMs, we can let $A(i)$ denote the set of VM requests allocated to machine PM_i. With this allocation, machine PM_i will have the total loads:

$$L_i = \sum_{j \in A(i)} c_j t_j \qquad (5.1)$$

where c_j is the capacity (e.g., CPU) request of VM_j and t_j is the span of request j (i.e., the length of processing time of request j). The goal of load balancing is to minimize the maximum load (capacity makespan) on any PM. Some other related metrics, such as imbalance value and load efficiency, are also considered and will be explained in the following section.

5.3.1 Metrics for real-time load balancing scheduling algorithms

In this section, a few existing metrics and new metrics for load balancing scheduling will be presented. Wood et al. [6] introduced a few VM migration techniques. One integrated load balance measurement is applied as follows:

$$V = \frac{1}{(1 - \text{CPU}_u)(1 - \text{Mem}_u)(1 - \text{NET}_u)} \qquad (5.2)$$

where CPU_u, Mem_u, NET_u are the average utilization of CPU, memory, and network bandwidth during each observed period, respectively. The higher the value of V, the higher the integrated utilization will be.

Zheng et al. in Ref. [19] introduced an integrated load balancing index and load balancing algorithm:

$$B = a \times \frac{N_{1i} \times C_i}{N_{1m} \times C_m} + b \times \frac{N_{2i} \times M_i}{N_{2m} \times M_m} + c \times \frac{N_{3i} \times D_i}{N_{3m} \times D_m} + d \times \frac{\text{NET}_i}{\text{NET}_m} \qquad (5.3)$$

where i is the index of PM and m is the ID of the referenced PM, N_i is the capability of CPU, N_2 is the parameter of memory, N_3 refers to the parameter of bandwidth, C and M are the utilization of CPU and memory, D is the transference rate of the hard disk, Net is the network throughput, a, b, c, d are the compared weighted values of CPU, memory, hard disk, and network, respectively, initialized as 1. The optimization goal seeks to allocate requests to the PM with the smallest B value. For the OLRSA algorithm, we take the following parameters into consideration:

1. PM resource: $PM_i(i, \text{PCPU}_i, \text{PMem}_i, \text{PStorage}_i)$, i is the index number of PM, PCPU_i, PMem_i, PStorage_i are the CPU, memory, and storage capacity that a PM can provide.
2. VM resource: $VM_j(j, \text{VCPU}_j, \text{VMem}_j, \text{VStorage}_j, T_j^{\text{start}}, T_j^{\text{end}})$, j is the VM type ID, VCPU_j, VMem_j, VStorage_j are the CPU, memory, storage requirements of VM_j, T_j^{start}, T_j^{end} are the start time and end time, which are used to represent the life cycle of a VM.

3. Time slot: we consider a time span from 0 to T divided into parts of the same length. Then n parts can be defined as $[(t_1 - t_0), (t_2 - t_1), \ldots, (t_n - t_{n-1})]$, each time slot T_k means the time span $(t_k - t_{k-1})$.

4. Average CPU utilization of PM$_i$ during slot 0 and T_n:

$$PCPU_i^U = \frac{\sum\limits_{k=0}^{n} PCPU_i^{T_k} \times T_k}{\sum\limits_{k=0}^{n} T_k} \tag{5.4}$$

And with memory $PMem_i^U$ and storage $PStorage_i^U$, utilization of both PMs and VMs can be computed in the same way. Similarly, average CPU utilization of a VM can be computed.

5. Integrated load imbalance value ILB$_i$ of PM$_i$. The variance is widely used as a measure of how far a set of values are spread out from each other in statistics. Using variance, an integrated load imbalance value IBL$_i$ of server i is defined

$$ILB_i = \frac{(Avg_i - CPU_u^A)^2}{3} + \frac{(Avg_i - Mem_u^A)^2}{3} + \frac{(Avg_i - Storage_u^A)^2}{3} \tag{5.5}$$

where

$$Avg_i = \frac{PCPU_i^U + PMem_i^U + PStorage_i^U}{3} \tag{5.6}$$

and $PCPU_i^U, PMem_i^U, PStorage_i^U$ are respectively the average utilization of CPU, memory, and storage in a Cloud data center. ILB$_i$ is applied to indicate load imbalance level, comparing utilization of CPU, memory, and network bandwidth of a single server, itself. This metric is very similar to the VMware DRS load balance metric with standard deviation, as presented in Ref. [20].

6. Makespan is the same as in the traditional definition, and therefore the capacity makespan of all PMs can be formulated as below:

$$capacity_{makespan} = max_i(L_i) \tag{5.7}$$

7. Load efficiency (skew of makespan) is defined as the minimal average load divided by the maximal average load on all machines:

$$skew(makespan) = \frac{min_i L_i}{max_i(L_i)} \tag{5.8}$$

where L_i is the load of PM$_i$. The Skew shows the load balance efficiency to some degree.

8. Imbalance Level (IBL) of CPU is defined as:

$$ILB_{cpu} = \frac{\sum\limits_{i=0}^{n} (CPU_i^u - PCPU_{avg})^2}{n} \tag{5.9}$$

where $PCPU_{avg}$ is the average utilization of all CPUs in a data center. The IBL of memory IBL_{Mem} and the IBL of storage $IBL_{Storage}$ can be obtained in the same way.

So the total IBL of a data center is:

$$IBL_{total} = IBL_{CPU} + IBL_{Mem} + IBL_{Storage} \qquad (5.10)$$

Based on the above definitions and equations, we have developed another metric: capacity skew of the load balancing algorithm for the new situation as follows:

9. Skew of capacity makespan is defined as the minimal capacity makespan over maximal capacity makespan on all machines (referring to Eq. (5.1)):

$$Skew(capacity - makespan) = \frac{\min \sum_{j \in A(i)} c_j t_j}{\max \sum_{j \in A(i)} c_j t_j} \qquad (5.11)$$

A higher value shows a better load balance to some degree.

From these equations, we notice that life cycle and capacity sharing are two major differences from traditional metrics such as makespan and skew. Traditionally, LS [18] is widely used for load balancing online multiprocessor scheduling. By considering both fixed process intervals and capacity sharing properties in a Cloud data center, we propose a new online algorithm as follows.

5.4   OLRSA algorithm

5.4.1   Algorithm description

Figure 5.2 shows the core process of the OLRSA algorithm. For each request, it first finds the PM with the lowest average capacity makespan. The PM with the next-lowest average capacity makespan would be turned on only if the resources on the first PM have already been utilized, so all requests can be allocated without rejection.

Theorem 5.2   The computational complexity of OLRSA algorithm is O(nlogm) using priority queue data structure where n is the number of VM requests and m is the total number of PMs used.

Proof   The priority queue is designed such that each element (PM) has a priority value (average capacity makespan), and such that each time the algorithm needs to select an element from it, the algorithm takes the one with the highest priority (the smaller the value of the average capacity makespan, the higher priority it is). Sorting a set of n numbers in a priority queue takes O(n) time, and a priority queue performs the insertion and the extraction of minima in O(logn) steps (detailed proof of the priority queue is shown in [16]). Therefore, by using a priority queue or related data structure, the algorithm can find the PM with the lowest average capacity makespan in O(logm) time. Altogether, for *n* requests, the OLRSA algorithm has time complexity O(nlogm).

Input: VM requests (each indicated by their required VM type ID, start time, finish time, and requested capacity), the interval of start time and finish time of request i is denoted as I_i
Output: Assign a PM ID to each request and allocate an interval for each request.

1. $d=0$;
2.   **for** j = from 1 to n **do**
3.   for all PMs, finding a PM with lowest average capacity_makespan, noted as PM_lowest (as in equation (6))
4.   **if**   the request j still can share capacity of PM_lowest **do**
5.   allocate I_j to the PM
6.   **else**
7.   finding a PM with next lowest average capacity_makespan;
8. $d=d+1$;
9.   allocate I_j to PM d
10.   **endif**
11. **endfor**

Figure 5.2 Pseudo code of OLRSA algorithm.

Theorem 5.3 The competitive ratio of OLRSA algorithm is $(2 - 1/m)$ where m is the total number of machines.

Proof Considering m machines and n requests:

$$n > m, m > 2 \tag{5.12}$$

CM_i is the capacity makespan of VM_i, c_i is the resource capacity VM_i needed, which could be CPU, memory, storage, or integrated resources:

$$CM_i = c_i * (T_i^{end} - T_i^{start}) \tag{5.13}$$

Let OPT and OLRSA represent the scheduling results of an optimal solution and an OLRSA solution respectively. Let L_i denote the load of machine M_i and let M^* be the most heavily loaded machine in the schedule by OLRSA. Let j_k be the last job assigned to M^*. We can easily deduce the following two equations:

$$OPT \geq \frac{1}{m} \sum_{i=1}^{n} CM_i \tag{5.14}$$

$$OPT \geq \max_i CM_i \tag{5.15}$$

All PMs must be loaded at least (OLRSA-CM_k) at the time of allocating CM_k because OLRSA already allocates a VM to a PM with the lowest capacity makespan. Since OLRSA $-$ CM_k represents the PM with the lowest capacity makespan, we have:

$$\sum_{u=1}^{i=n} CM_i - CM_k \geq m(\text{OLRSA} - CM_k) \tag{5.16}$$

The above equations can be transformed to:

$$\text{OLRSA} \quad \leq \frac{\sum\limits_{i=1}^{i=n} CM_i - CM_k}{m} + CM_k$$

$$= \frac{\sum\limits_{i=1}^{i=n} CM_i}{m} + \left(1 - \frac{1}{m}\right) CM_k$$

$$\leq \text{OPT} + \left(1 - \frac{1}{m}\right) \text{OPT}$$

$$= \left(2 - \frac{1}{m}\right) \text{OPT}$$

Observation The upper bound for the OLRSA algorithm is tight.

Remarks We have shown a general example to demonstrate that the upper bound holds. Consider m machines are providing resources and each machine can be allocated VMs with the total capacity g (total capacity of a machine is g). Suppose there are $(m-1) \times g + 1$ requests in total, the first $(m-1) \times g$ requests all start at time slot 0 and finish at time slot 1, while the last request starts at 0 and ends at g. In this case, for the OPT algorithm, the capacity makespan is:

$$\text{OPT} = \frac{(m-1)g + g}{m} = g$$

As for OLRSA, the first $(m-1)g$ would be allocated to m machines equally by the allocation rule (let $(m-1)g$ divide m), and the last one would also be allocated to the PM with the lowest capacity makespan value (in this case any PM would work). So

$$\text{OLRSA} = \frac{(m-1)g}{m} + g = g\left(1 - \frac{1}{m}\right) + g$$

Then, the competitive ratio of OLRSA over OPT is:

$$\frac{\text{OLRSA}}{\text{OPT}} = 1 - \frac{1}{m} + 1 = 2 - 1/m$$

5.4.2 Mythology and simulation settings

In this section, we will show simulation results for the OLRSA algorithm compared with other existing algorithms. A Java discrete simulator is developed for this purpose. All simulations are conducted on a Pentium dual-core computer with 3.2 GHz CPU and 2 GB memory. We compare the simulation results of our proposed algorithm with four existing algorithms:

1. **Random Algorithm (Random):** a general scheduling algorithm that randomly allocates the VM requests to the PM that can provide the resource required.
2. **Round Robin (Round):** a traditional load balance scheduling algorithm allocates the VM requests one-by-one to each PM in turn that can provide the resources required.
3. **ZHJZ algorithm:** as defined in Ref. [19] selects a referenced PM, calculates the value, and chooses the PMs with the lowest B value (as defined in Eq. (5.3)) and available resources to which to allocate VMs.
4. **LS algorithm [16]:** One of the best-known online traditional load-balancing algorithms, it selects the available PM with the lowest current load to which to allocate the VM.

For a simulation to be realistic, we adopt the log data from Lawrence Livermore National Lab (LLNL) [21]. That log contains months of records collected by a large Linux cluster. Each line of data in that log file includes 18 elements, while in our simulation; we only need the requestID, start time, duration, and relevant processor. To enable that data to fit within our simulation, some conversions are needed. For example, we can convert the units from seconds from the LLNL log file into minutes, because we set a minute as a time slot length as mentioned in the previous section. Another conversion changes the processor number needed in the LLNL log file to eight types of VM requests. To simplify the simulation, three types of heterogeneous PMs and eight types of VMs are considered (they can be dynamically configured and extended). We simulate with enough PMs to satisfy all VM requests (e.g., with 200 VMs and durations larger than 30, the number of PMs is 18 type-1, 20 type-2, and 12 type-3, respectively). VM numbers vary from 200 to 800 (each type equaling approximately 1/8 of the total). The simulations for different algorithms use the same environment with the same VM requests. The only difference lies in the scheduling process of each algorithm: OLRSA PMs are turned on one by one according to the VM requests, while all other PMs are turned on at the beginning.For the sake of easy comparison, if the actual total number of PMs turned on are not the same for different algorithms, all metrics—such as capacity makespan, skew, and imbalance value—are adjusted with a timing coefficient (the actual total number of PMs turned on divided by the maximum number of PMs used by all algorithms).

5.4.3 Simulation results and analysis for OLRSA

5.4.3.1 Divisible capacity configuration of VMs and PMs

Strongly divisible capacity of jobs and machines: the capacity of all jobs form a divisible sequence (i.e., the sequence of distinct capacities $c_1 \geq c_2 \geq \ldots \geq c_i \geq c_{i+1} \geq \ldots$) taken on by jobs (the number of jobs of each capacity is arbitrary) such that all $i > 1$, c_i is divisible by c_{i+1}, and capacity C is divisible by the largest item capacity c_i in L. See Ref. [17] for a detailed discussion.

In this paper, we also adopt the following divisible capacity configuration of VMs and PMs as shown in Tables 5.1 and 5.2. Note that one Compute Unit (CU) has the equivalent CPU capacity of a 1.0–1.2 GHz 2007 Opteron or 2007 Xeon processor [22].

To simplify the corresponding relationship, we use VM types 1, 2, and 3 for PM Type 1; VM types 4, 5, and 6 for PM Type 2; and VM types 7 and 8 for PM Type 3.

Figures 5.3–5.7 show the IBLs, makespans and skews of makespans, and capacity makespans and skews of capacity makespans, respectively when keeping the total number of VM requests as 200 but varying the maximum duration of VMs. The results are an average value of five different simulations of the same inputs (data is from an LLNL log file). From these figures, we notice that the OLRSA algorithm shows the best performance in IBLs, makespans, capacity makespans, and skews of capacity makespans; everything except for skews of makespans when compared with the other four algorithms. Notice that the skew of the makespan is a traditional index for measuring load balance scheduling without considering capacity-sharing and fixed-interval constraints.

Table 5.1 **Eight types of VMs in Amazon EC2**

CPU units	Mem	Storage	VM type
1 unit	1.7 GB	160 GB	1-1(1)
4 units	7.5 GB	850 GB	1-2(2)
8 units	15 GB	1690 GB	1-3(3)
6.5 units	17.1 GB	420 GB	2-1(4)
13 units	34.2 GB	850 GB	2-2(5)
26 units	68.4 GB	1690 GB	2-3(6)
5 units	1.7 GB	350 GB	3-1(7)
20 units	7 GB	1690 GB	3-2(8)

Table 5.2 **Three types of recommended PMs**

PM pool type	CPU units	Mem	Storage
Type 1	16 units	30 GB	3380 GB
Type 2	52 units	136 GB	33S0 GB
Type 3	40 units	14 GB	3380 GB

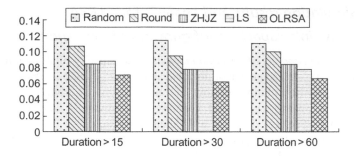

Figure 5.3 IBL comparisons when varying duration of VMs.

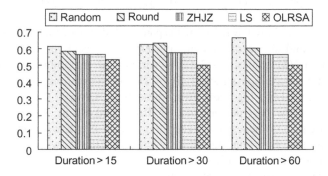

Figure 5.4 Makespan comparisons when varying duration of VMs.

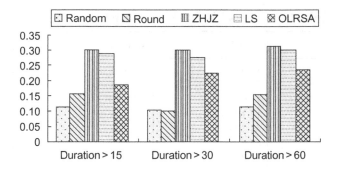

Figure 5.5 Skews of makespan comparisons when varying duration of VMs.

5.5 LIF algorithm

In this section, we introduce another OLRSA: the Lowest Integrated-load First (LIF) algorithm. The objective of the LIF algorithm is to globally minimize the current total imbalance value of all servers in a Cloud data center (i.e., min $\sum_{i=1}^{N} \text{ILB}_i$). The LIF is a dynamic scheduler with past and current requirement

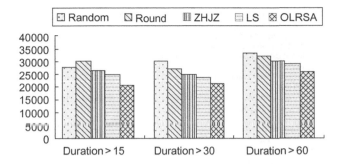

Figure 5.6 Capacity-makespan comparisons when varying duration of VMs.

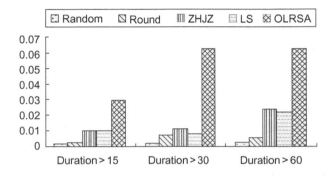

Figure 5.7 Skews of capacity-makespan comparisons when varying duration of VMs.

information, but without future incoming request information. In long run, it will cause the lowest total imbalance value of all servers when the number of requests is large compared to the total number of physical servers. Results in the simulation section validate this observation.

5.5.1 Description of LIF algorithms

Figure 5.8 shows the detailed steps of an LIF algorithm. Inputs into the algorithm include current the VM request r, the status of current active tasks, and PMs. For dynamic scheduling, the output is a placement scheme for request r. Basically, the algorithm dynamically finds the data center's lowest total imbalance value when placing a new VM request by comparing different imbalance values that would be created if the request is allocated to different PMs. In actuality, the algorithm finds the PM with the lowest integrated-load (referred to in Eq. (5.5)).

Theorem 5.1 For all of the PMs in a Cloud data center, allocating the current VM request to the PM with the lowest integrated load (the lowest average multidimensional utilization value, as defined in Eq. (5.5)) leads to the lowest total imbalance value of all servers in a Cloud data center.

```
Algorithm : Lowest-Integrated-Load-First( )
Input: placement request r = (id, vC, vM, vN);
          status of current active tasks and PMs
Output: placement scheme for r and IBL_tot.
1) initialization: LowestAvg = large number;
2) For i=1:N Do
3)    If request r can be placed on PM_i
4)    Then
5)      compute Avg_i utilization value of PM_i it using equations (4)-(6);
6)        If Avg_i <LowestAvg
7)        Then
8)    LowestAvg=Avg_i;
9)            Else
10)       Endif
11)     Else //find next PM
12)  Endfor
13)  IF LowestAvg== large number L // cannot allocate
14)     Then put r into waiting queue or reject
15)  Else
16)         allocatedPMID=i;
17)         place r on PM with allocatedPMID and compute IBL_tot
```

Figure 5.8 LIF algorithm.

Proof Let's set the current VM_i with CPU, memory, and network bandwidth requests (vC, vM, vN) for N PMs. If the VM can be satisfied, then the average utilization of CPU, memory, and network bandwidth of the data center will be $(CPU_u^A, Mem_u^A, NET_u^A)$, respectively. Using Eq. (5.10), the total imbalance values of all PMs in a Cloud data center is the sum of individual imbalance values of each PM. After allocating for the current VM_i, data center—wide average utilization of CPU, memory, and network bandwidth is fixed for all PMs. Only one PM—which hosts the current VM request—will change its Avg_i as defined in Eq. (5.6). For the sake of generalization, let us state that there are N PMs, each with average multidimensional utilization Avg_i as defined in Eq. (5.6). Therefore, there are N possible allocations if all PMs can host VM_i, with corresponding total imbalance values as IBL_{tot}^j. Let us set average utilization of CPU, memory, and network bandwidth as (U_C, U_M, U_N) after allocating VM_i. Supposing that PM_i and PM_k are the two PMs on which the scheduler is trying to allocate VM_i, ILB_i, and ILB_k are the imbalance values of physical server i before allocating VM_i and after allocating VM_i, respectively. ILB_k and ILB_k are imbalance values of physical server k before allocating VM_i and after allocating VM_i, respectively. Let the total imbalance value IBL_i denote the total imbalance values of all servers if VM_i is allocated on PM_i and, similarly, IBL_{tot}^k denote the total imbalance values of all servers if VM_i is allocated on PM_k, then:

$$IBL_{tot}^i = IBL_i + ILB_2 + \cdots + ILB_i + \cdots + ILB_k + \cdots + ILB_N \tag{5.17}$$

and

$$IBL_{tot}^k = ILN_1 + ILB_2 + \cdots + ILB_i + \cdots + ILB_k + \cdots + ILB_N \tag{5.18}$$

Comparing the above two equations, only $E_1 = (\text{ILB}_i + \text{ILB}_k)$ and $E_2 = (\text{ILB}_j + \text{ILB}_k)$ will affect the total imbalance values because the other parts are the same for both equations. This assumes that all PMs are homogeneous. If PMs are heterogeneous, then classification of different PMs is necessary to convert the heterogeneous problem into a homogeneous problem. For example, if different types of PMs can be put into different clusters (data centers), then all PMs in each cluster (data center) are treated as homogeneous. Next, we compare E_1 and E_2. Set $\alpha = \text{Avg}_i$; $\hat{\alpha} = \text{Avg}_i = \alpha + \delta$, where δ is the average utilization increase of PM$_j$ if VM$_i$ is allocated to it; and $\beta = \text{Avg}_k$; $\hat{\beta} = \beta + \delta$, where δ is the average utilization increase of PM$_k$ if VM$_i$ is allocated to it. Set U_C, U_M, U_N as average CPU, memory, and network (or storage) utilization in a Cloud data center as defined in Eq. (5.5). We prove that $E_1 << E_2$ is equivalent to the following:

$$\equiv (\hat{\alpha}-U_C)^2 + (\hat{\alpha}-U_M)^2 + (\hat{\alpha}-U_N)^2 + (\beta-U_C)^2 + (\beta-U_M)^2 + (\beta-U_N)^2 <$$
$$(\alpha-U_C)^2 + (\alpha-U_M)^2 + (\alpha-U_N)^2 + (\hat{\beta}-U_C)^2 + (\hat{\beta}-U_M)^2 + (\hat{\beta}-U_N)^2$$
$$\equiv 3\hat{\alpha}^2 - 2\hat{\alpha}(U_C + U_M + U_N) + 3\beta^2 - 2\beta(U_C + U_M + U_N) < 3\alpha^2 - 2\alpha(U_C + U_M + U_N)$$
$$+ 3\hat{\beta}^2 - 2\hat{\beta}(U_C + U_M + U_N)$$
$$\equiv 3\hat{\alpha}^2 - 3\alpha^2 - 2(\hat{\alpha} - \alpha)(U_C + U_M + U_N) + 3\beta^2 - 3\hat{\beta}^2 + 2(\hat{\beta} - \beta)(U_C + U_M + U_N) < 0$$
$$\equiv 3(\hat{\alpha} - \alpha)(\hat{\alpha} + \alpha) + 2(\hat{\beta} - \beta - \hat{\alpha} + \alpha)(U_C + U_M + U_N) + 3(\beta - \hat{\beta})(\hat{\beta} + \beta) < 0$$
$$\equiv \delta\left(2\alpha + \frac{\delta}{3}\right) + \left(2\frac{\delta}{3} - 2\frac{\delta}{3}\right)(U_C + U_M + U_N) - \delta\left(2\beta + \frac{\delta}{3}\right) < 0$$
$$\equiv 2\alpha\delta - 2\beta\delta < 0$$
$$\equiv \alpha < \beta$$
$$\equiv \text{Avg}_i < \text{Avg}_k$$

This means that allocating current VM requests to the PM with the lowest integrated load creates the lowest total imbalance value of all of the servers, which completes the proof.

5.5.2 Simulation results

In this section, we provide simulation results for the comparison of the five different scheduling algorithms introduced in this paper. For convenience, a short name is given for each algorithm as follows:

1. **ZHCJ algorithm:** as introduced in [6], the algorithm always chooses PMs with the lowest V value (as defined in Eq. (5.2)) and available resources to which to allocate VMs.
2. **ZHJZ algorithm:** selects a referring PM [19], calculates the value, and chooses the PM with the lowest B value (as defined in Eq. (5.3)) and available resources to which to allocate VMs.
3. **LIF algorithm:** as described in Figure 5.8, based on-demand characteristics (e.g., CPU, memory, network bandwidth requirements, etc.), always selects the PMs with the lowest integrated load (or average multidimensional utilization) and available resources to which to allocate VMs.
4. **Rand algorithm:** randomly assigns requests (VMs) to PMs that have available resources.

5. Round-Robin (Round) algorithm: one of the simplest scheduling algorithms, which assigns tasks to each PM in equal portions and in circular order, handling all tasks without priority (also known as the cyclic executive). In the following, we only consider random configuration cases, which are more general. For the simulations, three types of heterogeneous PM pools (clusters) are considered; each PM pool consists of some number of PMs (which can be dynamically configured and extended). For the simulation of a large number of VM requests, both CPU and memory are configured with large sizes that can be set dynamically:

  type 1: CPU = 12 GHz, memory = 24 G, bandwidth = 200 M
  type 2: CPU = 24 GHz, memory = 36 G, bandwidth = 300 M
  type 3: CPU = 32 GHz, memory = 48 G, bandwidth = 400 M.

Similarly, the following eight Amazon EC2 examples have high CPU values, high-memory, and standard configurations (but not exactly the same), and eight types of VMs with an equal probability of requests that are generated randomly as follows (can be dynamically configured):

  type 1: CPU = 2.0 GHz, memory = 1.0 G, bandwidth = 2.0 M
  type 2: CPU = 10.0 GHz, memory = 4.0 G, bandwidth = 8.0 M
  type 3: CPU = 16.0 GHz, memory = 12.0 G, bandwidth = 15.0 M
  type 4: CPU = 3.0 GHz, memory = 9.0 G, bandwidth = 5.0 M
  type 5: CPU = 6.0 GHz, memory = 20.0 G, bandwidth = 15.0 M
  type 6: CPU = 13.0 GHz, memory = 36.0 G, bandwidth = 25.0 M
  type 7: CPU = 1.0 GHz, memory = 1.0 G, bandwidth = 25.0 M
  type 8: CPU = 2.0 GHz, memory = 4.0 G, bandwidth = 50.0 M.

For all of the simulations, the number of PMs ranges from 100 to 600 (with an equal probability); the number of requests of VMs is randomly generated and varies from 1000 to 6000; and a Pentium PC with 2 GHz CPU, 2 G memory is used for all of the simulations. All simulations use the same set of randomly generated requests. The average imbalance value of a Cloud data center and all PMs are two major metrics we computed.

Figure 5.9 shows the average imbalance value (defined in Eq. (5.10)) of a Cloud data center. In this simulation, the five scheduling algorithms ZHJZ, ZHCJ, Rand, Round Robin, and LIF are compared when both the total number of PMs and the total number of VM requests are changing. It can be seen that the LIF algorithm has the lowest average imbalance value of a Cloud data center when both the total number of PMs and the total number of VM requests change (i.e., the total number of PMs change from 100 to 600 and the total number of VM requests change from 1000 to 6000 correspondingly). Note that the same eight types of VMs with an equal probability of requests are used for all of the simulations.

Figure 5.10 shows the average imbalance value of all physical servers (defined in Eq. (5.5)). Here, the simulation settings are the same as in Figure 5.9. The LIF algorithm has the lowest average imbalance value for all PMs.

Figure 5.11 shows the average imbalance value (defined in Eq. (5.10)) of a Cloud data center when the total number of PMs is fixed, but the number of VMs varies. Here the total number of PMs is fixed at 100, but the total number of VMs varies between 250, 500, 700, 1000, and 1500. It can be seen that the LIF algorithm has the lowest average imbalance value of a Cloud data center.

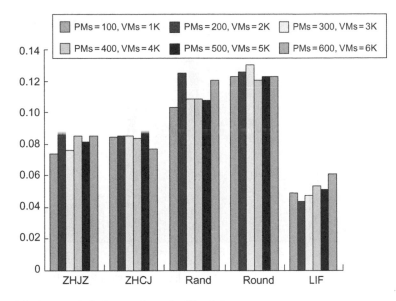

Figure 5.9 Average imbalance value of a Cloud data center.

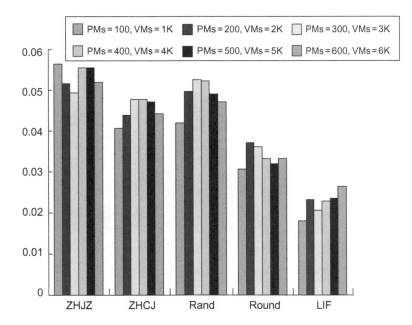

Figure 5.10 Average imbalance value of all physical servers.

Figure 5.12 shows the average imbalance value for all physical servers (as defined in Eq. (5.5)) when the total number of PMs is fixed but the number of VMs varies. Here the total number of PMs is fixed at 100, but the total number of VMs

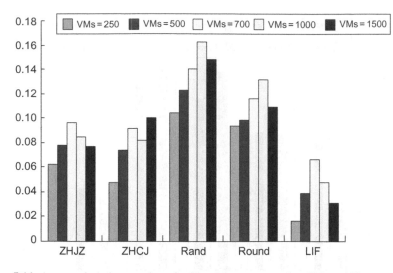

Figure 5.11 Average imbalance value of a Cloud data center when PMs = 100.

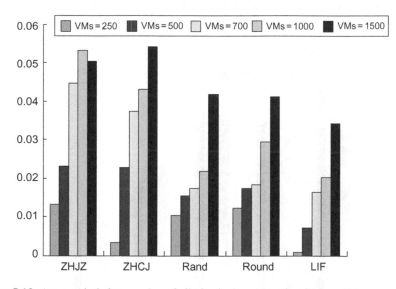

Figure 5.12 Average imbalance value of all physical servers when PMs = 100.

varies betweens 250, 500, 700, 1000, and 1500. The LIF algorithm has the lowest average imbalance value in this case.

Through extensive simulation, similar results are observed. Because of page limitations, other simulation results—such as those from varying the probability of each VM request, fixing the total number of PMs, and varying the number of VMs—are not provided here.

5.6   Discussion and conclusion

In this chapter, to reflect capacity sharing property and fixed-interval constraints in Cloud data centers, we propose an Online Resource Scheduling Algorithm (OLRSA) with new metrics, such as capacity makespan and skew of capacity makespan. Simulations have shown that OLRSA has better performance results than the few existing algorithms when it comes to IBL, capacity makespan, and skew of capacity makespan. A theoretical competitive ratio upper bound $\left(2 - \frac{1}{m}\right)$ is provided and the proof is also given where m is the number of PMs.

We also introduce a dynamic resource scheduling algorithm (LIF) for Cloud data centers by considering multidimensional resources. Simulation results show that the LIF algorithm works well when considering the total imbalance value of a Cloud data center and all servers, and the average imbalance value of a Cloud data center and each server.

References

[1] Andre L, et al. The datacenter as a computer: an introduction to the design of ware-house-scalemachines, Ebook, 2009.

[2] Armbrust M, et al. Above the Clouds: a Berkeley view of Cloud computing, Technical Report, 2009.

[3] Foster I, Zhao Y, Raicu I, Lu S. Cloud computing and grid computing 360-degree compared. In: IEEE international workshop on grid computing environments (GCE) 2008, Co-located with IEEE/ACM supercomputing, 2008.

[4] Buyya R, Ranjan R, Calheiros RN. Modeling and simulation of scalable cloud computing environments and the CloudSim toolkit: challenges and opportunities. In: Proceedings of the seventh high performance computing and simulation conference, HPCS 2009, Leipzig, Germany, June 21–24, 2009.

[5] Wickremasinghe B, et al. CloudAnalyst: a CloudSim-based tool for modelling and analysis of large scale cloud computing environments. In: Proceedings of the 24th IEEE international conference on advanced information networking and applications (AINA 2010), Perth, Australia, April 20–23, 2010.

[6] Wood T, et al. Black-box and gray-box strategies for virtual machine migration. In: Proceedings of symposium on networked systems design and implementation (NSDI), 2007.

[7] Zhang W. Research and implementation of elastic network service, PhD dissertation, National University of Defense Technology, China, 2000 (in Chinese).

[8] Singh A, Korupolu M, Mohapatra D. Server-storage virtualization: integration and load balancing in data centers, International conference for high performance computing, networking, storage and analysis, 2008.

[9] Arzuaga E, Kaeli DR. Quantifying load imbalance on virtualized enterprise servers. In: Proceedings of WOSP/SIPEW 10, San Jose, CA, January 28–30, 2010.

[10] Tian W. Adaptive dimensioning of cloud data centers. In: Proceeding of the eighth IEEE international conference on dependable, automatic and secure computing, DACS, 2009.

[11] Sun X, Xu P, Shuang K, et al. Multi-dimensional aware scheduling for co-optimizing utilization in data center. China Commun 2011;8(6):19−27.
[12] Tian W, Jing C, Hu J. Analysis of resource allocation and scheduling policies in Cloud datacenter. In: Proceedings of the IEEE third international conference on networks security wireless communications and trusted computing, March 2011.
[13] Li K, Xu G, Zhao G, et al. Cloud task scheduling based on load balancing ant colony optimization, 2011 sixth annual China grid conference, 2011, p. 3−9.
[14] Galloway JM, Smith KL, Vrbsky SS. Power aware load balancing for cloud computing. In: Proceedings of the world congress on engineering and computer science 2011, WCECS 2011, vol. I, October 19−21, 2011.
[15] Hu J, Gu J, Sun G, et al. A scheduling strategy on load balancing of virtual machine resources in cloud computing environment, 2010 third international symposium on parallel architectures, algorithms and programming (PAAP), December 18−20, 2010, p. 89−96.
[16] Kleinberg J, Tardos E. Algorithm design. Pearson Education Inc.; 2005.
[17] Coffman Jr. EG, Garey MR, Johnson DS. Bin-packing with divisible item sizes. J Complexity 1987;3:406−28.
[18] Graham RL. Bounds on multiprocessing timing anomalies. SIAM J Appl Math 1969; 17(2):416−29.
[19] Zheng H, Zhou L, Wu J. Design and implementation of load balancing in web server cluster system. J Nanjing Univ Aeronaut Astronaut 2006;38(3):.
[20] Gulati A, Shanmuganathan G, Holler A, Ahmad I. Cloud-scale resource management: challenges and techniques. VMware Tech J 2011.
[21] Hebrew University, Experimental Systems Lab, <www.cs.huji.ac.il/labs/parallel/workload>; 2007.
[22] Amazon, Amazon Elastic Compute Cloud, <http://aws.amazon.com/ec2/>; 2012.

Energy-efficient Allocation of Real-time Virtual Machines in Cloud Data Centers Using Interval-packing Techniques

Main Contents of this Chapter

- Background of energy efficiency in Cloud computing
- The green architecture of Cloud computing
- Energy-efficient scheduling
- Performance evaluation of energy-efficient scheduling

6.1 Introduction

Cloud computing is developing based on various recent advancements in virtualization, Grid computing, Web computing, utility computing, and related technologies. Cloud computing provides both platforms and applications on demand through the Internet or intranet [1]. Some examples of emerging Cloud computing platforms are Google App Engine [2], IBM blue Cloud [3], Amazon EC2 [4], and Microsoft Azure [5]. Cloud computing allows the sharing, allocation, and aggregation of software; and computational and storage network resources on demand. Some of the key benefits of Cloud computing include the hiding and abstraction of complexity, virtualized resources, and efficient use of distributed resources. Cloud computing is still considered to be in its infancy as there are many challenging issues to be resolved [1,6−8]. Youseff et al. [9] establish a detailed ontology of dissecting Cloud computing into five main layers from the top down: Cloud applications (SaaS), the Cloud software environment (PaaS), Cloud software infrastructure (IaaS), the software kernel, and hardware (HaaS), and illustrates their interrelations as well as their interdependency on preceding technologies. In this paper, we focus on Infrastructure as a Service (IaaS) in Cloud data centers.

There is extensive research on issues related to Cloud data centers. Armbrust et al. [1] summarize the key issues and solutions in Cloud computing. Foster et al. [8] compare Cloud computing to Grid computing. Tian [10] presents multi-dimensional algorithms for Cloud data centers by considering dynamic traffic models. IaaS is one of the key services in Cloud computing. It is very important to develop an on-demand resource management system for IaaS in Cloud environments.

As for Cloud architecture, Liu et al. [11] present GreenCloud architecture, which aims to reduce data center power consumption while guaranteeing performance from a user's perspective. Using the recommendations developed in its open-source Cloud standards' incubator, DMTF [12] focuses on standardizing interactions among Cloud environments. Nurmi et al. [13] introduce the Eucalyptus open-source Cloud-computing system. Tian et al. [14] propose a dynamic and integrated load-balancing algorithm for resource scheduling in Cloud data centers.

Garg et al. [15] introduce a GreenCloud framework for improving the carbon efficiency of Clouds; Beloglazov et al. [6] propose a taxonomy and survey of energy-efficient data centers and Cloud computing. Jing et al. [16] provide a state-of-the-art research study for GreenCloud computing and point out three hot research areas. Srikantaiah et al. [17] study the interrelationships among energy consumption, resource utilization, and performance of consolidated workloads. Lee et al. [18] introduce two online heuristic algorithms for energy-efficient utilization of resources in Cloud computing systems by consolidating active tasks. Beloglazov et al. [19] consider offline allocation of virtual machines (VMs) by modified best-fit bin-packing heuristics and also minimizing the total number of migrations. Liu et al. [20] study performance and energy modeling for live migration of VMs and evaluate models using five representative workloads on a Xen virtualized environment. Guazzone et al. [21] consider a two-level control model to automatically allocate resources to reduce energy consumption of web-service applications. Kim et al. [22] model a real-time service as a real-time VM request, and use dynamic voltage frequency scaling schemes for provisioning VMs in Cloud data centers. Other than dynamic voltage frequency scaling schemes, there is still a lack of research on real-time VM scheduling considering fixed processing intervals.

Resource scheduling plays an important role in Cloud data centers. One of the challenging scheduling problems in Cloud data centers is the consideration of the allocation and migration of VMs with full life cycle constraints, which is often neglected [23].

In this chapter, we introduce a framework for energy-efficient scheduling of real-time VMs considering fixed processing intervals in IaaS to address the above mentioned key issues. The main aims of this chapter are as follows:

- Providing a uniform view to facilitate the management of different heterogeneous types of physical machines (PMs) and VMs with various combinations. Then both managers and users can more easily control and monitor their increasing collections of VMs through this single access point.
- Considering the allocation of VMs with their fixed processing intervals (full life cycles). This is often neglected by most research work. Taking into account both critical capacity and real-time constraints increases the difficulty of the problem.
- Designing scheduling schemes for offline and online contexts by taking advantage of classical interval scheduling and bin-packing techniques. Our models are different from traditional interval scheduling problems (ISPs) by considering multiple intervals sharing the total capacity of a PM during some periods if the capacity constraint is satisfied. Our models are different from traditional bin-packing problems (BPPs) by considering the life cycle of the VMs.

- For the offline context in which the scheduler knows all requests in advance, optimal and approximate algorithms that minimize energy consumption are derived with theoretic proofs.
- Observing that the total number of PMs and their power-on time affect total power consumption, approximate algorithms with delay and minimum migration are proposed for the online context when the scheduler knows only the current requests.
- Considering the energy impact under different configurations and energy models, there are some existing results that are based on a single and simple set of VM and PM configurations. We show through simulations that energy consumption can be different under different configurations and models. Especially important is the proposed divisible capacity configuration of VMs and PMs to simplify the scheduling problem and reduce energy consumption.

The remaining content of this chapter is structured as follows: Section 6.2 presents the proposed GreenCloud architecture and main components for resource scheduling in Cloud data centers. Section 6.3 formulates the problem and introduces proposed scheduling algorithms. Section 6.4 shows the performance evaluation of different algorithms under different configurations. Section 6.5 presents related work in energy-efficient scheduling. Section 6.6 concludes.

6.2 GreenCloud architecture

The layered architecture for GreenCloud is proposed in Figure 6.1. There is a web portal at the top layer for the user to select resources and send requests: basically, it's a uniform view of the few types of VMs that are preconfigured for users to choose. Once user requests are initiated, they go to the next level—CloudSched—which is

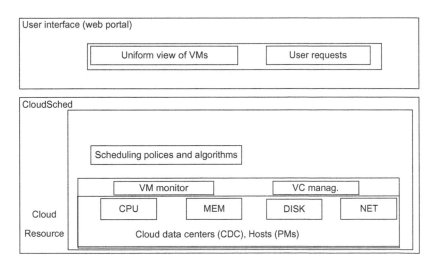

Figure 6.1 Proposed GreenCloud architecture.

responsible for choosing appropriate data centers and PMs based on user requests. This layer can manage a large number of Cloud data centers, consisting of thousands of PMs. At this layer, different scheduling algorithms can be applied in different data centers based on customer characteristics. At the lowest layer, there are Cloud resources that include PMs and VMs, both consisting of a certain amount of CPU, memory, storage, and bandwidth. At the Cloud resource layer, virtual management is mainly responsible for keeping track of all VMs in the system, including their status, required capacities, hosts, arrival times, and departure times.

6.2.1   Cloud data center resources

In this chapter, only computing resources are considered. A data center is composed of a set of hosts (PMs), which are responsible for managing VMs during their life cycles. A host is a component that represents a physical computing node in a Cloud. It is assigned a preconfigured processing capability (e.g., that expressed in Million Instructions Per Second or GHz), memory, storage, and a scheduling policy for allocating VMs. A number of hosts can also be interconnected to form a cluster or a data center.

6.2.2   A uniform view for different types of VMs

There can be too many different types of PMs, VMs, and their combinations altogether. Cloud providers will face a huge number of problems if a uniform view is not provided. Taking the widely used example of Amazon EC2, we show that a uniform view of different types of VMs is possible. Table 6.1 shows the eight types of VMs as found in Amazon EC2 online information. Amazon EC2 does not provide information on its hardware configuration. However, we can still form three types of different PMs based on compute units. In a real Cloud data center, for example,

Table 6.1 8 types of VMs in Amazon EC2

Memory (GB)	Compute units	Storage (GB)	API name	VM type
1.875	1 (1 cores × 1 units)	211.25	m1.small	1-1(1)
7.5	4 (2 cores × 2 units)	845	m1.large	1-2(2)
15.0	8 (4 cores × 2 units)	1690	m1.xlarge	1-3(3)
17.1	6.5 (2 cores × 3.25 units)	420	m2.xlarge	2-1(4)
34.2	13 (4 cores × 3.25 units)	845	m2.2xlarge	2-2(5)
68.4	26 (8 cores × 3.25 units)	1690	m2.4xlarge	2-3(6)
1.7	5 (2 cores × 2.5 units)	422.5	c1.medium	3-1(7)
7.0	20 (8 cores × 2.5 units)	1690	c1.xlarge	3-2(8)

Table 6.2 **Divisible configuration of three types of PMs (an example)**

PM type	CPU (compute units)	Memory (GB)	Storage (GB)
Type1	16	30.0	3380
Type2	52	136.8	3380
Type3	40	14.0	3380

Table 6.3 **Random configuration of three types of PMs (an example)**

PM type	CPU (compute units)	Memory (GB)	Storage (GB)
Type1	13	37.0	3000
Type2	53	137.8	4000
Type3	47	17.0	2000

in a PM with 2×68.4 GB memory, 16 cores $\times 3.25$ units, and 2×1690 GB storage can be provided. In this or a similar way, it is possible to form a uniform view of different types of VMs. This kind of classification provides a uniform view of virtualized resources for heterogeneous virtualization platforms (e.g., Xen, KVM, VMWare) and brings great benefits to VM management and allocation. Customers only need to select suitable types of VMs based on their requirements. Tables 6.2 and 6.3 are possible divisible and random capacity configurations of PMs, respectively, comparing with VM capacity in Table 6.1. We will define "divisible" and "random" capacity of VMs and PMs formally in Section 6.3.

6.2.3   Real-time VM request model

The Cloud computing environment is a suitable solution for real-time VM service because it leverages virtualization [22]. When users request execution of their real-time VMs in a Cloud data center, appropriate VMs are allocated.

Example 1 A real-time VM request can be represented in an interval vector: vmRequestID(VM typeID, start time, finish time, requested capacity). In Figure 6.2, vm1(1, 0, 6, 0.25) shows that for VM request ID vm1, the VM requested is of Type1 (corresponding to integer 1) with a start time of 0 and a finish time of 6 (i.e., finished at the 6th slot after start time of 0), and 25% of the total capacity of Type1 PM. Other requests can be represented in similar ways. Figure 6.2 shows the life cycles of VM allocation in a slotted-time window format using two PMs, where PM#1 hosts vm1, vm2, and vm3 while PM#2 hosts vm4, vm5, and vm6. Notice that the total capacity restriction has to be met in each interval.

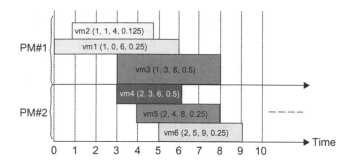

Figure 6.2 VM allocations using two PMs.

Figure 6.3 Time in slotted format.

6.3 Energy-efficient real-time scheduling

6.3.1 Problem description

We model the problem of real-time scheduling of VMs as a modified ISP. More explanation and analysis about fixed ISPs can be found in Ref. [24] and references therein. We present a formulation of the modified interval scheduling problem and evaluate its results compared to well-known existing algorithms.

A set of requests $\{1, 2,..., n\}$ where the ith request corresponds to an interval of time starting at s_i and finishing at f_i, associated with a capacity requirement c_i. For energy-efficient scheduling, the goal is to meet all requirements with the minimum number of running PMs and total running times based on the following assumptions:

1. All data are deterministic and—unless otherwise specified—the time is formatted in slotted windows. As shown in Figure 6.3, we partition the total time period $[0,T]$ into slots with equal length (s_0), with the total number of slots $k = T/s_0$ (in integer form). The start time s_i and finish time f_i are integer numbers of one slot. Then the interval of a request can be represented in slot format with (start time, finish time). For example, if $s_0 = 5$ min, an interval $[16,19]$ means that it has start time and finish time at the 3rd slot and 10th slot, respectively. The actual duration of this request is $(10 - 3) \times 5 = 35$ min.
2. All tasks are independent. There are no precedence constraints other than those implied by the start and finish times.
3. The required capacity of each request is a positive real number between $(0,1]$. Notice that the capacity of a single PM is normalized to be 1. When considering multiple resources—such as CPU, memory, or storage, for example—it can become multidimensional.
4. Assume that—when processed—each VM request is assigned to a single PM. Thus, interrupting a request and resuming it on another machine is not allowed, unless explicitly stated otherwise (such as when using migration).
5. Each PM is always available (i.e., each machine is continuously available in $[0, \infty)$).
6. Assume each VM request consumes the maximum required capacity (the worst case scenario) when allocated. For example, if the total capacity of a PM is normalized to be

1—all capacity of (CPU, memory, storage) = [1,1,1], when a VM request VM_i = (CPU, memory, storage) = [0.25,0.25,0.25] during interval [0,5]—then the scheduler allocates 0.25 of the total capacity of a PM to VM_i (i.e., the system presumes that the VM_i occupies 25% of the total capacity of a PM during interval [0,5]).

To help formally understand the problem, the following definitions are given:

[Definition 1. Traditional interval scheduling with fixed processing time]. A set of requests {1, 2,...,n} where the ith request corresponds to an interval of time starting at s_i and finishing at f_i. Each request needs a capacity of 1 (i.e., occupying the whole capacity of a machine during the fixed processing time).

[Definition 2. Interval scheduling with capacity sharing (ISWCS)]. The only difference from traditional interval scheduling is that a resource (to be specific, a PM) can be shared by different requests if the total capacity of all requests allocated on the single resource at any time does not surpass the total capacity that the resource can provide.

[Definition 3. Sharing compatible intervals for ISWCS]. A subset of intervals with the total required capacity do not surpass the total capacity of a PM at any time, therefore they can share the capacity of the PM.

The energy consumption of all VMs and PMs are closely related to the power model, capacity configuration of VMs and PMs, and the power usage policies. These are introduced as follows.

6.3.1.1 The linear power consumption model of a server

Most of the power consumption in data centers is from computation processing, disk storage, networking, and cooling systems. In Ref. [25] authors propose a power consumption model for blade servers:

$$P = 14.45 + 0.236U_{cpu} + (4.47E - 8)U_{mem} + 0.0028U_{disk} + (3.1E - 8)U_{net} \quad (6.1)$$

where U_{cpu}, U_{mem}, U_{disk}, and U_{net} are utilization of CPU, memory, hard disk, and network interface, respectively. It can be seen that other factors such as memory, hard disk, and network interface have a very small impact on total power consumption. In Ref. [19], authors find that CPU utilization is typically proportional to the overall system load and propose a power model defined in Eq. (6.2):

$$P(u) = kP_{max} + (1 - k)P_{max}u \quad (6.2)$$

where P_{max} is the maximum power consumed when the server is fully utilized; k is the fraction of power consumed by the idle server (studies show that on average it is about 70%); and u is CPU utilization. This chapter focuses on CPU power consumption, which accounts for the main part of energy consumption compared to other resources, such as: memory, disk storage, and network devices. In this work, we use the power model defined in Eq. (6.2). Equation (6.2) is further reduced to Eq. (6.3):

$$P = P_{min} + (P_{max} - P_{min})u \quad (6.3)$$

where P_{min} is the power consumption of the given PM when its CPU utilization is zero (when the PM is idle without any VM running). In a real environment, the utilization of the CPU may change over time due to workload variability. Thus, CPU utilization is a function of time and is represented as $u(t)$. Therefore, the total energy consumption by a PM (E_i) can be defined as an integral of the power consumption function over a period of time as in Eq. (6.4):

$$E_i = \int_{t_0}^{t_1} P(u(t)) dt \tag{6.4}$$

If $u(t)$ is constant over time, for example, if average utilization is adopted, $u(t) = u$, then $E_i = P(u)(t_1 - t_0)$.

1. The total energy consumption of a Cloud data center is computed as Eq. (6.5):

$$E_{DC} = \sum_{i=1}^{n} E_i \tag{6.5}$$

   It is the sum of energy consumed by all PMs. Note that energy consumption of all VMs on PMs is included.
2. The total length of power-on time of all PMs during the testing period is

$$Total\_Time = \sum_{i=0}^{n} PM_i\_Poweron\_Time \tag{6.6}$$

where $PM_i\_$Power-on Time is total power-on time of the ith PM.

For comparison purposes, we will assume that all VMs consume 100% of their requested CPU capacities.

Suppose current CPU utilization of a PM is u, and becomes u' after allocating a VM, then the energy increase caused by the VM is denoted as E_{vm}, and can be computed as in Eq. (6.7), where Δu is the CPU utilization increase after allocating a VM:

$$\begin{aligned} E_{vm} &= P \times (t_1 - t_0) - P' \times (t_1 - t_0) \\ &= (P' - P) \times (t_1 - t_0) \\ &= (P_{min} + (P_{max} - P_{min})u' - (P_{min} - (P_{max} - P_{min})u)) \\ &(P_{max} - P_{min}) \times (u' - u) \times (t_1 - t_0) \\ &(P_{max} - P_{min}) \times \Delta u \times (t_1 - t_0) \end{aligned} \tag{6.7}$$

Formally, our problem of real-time scheduling VMs to minimize total energy consumption (Min $\Sigma_i E_i$) becomes a multidimensional combinatorial optimization problem with constraint satisfaction (satisfying capacity and time constraints), which makes it an NP-complete problem [26,27].

Theorem 1 *The decision version of a real-time VM scheduling problem in a heterogeneous case is NP-complete.*

Remark In the case of a heterogeneous configuration, different types of PMs and VMs are considered. It is proven in Ref. [23] that the decision version (determining whether a feasible scheduling exists) of this problem is NP-complete.

To reduce the complexity, we consider the heterogeneous case but mapping different types of VMs to corresponding types of PMs (i.e., we simplify the heterogeneous case to a homogeneous case as given in Tables 6.1−6.3). In the following, all discussion and results are based on a homogeneous case.

6.3.1.2　Capacity configuration of VMs and PMs

Observing that different capacity configurations of VMs and PMs affect the problem's complexity and the total energy consumption, in the following, we consider two different capacity configurations.

6.3.1.2.1　Random capacity configuration of VMs and PMs
In this case—called the random capacity case—the capacities (CPU, memory, storage, and other factors) of VMs and PMs are randomly set. If we need to consider CPU, memory, storage, life cycles, and other factors of VMs and PMs, this problem can be transformed into a dynamic multidimensional BPP or interval-packing problem, which is known to be an NP-complete problem. See for example Refs. [5,26,27].

Lemma 1 In a random capacity case, there is no optimal solution for minimizing the total number of power-on PMs in offline scheduling—as shown in the literature.

Remark In this case, our real-time VM scheduling problem can be transformed into a classic multidimensional (interval) BPP by considering CPU, memory, storage, life cycle, and other factors. By reducing a well-known NP-complete problem —the multidimensional BPP—to our problem, it is easy to prove that the real-time VM scheduling problem is an NP-complete problem [5,26,27]. No optimal solution can be obtained in polynomial time, but some approximate solutions can be reached to minimize the total number of power-on PMs.

6.3.1.2.2　Divisible capacity configuration of VMs and PMs
In this case, (CPU, memory, storage) capacities are treated as a whole, as given in Tables 6.1 and 6.2. For example, the total capacity (CPU, memory, storage) of VM Types 1-1, 1-2, and 1-3 is 1/16, 1/4, and 1/2 of the total capacity (CPU, memory, storage) of PM Type1, respectively. Similarly, the total capacity of VM Type 2-1 and 2-2 is 1/8 and 1/4 of the total capacity of PM Type2, respectively. The total capacity of VM Type 3-1 and 3-2 is 1/8 and 1/2 of the total capacity of PM Type3, respectively. This is called the strongly divisible capacity case.

[Definition 4 Strongly divisible capacity of VMs and PMs]. The capacity of VMs form a divisible sequence, that is, the sequence of distinct capacities $s_1 > s_2 > \ldots > s_i > s_{i+1} > \ldots$ taken on by VMs (the number of VMs of each capacity is arbitrary) is such that for all $i > 1$, s_{i+1} exactly divides s_i. Let's say that a list L of items has a divisible item capacity if the capacities of the items in L form a divisible sequence. Also, if L is a list of items and C is a total capacity of a PM, we say that the pair (L, C) is weakly divisible if L has divisible item capacities and strongly divisible if, in addition, the largest item capacity s_1 in L exactly divides the capacity C [5].

Lemma 2 In a strongly divisible capacity case, there is an optimal solution for minimizing total number of power-on PMs in offline scheduling.

Proof In the strongly divisible capacity case, as given in Tables 6.1 and 6.2, the total capacity of a VM is (1/16 or 1/8 or 1/4 or 1/2) of the total capacity of a PM and the capacities of all VMs of the same type form a strongly divisible sequence. Our real-time VM scheduling problem therefore can be transformed into a classic one-dimensional interval-packing problem or BPP; the First-Fit Decreasing (FFD) or Best-Fit Decreasing (BFD) algorithm produces the optimal result [5] for offline scheduling. Also, in this case, the problem can be transformed into an ISP, which proves that the minimum number of PMs to host all requests exists [27].

Lemma 3 In the strongly divisible capacity case, the asymptotic worst case approximation ratio (compared to the offline optimal solution) of minimizing the total number of power-on PMs in online scheduling is 2.384.

Remark The proof of *Lemma 3* can be obtained from proofs given in Coffman et al. [28].

In the strongly divisible capacity case, the multidimensional problem (considering CPU, memory, storage, and other factors) is reduced to a one-dimensional BPP or interval-packing problem; therefore many existing results can be applied. The following discussion and simulation are based on this.

6.3.1.3   The power usage policies

6.3.1.3.1   Strategy one: idle servers turned off

To reduce energy consumption, assume a PM is turned off when it is idle during a testing period. It may happen that each PM can be turned on or off many times during the testing period.

Example 2 Given a testing period (0,1000), a PM is turned on during three intervals (2, 100), (209, 235), (789, 1000), respectively, with average utilization 0.5 during all intervals, $P_{max} = 300$ W, $P_{min} = 200$ W, then its total length of power-on time is $100 - 2 + 235 - 209 + 1000 - 789 = 335$ slots. Assuming each slot is

5 min, then the total energy consumption is $(200 + (300 - 200) \times 0.5) \times 335 \times 5/60/1000 = 6.979$ kW h.

Lemma 4 Minimizing the total number of PMs does not necessarily mean that the total energy is minimized when turning off idle servers.

Proof From the linear power model of Eqs. (6.3)–(6.7), it can be seen that the total energy consumption of a PM depends on the average utilization and its power-on times, but not solely on the total number of PMs used. When VM requests are the same and therefore average utilization of all PMs are the same, the total power consumption also depends on the total power-on time of all PMs. Therefore, the objective of minimizing total energy consumption is to minimize both the total number of PMs used and their power-on time.

Remark It is an NP-complete problem to minimize the total busy time of all machines (PMs) [26,27]. No optimal scheduling is known yet in this case, so we propose an approximate algorithm, called the modified interval scheduling algorithm (MFFI).

6.3.1.3.2 Strategy two: idle servers not turned off
Considering server reliability and to avoid too many server transitions or traffic vibrations, in this case idle servers are not turned off but can be put into sleep mode to save energy.

In Example 2, assume servers in idle states consume power P_{min} and are never turned off. Then the total power-on time is 1000 slots, and average utilization is $335 \times 0.5/1000 = 0.1675$. The total energy consumption is $(200 + (300 - 200) \times 0.1675) \times 1000 \times 5/60/1000 = 18.06$ kW h.

From Example 2, it can be seen that the total energy consumption can also be affected by different strategies on how to deal with idle servers.

Lemma 5 The problem of minimizing the total energy consumption reduces to finding the minimum number of PMs, assuming idle servers are not turned off.

Proof (1). Assume that idle servers are turned on (but can be put into sleep mode) during the scheduling process. From Eqs. (6.3)–(6.7), the total energy consumption depends on average utilization and running times because P_{min} values are the same. (2). Set $E_i = (P_{min} + (P_{max} - P_{min})u)t = (\alpha + \beta u_i)t$, where u_i is the average utilization of $\underline{PM_i}$. Assuming there are m homogeneous PMs, then the total energy consumption is $E = \Sigma_i E_i = m\alpha t + \beta(\Sigma_i u_i)t$. (3). If two scheduling results use the same number of PMs, we know the total time t (the length of time from start-up to the present) is the same for all scheduling because $m\alpha t$ is the same. $\beta(\Sigma_i u_i)t$ is the same because there are the same number of VM requests resulting in the same utilization for all PMs. (4). If two scheduling processes use different numbers of PMs— say scheduling#1 uses m homogeneous PMs and scheduling#2 uses $m + 1$

```
Input: VM requests (indicated by their required VM type ID,
start time, finish time, and requested capacity), interval of
start time and finish time of request i is denoted as Iᵢ
Output: Assign a PM ID to each request and allocate an
interval for each request.
1.    d=0;
2.    for j = from 1 to n do
3.        foreach Iᵢ that precedes Iⱼ
4.            if they are not overlapped or overlapped but still
can share resources of an allocated PM do
5.                allocate Iᵢ to the PM
6.            else
7.                start a new PM;
8.                d=d+1;
9.                allocate Iᵢ to PM d
10.           endif
11.       endforeach
12.   endfor
```

Figure 6.4 Modified interval partitioning first-fit algorithm (MFF).

homogeneous PMs—then the only difference is $m\alpha t$, $(m+1)\alpha t$, obviously $m\alpha t$ $<(m+1)\alpha t$ when $\alpha t>0$ (which is true). This means that using more PMs will cause the total energy consumption to be larger (notice that this is not true if assumption is that idle servers are turned off). This completes the proof.

6.3.2   Four offline and online scheduling algorithms

We propose four offline and online scheduling algorithms as follows:

> **[Definition 5. Modified Interval Partitioning First-Fit Algorithm (MFF)].** The algorithm places the requests in arbitrary order. It attempts to place each request in the first PM (with the lowest index) that can accommodate it. If no nonempty PM is found, it starts a new PM and places the VM on it. Note that MFF is online with respect to the VM requests, in that it does not use any information about other requests that follow the current request.
> **[Definition 6. Modified Interval Partitioning First-Fit Increasing Algorithm (MFFI)].** For the ISWCS problem, the VM requests are preceded by sorting based on the increasing order of their start times before MFF is applied. MFFI is an offline scheduling algorithm.
>   Figures 6.4 and 6.5 show the pseudo code of MFF and MFFI algorithms, respectively, also called ONWID and OFWID in this chapter.

Lemma 6 The time complexity of the MFFI algorithm as shown in Figure 6.5 is O $(n \max(m, \log n))$, where n is the number of VM requests and m is the number of PMs.

Remark The proof of *Lemma 6* is straightforward following the pseudo code in Figure 6.5.

Lemma 7 The time complexity of the MFF algorithm as shown in Figure 6.4 is O (nm), where n is the number of VM requests and m is the number of PMs.

```
Input: VM requests indicated by their (required VM
type IDs, start times, ending times, requested
capacity), the interval of start time and ending time
of request i is denoted as I_i
Output: Assign PM IDs to all requests and allocated
intervals for all requests
1.  Sort intervals by start-times in increasing order,
    breaking ties arbitrarily
2.    Let I_1, I_2.... I_n denote the intervals in this order
3.    d=0;
4.  for j = from 1 to n do
5.    foreach I_i that precedes I_j in sorted order
6.    if they are not overlapped or overlapped but still
      can share resources of an          allocated PM do
7.        allocate I_j to the PM hosts I_i
8.      else
9.        start a new PM; d=d+1; allocate I_j to PM d
10.     end
11.    endeach
12.  endfor
```

Figure 6.5 Modified interval partitioning first-fit increasing (MFFI).

Remark The proof for *Lemma 7* is straightforward, so details are omitted.

[**Definition 7. Offline MFFI with delay (OFWD)**]. Observing that requests can conflict with respect to time and capacity restrictions, postponing starting times of some requests can reduce the total number of PMs. For the most part this algorithm is the same as MFFI (OFWID), but OFWD can delay the starting time of VM requests for some times (with a threshold) and then use MFFI.

[**Definition 8. Online MFF with delay and migration (ONWD)**]. Similar to ONWID, but this algorithm allows postponing starting times of some VMs and the migration of VMs between PMs. This is helpful for reducing the total number of PMs and their power-on times. Migration takes place only when the total workload of the system is low: always choosing VMs from the PMs with the lowest (or second-lowest) loads and relocating the chosen VMs to other PMs using the MFF algorithm.

6.4 Performance evaluation

In this section, we introduce how to evaluate different scheduling algorithms; analysis of methodologies, metrics, algorithms, and results are provided as follows.

6.4.1 Methodology

There is no existing tool suitable for performing the comparisons proposed in this chapter. A java discrete simulator is therefore implemented for performing comparisons. The same set of inputs (VM requests) is applied to all compared algorithms. The set of inputs are first generated by a program and then written into a text file. Offline algorithms then use all of these inputs at once, while online algorithms read one record (request) at a time. In the simulations, all results are based on divisible capacity configurations of VMs and PMs, as given in Tables 6.1 and 6.2.

6.4.2   Metrics

1. Although the linear energy model (Eqs. (6.3)–(6.7)) is applied in all simulations, our algorithmic results hold for any power function that is convex.
2. The total energy consumption of a Cloud data center.
3. The total number of PMs, which are powered on during the testing period.
4. The total length of power-on time of all PMs during the testing period.

6.4.3   Algorithms

The four proposed algorithms are already explained in Section 6.3. The other two algorithms are as follows:

> *Round Robin (Round)*: the Round Robin is one of most commonly used scheduling algorithms (e.g., by Eucalyptus [13] and Amazon EC2 [4]), which allocates VM requests in turn to each PM. The advantage of this algorithm is that it is simple to implement.
> *Modified Best-Fit Decreasing (MBFD)*: The MBFD algorithm is a bin-packing algorithm. BFD is shown to use no more than 11/9 OPT +1 bins (where OPT is the number of bins given by the optimal solution) for the one-dimensional BPP [19]. The MBFD algorithm first sorts all VMs in decreasing order of their CPU utilization and then allocates each VM to a host that provides the smallest increase of power consumption due to the allocation.

6.4.4   Inputs settings and results analysis

The configurations of VMs and PMs are given in Tables 6.1 and 6.2, which we consider to be strongly divisible capacity cases. Table 6.4 also provides a different P_{min} and P_{max} for different type of PMs.

For comparison, we assume all VMs occupy the total amount of requested capacity (as the worst case scenario). In this case, eight types of VMs are considered—as shown in Table 6.1—which is based on Amazon EC2. The total number of arrivals (requests) is 1000 and each type of VM has an equal number (i.e., 125). All requests follow the Poisson arrival process and have exponential service times. The mean inter-arrival period is set as 5 slots; the maximum intermediate period is set as 50 slots; the maximum duration of requests is set as 50, 100, 200, 400, and 800 slots, respectively. Each slot is equal to 5 min. For example, if the requested duration (service time) of a VM is 20 slots, its actual duration is $20 \times 5 = 100$ min. For each set of inputs (requests), simulations are run six times and all of the results

Table 6.4 **Three types of PMs with power consumptions**

PM type	CPU (compute units)	Memory (GB)	Storage (GB)	P_{min} (W)	P_{max} (W)
Type1	16	30.0	3380	210	300
Type2	52	136.8	3380	420	600
Type3	40	14.0	3380	350	500

Table 6.5 **Total energy consumption (idle servers turned off)**

Total energy consumed in a DC (kW h)	RR	OFWID	OFWD	MBFD	ONWID	ONID	Migrations
maxdur. = 50	655.6	465.9	438.4	495.1	476.0	459.8	0
maxdur. = 100	1210.7	813.3	781.7	890.8	824.7	796.8	1
maxdur. = 200	2312.1	1478.3	1444.4	1620.0	1492.3	1158.8	4
maxdur. = 400	4011.4	2731.3	2676.0	2957.3	2762.3	2708.3	12
maxdur. = 800	7508.2	5190.9	5117.2	5559.6	5209.8	5168.9	21

Table 6.6 **Total energy consumption (idle servers NOT turned off)**

Total energy consumed (kW h)	Round	ONWID	OFWID	MBFD	OFWD	ONWD	Migrations
maxdur. = 50	2793.4	1918.4	1918.4	1918.4	1305.9	1305.9	0
maxdur. = 100	3534.5	2790.7	2659.5	2397.0	1784.5	1784.5	2
maxdur. = 200	5029.9	3542.4	3411.2	3411.2	3017.4	3017.4	5
maxdur. = 400	8353.4	6034.7	6034.7	6034.7	5290.9	5290.9	16
maxdur. = 800	16918.7	9962.5	9831.2	9568.7	9568.7	9568.7	30

shown in this chapter are the average of the six runs. We restrict the maximum delay to 50 slots.

6.4.4.1 Assuming idle servers turned off

Tables 6.5 and 6.6 present total energy consumption assuming idle servers turned off and idle servers not turned off, respectively. The last column in both tables is the total migration number; only the online scheduling algorithm ONWD applies migration.

Figure 6.6 shows the total energy consumption (in percentages compared to Round Robin) of the six algorithms as the maximum duration of VMs varies from 50 to 800 slots, while all other parameters are the same. The total energy consumption of other algorithms are compared to Round Robin: setting the total energy consumption of Round Robin as 100% as the baseline. Then total energy consumption of other algorithms are compared with Round Robin. For all cases, Round > MBFD > ONWID > OFWID > ONWD > OFWD for the total energy consumption calculated using Equations 6.3–6.7. In general, ONWID, ONWD, OFWD. and OFWID consume about 2−8% less power than MBFD and 30% less power than Round Robin. The reason ONWID, ONWD, OFWD, and OFWID perform

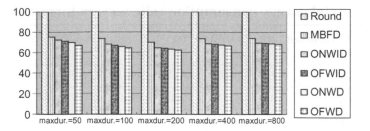

Figure 6.6 Total energy consumption comparing to Round Robin (%) when varying maximum duration of VM requests (idle servers turned off).

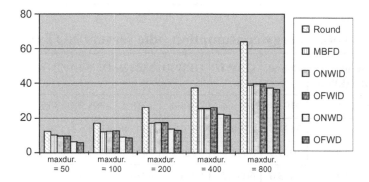

Figure 6.7 Total number of PMs used (idle servers turned on).

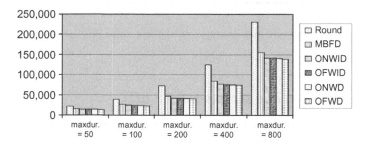

Figure 6.8 Total power-on time (minutes) of all PMs (idle servers turned off).

better than MBFD is that ONWID and OFWID use the best possible capacity sharing and take less total power-on time.

Figure 6.7 shows the total number of PMs used in six algorithms, observing that the order is not strictly like the total energy consumption.

Figure 6.8 shows the total power-on time (in minutes) of six algorithms. Note that in all simulations, a PM is assumed to be turned off if it is idle during some intervals. The total power-on time of all PMs is computed using Eq. (6.6). It can be seen that in all cases, Round > MBFD > ONWID > OFWID > ONWD > OFWD with respect to total power-on time. This explains why the total energy consumption follows the same pattern and is consistent with the theoretical results and proof of *Lemma 3*.

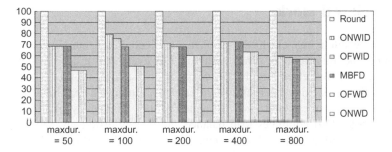

Figure 6.9 Total energy consumption comparing to Round Robin in percentages (idle servers not turned off).

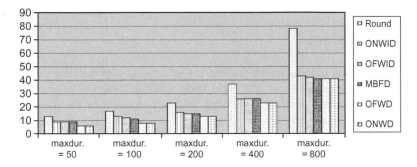

Figure 6.10 Total number of PMs used (idle servers not turned off).

6.4.4.2 Assuming idle servers not turned off

Figure 6.9 shows the total energy consumption (in percentages compared to Round Robin) of the six algorithms as the maximum duration of VMs varies from 50 to 800 slots, while all other parameters are the same. For all cases, Round > ONWID > OFWID > MBFD > OFWD > ONWD regarding total energy consumption calculated using Eqs. (6.3)−(6.7). In general, ONWD and OFWD consume about 5−20% less power than MBFD, and 40% less power than Round Robin. The reason ONWD and OFWD perform better is that delay or migrations are adopted so a smaller total number of PMs are used. Figure 6.10 shows the total number of PMs used in different algorithms; these results validate the theoretical results and proof of *Lemma 4*.

6.4.4.3 Impact of varying the total number of VM requests

We also fixed the total number of each type of PM, but varied the total number of VM requests. The system load was defined as the average arrival rate divided by the average service rate. Similar results were observed as before. Because of page limits, these results are not provided here.

6.5   Related work

One of the challenging scheduling problems in Cloud data centers is to consider the allocation and migration of VMs with full life cycle constraints, which is often neglected [23]. Beloglazov et al. [19] consider offline allocation of VMs by modified best-fit bin-packing heuristics. Kim et al. [22] model a real-time service as a real-time VM request and use dynamic voltage frequency scaling schemes. Matthew et al. [29] combines load balance and energy efficiency and proposes an optimal offline algorithm and an optimal online algorithm. Rao et al. [30] models the problem as constrained mixed-integer programming and proposes an approximate solution. Lin et al. [31] proposes online and offline algorithms for data centers by turning off idle servers to minimize total cost.

6.6   Conclusions

In this chapter, we introduce energy-efficient scheduling schemes that consider the full life cycle of heterogeneous VM types using modified interval partitioning models. We have shown that these scheduling schemes can reduce the overall energy consumption of Cloud data centers. There are a few more research directions that need further investigation:

1. the consideration of energy consumption during migration transitions;
2. the collection and analysis of energy consumption data in real Cloud data centers;
3. the combination of energy efficiency, load balance, and other features together.

Our future work will investigate scheduling schemes that consider these points.

References

[1] Armbrust M, Fox A, Griffith J, Anthony DK, Randy HK, Andrew L, et al. Above the Clouds: a Berkeley view of Cloud computing. Berkeley: EECS Department, University of California; 2009.
[2] Google App Engine. <http://code.google.com/intl/zh-CN/appengine/>.
[3] IBM (2007) blue cloud, <http://www.ibm.com/grid/>.
[4] Amazon EC2. <http://aws.amazon.com/ec2/>.
[5] Microsoft Inc., Windows Azure, < http://www.microsoft.com/windowsazure >; December 2013.
[6] Beloglazov A, Buyya R, Lee YC, Zomaya A. In: Zelkowitz M, editor. A taxonomy and survey of energy-efficient data centers and Cloud computing systems, advances in computers, vol. 82. Amsterdam, The Netherlands: Elsevier; 2011. ISBN: 978-0-12-385512-1.
[7] Boss G, et al. Cloud computing, IBM Corporation white paper, < http://download.boulder.ibm.com/ibmdl/pub/software/dw/wes/hipods/Cloud_computing_wp_final_8Oct.pdf >; November 2007.

[8] Foster I, et al. Cloud computing and grid computing 360-degree compared [R]. IEEE International Workshop on Grid Computing Environments (GCE) 2008, co-located with IEEE/ACM Supercomputing, 2008.

[9] Youseff L, et al. Toward a unified ontology of Cloud computing. In: The proceedings of grid computing environments workshop, GCE'08, 2008.

[10] Tian WH. Adaptive dimensioning of Cloud datacenters. In: The proceedings of IEEE the eighth international conference on dependable, autonomic and secure computing (DASC-09), Chengdu, China; December 12—14, 2009.

[11] Liu L, Wang H, Liu X, Jin X, He WB, Wang QB, et al. GreenCloud: a new architecture for green data center. Proceedings of the sixth international conference session on autonomic computing and communications industry session, ICAC-INDST'09. New York, NY: ACM; 2009. p. 29—38.

[12] Distributed Management Task Force Inc., Interoperable Clouds: A white paper from the open cloud standards Incubator, < www.dmtf.org/about/policies/disclosures.php > ; November 2009.

[13] Nurmi D, et al. The Eucalyptus open-source Cloud-computing system. In: Proceedings of ninth IEEE international symposium on cluster computing and the grid, Shanghai, China, 2008.

[14] Tian WH, Zhao Y, Zhong YL, Xu MX, Jing C. A dynamic and integrated load-balancing scheduling algorithm for Cloud data centers. In: the proceedings of CCIS 2011, Beijing.

[15] Garg SK, Yeo CS, Buyya R. GreenCloud framework for improving carbon efficiency of Clouds. In: Proceedings of the 17th international European conference on parallel and distributed computing (EuroPar 2011, LNCS, Springer, Germany), Bordeaux, France; August 29—September 2, 2011.

[16] Jing S, Ali S, She K, Zhong Y. State-of-the-art research study for green Cloud computing. J Supercomputing, Special Issue on Cloud Computing 2011. 2013;65(1):445—68.

[17] Srikantaiah S, Kansal A, Zhao F. Energy aware consolidation for Cloud computing. In: Proceedings of the 2008 conference on power aware computing and systems.

[18] Lee Y, Zomaya AY. Energy efficient utilization of resource in Cloud computing systems. J Supercomput May 2012;60(2):268—80.

[19] Beloglazov A, Abawajy J, Buyya R. Energy-aware resource allocation heuristics for efficient management of data centers for Cloud computing. Future Gener Comput Syst May 2012;28(5):755—68.

[20] Liu H, Xu C, Jin H, Gong J, Liao X. Performance and energy modeling for live migration of virtual machines. In: The proceedings of HPDC'11, June 8—11, San Jose, CA; 2011.

[21] Guazzone M, Anglano C, Canonico M. Energy-Efficient Resource Management for Cloud Computing Infrastructures. In the proceedings of CloudCom, 2011.

[22] Kim K, Beloglazov A, Buyya R. Power-aware provisioning of virtual machines for real-time Cloud services, Concurrency and Computation: Practice and Experience, vol. 23, Number 13, New York, NY: Wiley Press; September 10, 2011. p. 1491—505. ISSN: 1532-0626.

[23] Kolen AWJ, Lenstra JK, Papadimitriou CH, Spieksma FCR. Interval scheduling: a survey, Published online 16 March 2007 in Wiley InterScience (<www.interscience. wiley.com>).

[24] Kovalyov MY, Ng CT, Cheng E. Fixed interval scheduling: models, applications, computational complexity and algorithms. Eur J Operational Res 2007;178(2):331—42.

[25] Economou D, Rivoire S, Kozyrakis C, Ranganathan P. Full-system power analysis and modeling for server environments, 2006. Stanford University/HP Labs workshop on modeling, benchmarking, and simulation (MoBS) June 18, 2006.

[26] Garey R, Johnson DS. Computing and intractability: a guide to the theory of NP-completeness. San Francisco, CA: W.H. Freeman; 1978.

[27] Kleinberg J, Tardos E. Algorithm design. Pearson Education; 2005. ISBN: 0321295358.

[28] Coffman Jr. EG, Garey MR, Johnson DS. Bin-packing with divisible item sizes. J Complexity 1987;3:406−28.

[29] Mathew V, Sitaraman RK, Shenoy P. Energy-aware load balancing in content delivery networks. In: The proceedings of INFOCOM, 2012.

[30] Rao L, Liu X, Xie L, Liu WY. Minimizing electricity cost: optimization of distributed Internet data centers in a multi-electricity-market environment. In INFOCOM, 2010.

[31] Lin M, Wierman A, Andrew LLH, Thereska E. Dynamic right- sizing for power-proportional data centers. In: Proceedings of the IEEE INFOCOM, Shanghai, China; 2011. p. 10−5.

Energy Efficiency by Minimizing Total Busy Time of Offline Parallel Scheduling in Cloud Computing

Main Contents of this Chapter:

- Approximation algorithm and its approximation ratio bound
- Application to energy efficiency in Cloud computing
- Performance evaluation

7.1 Introduction

We follow a three-field notation scheme for the job scheduling problem in machines. This notation is proposed in Ref. [1] as $\alpha|\beta|\gamma$, which specifies the processor environment, task characteristics, and objective function, respectively. For example, $P|r_j, e_j|C_{\max}$ refers to the multiprocessor problem of minimizing the completion time (makespan), when each task has a release date and deadline specified. $P_m|r_j, e_j|\sum C_j$ denotes the multiprocessor problem of minimizing the total completion time, when each task has a release date and deadline specified, and m number of processors is specified as part of the problem type.

In this chapter, the notation is $P_g|s_j, e_j|\sum_i b_i$, where multiple machines (each with capacity g) are considered. Each job has a start-time and end-time specified during which interval it should be processed, and the objective is to minimize the total busy time of all used machines. Formally, the input is a set of n jobs $J = J_1, \ldots, J_n$. Each job J_j is associated with an interval $[s_j, e_j]$ in which it should be processed; $p_j = e_j - s_j + 1$ is the process time of job J_j. Also given is the capacity parameter $g \geq 1$, which is the maximal capacity a single machine provides. The busy time of a machine i is denoted by its working time interval length b_i. The goal is to assign jobs to machines such that the total busy time of all machines, given by $B = \sum_i b_i$ is minimized. Note that the number of machines ($m > 1$) to be used is part of the output of the algorithm and takes an integral value. To the best of our knowledge, Khandekar et al. [2] are among the first to discuss this issue, while Brucker [3] reviews the problem and related references therein. Unless otherwise specified, lower case letters are used for indices, while upper case letters are used for a set of jobs, time intervals, and machines.

Cloud computing allows for the sharing, allocating, and aggregating of software, computational, and storage network resources on demand. Some of the key benefits of Cloud computing include the hiding and abstraction of complexity, virtualized resources, and the efficient use of distributed resources. Maximizing the energy efficiency of Cloud data centers is a significant challenge. Beloglazov et al. [4] propose a taxonomy and survey of energy-efficient data centers for Cloud computing, while Jing et al. [5] conduct a state-of-the-art research study for green Cloud computing and point out three hot research areas.

A Cloud Infrastructure as a Service provider, such as Amazon EC2 [6], offers virtual machine (VM) resources with specified computing units. A customer requests certain computing units of resources for a period of time and then pays based on the total provisioned time of these computing units. For a provider, the total energy cost of computing resources is closely related to the total power-on (busy) time of all computing resources. Hence, a provider aims to minimize the total busy time to save on energy costs. Therefore, in this chapter, we propose and prove a 3-approximation algorithm, modified first-fit-decreasing-earliest (MFFDE) that can be applied to VM scheduling in Cloud data centers to minimize energy consumption.

7.1.1 Related work

There is extensive research on job scheduling on parallel machines. In traditional interval scheduling [7−9], jobs are given as intervals in real time, each job has to be processed on some machine, and that machine can process only one job at any time.

There are many studies on scheduling with fixed intervals, in which each job has to be processed on some machine during a time interval between its release time and due date, or each job has to be processed during the fixed interval between its start-time and end-time assuming a machine can process a single job at any given time. In addition, there are studies of real-time scheduling with capacity demands in which each machine has some capacity; however, to the best of our knowledge, Khandekar et al. [2] are among the first to discuss the objective of minimizing the total busy time. There has also been earlier work on the problem of scheduling jobs to a set of machines so as to minimize the total cost [10], but in these works the cost of scheduling each job is fixed. On the other hand, in our problem, the cost of scheduling each job depends on the other jobs that are scheduled on the same machine in the corresponding time interval; thus, it may change over time and across different machines. As pointed out in [2], our scheduling problem is different from the batch scheduling of conflicting jobs [3].

In the general case, the scheduling problem is NP-hard [11]. Chapter 6 shows that the problem is NP-hard for $g = 2$, when the jobs are intervals on the line. Flammini et al. [12] consider the scheduling problem, in which jobs are given as intervals on the line with unit demand. For this version of the problem, Flammini et al. give a 4-approximation algorithm for general inputs and better bounds for some subclasses of inputs. In particular, Flammini et al. present a 2-approximation algorithm for instances in which no interval is properly contained in another interval (i.e., the input forms a proper interval graph) and in which any two intervals intersect (i.e., the input forms a clique (see also Ref. [2])). Flammini et al. also provide a 2-approximation for bounded lengths of time, i.e., the length (or process time) of any job is bounded by some fixed integer d.

Khandekar et al. [2] propose a 5-approximation algorithm for the scheduling problem by separating all jobs into wide and narrow jobs based on their demands when $\alpha = 0.25$, which is a demand parameter of narrow jobs as compared to the total capacity of a machine. The results obtained based on $\alpha = 0.25$ are only good for this special case. In this chapter, we improve upon and extend the results of Ref. [2] by proposing a 3-approximation algorithm for our scheduling problem.

As for energy efficiency in Cloud computing, one of the challenging scheduling problems in Cloud data centers is to consider the allocation and migration of VMs with full life cycle constraints, which is often neglected [13]. Srikantaiah et al. [14] examine the interrelationships between power consumption, resource utilization, and performance of consolidated workloads. Lee and Zomaya [15] introduce two online heuristic algorithms for energy-efficient utilization of resources in Cloud computing systems by consolidating active tasks. Liu et al. [16] study the performance and energy modeling for live migration of VMs and evaluate the models using five representative workloads in a Xen virtualized environment. Beloglazov et al. [10] consider the offline allocation of VMs by minimizing the total number of machines used and minimizing the total number of migrations through modified best-fit bin packing heuristics. Kim et al. [17] model a real-time service as a real-time VM request and use dynamic voltage frequency scaling schemes. Mathew et al. [18] combine load balancing and energy efficiency by proposing an optimal offline algorithm and an online algorithm for content delivery networks. Rao et al. [19] model the problem as constrained mixed-integer programming and propose an approximate solution. Lin et al. [20] propose online and offline algorithms for data centers by turning off idle servers to minimize the total cost. However, there is still a lack of research on VM scheduling that considers fixed processing intervals. Hence, in this chapter, we demonstrate how our proposed 3-approximation algorithm can be applied to VM scheduling in Cloud computing. Mertzios et al. [21] consider a similar problem model, but only consider it with respect to various special cases. They mainly provide constant factor approximation algorithms for both total busy time minimization and throughput maximization problems, while we focus on energy efficiency in Cloud data centers.

7.1.2 Preliminaries

For energy-efficient scheduling, the goal is to meet all requirements with the minimum number of machines and their total busy times based on the following assumptions:

- All data are deterministic and unless otherwise specified, the time is formatted in slotted windows. We partition the total time period $[0, T]$ into slots of equal length (l_0) in discrete time, thus the total number of slots is $k = T/l_0$ (always making it a positive integer). The start-time of the system is set as $s_0 = 0$. Then the interval of a request j can be represented in slot format as [StartTime, EndTime, RequestedCapacity] $= [s_i, e_i, d_i]$ with both start-time s_i and end-time e_i being nonnegative integers.

- All job tasks are independent. There are no precedence constraints other than those implied by the start-time and end-time. Preemption is also not considered in this chapter.
- The required capacity of each request is a positive integer between $[1, g]$.
- Assuming that each request is assigned to a single machine when processed, interrupting a request and resuming it on another machine is not allowed, unless explicitly stated otherwise.

From the aforementioned assumptions, we have the following key definitions and observations:

Definition 1 Given a time interval $I_i = [s, t]$ where s and t is the start-time and end-time, respectively, the length of I_i is $|I_i| = t - s + 1$. The length of a set of pairwise intervals $I = \cup_{i=1}^{k} I_i$, is defined as $\text{len}(I) = |I| = \sum_{i=1}^{k} |I_i|$, i.e., the length of a set of intervals is the sum of the length of each individual interval.

Definition 2 span(I) is defined as the length of the union of all intervals considered, i.e., span(I) = $| \cup I|$.

Example 1 If $I = \{[1, 4], [2, 4], [5, 6]\}$, then span($I$) = $|[1, 4]| + |[5, 6]| = (4 - 1) + 1 + (6 - 5) + 1 = 6$, and len($I$) = $|[1, 4]| + |[2, 4]| + |[5, 6]| = 9$. Note that span($I$) $\leq$ len(I) and equality holds if and only if I is a set of pairwise nonoverlapping intervals.

Definition 3 For any instance I and capacity parameter $g \geq 1$, let OPT(I) denote the minimized total busy time of all machines. Here, strictly speaking, busy time means the power-on time of all machines. From Definition 2 of span(I), to minimize the total busy time is to minimize the sum of makespan on all machines.

Note that the total power-on time of a machine is the sum of all intervals during which the machine is power-on. As in Example 1, a machine is busy (power-on) during intervals $[1, 5]$ and $[5, 6]$. Based on Definition 1 of the interval for each job, the total busy time of this machine is $(5 - 1) + (6 - 5) = 5$ time units (or slots). The interval $[0, 1]$ is not included in the total busy time of the machine.

Definition 4 Approximation ratio: An offline deterministic algorithm is said to be a C-approximation for the objective of minimizing the total busy time if the total busy time is at most C times that of an optimal solution.

Definition 5 Time in slotted window: Assuming that the start-time and end-time of all jobs are nonnegative integers, the required capacity of each job d_i is a natural number between 1 and g, i.e., $1 \leq d_i \leq g$.

Definition 6 For any job j, its required workload is $w(j)$, which is its capacity demand multiplied by its process time, i.e., $w(j) = d_j p_j$. Then the total workload of all jobs J is $W(J) = \sum_{j=1}^{n} w(j)$.

The following observations are given in Ref. [2].

Observation 1 For any instance J and capacity parameter $g \geq 1$, the following bounds hold:

  i. Capacity bound: $\text{OPT}(J) \geq W(J)/g$;
  ii. Span bound: $\text{OPT}(J) \geq \text{span}(J)$.

The capacity bound holds because g is the maximum capacity that can be achieved in any solution. The span bound holds because only one machine is sufficient when $g = 1$.

Observation 2 The upper bound for the optimal total busy time is $\text{OPT}(J) \leq \text{len}(J)$. The equality holds when $g = 1$, or all intervals are not overlapped when $g > 1$.

For analyzing any scheduler S, the machines are numbered as $M_1, M_2, \ldots$ and J_i is the set of jobs assigned to machine M_i with the scheduler S. The total busy period of a machine M_i is the length of its busy intervals, i.e., $b_i = \text{span}(J_i)$ for all $i \geq 1$, where $\text{span}(J_i)$ is the span of the set of job intervals scheduled on M_i.

7.1.3 Results

For the objective of minimizing the total busy time of multiple identical machines without preemption subject to fixed interval and capacity constraints (referred to as MinTBT), we obtain the following results:

- Minimizing the total busy time of multiple identical machines in scheduling without preemption and with capacity constraint (MinTBT) is an NP-complete problem in the general case (Theorem 1).
- There exist algorithms to find an optimal solution for the MinTBT problem in polynomial time when the demand is one unit and the total capacity of each machine is also one unit, so in this case, $\text{MFFDE}(I) = \text{OPT}(I) = \text{len}(I)$ (Theorem 2). This shows the result in the special case, which can be applied to energy-efficient Cloud data centers.
- The approximation ratio of our proposed MFFDE algorithm for the MinTBT problem has an upper bound 3 (Theorem 3). This is one of our main results, which guides us in the approximation of the algorithm design.
- The case in which $d_i = 1$, as shown in Ref. [12]—called the unit demand case—there is a special case of $1 \leq d_i \leq g$ (let us call it a general demand case). As for minimizing the total busy time, the unit demand case represents the worst-case scenario for first-fit-decreasing (FFD) and MFFDE algorithms (Observation 3).
- For the cases in which the capacities of all requests form a strongly divisible sequence, there exist algorithms to find an optimal solution of the minimum number of machines for the MinTBT problem in polynomial time (Theorem 4). This enables the design of approximate and near-optimal algorithms.
- For the cases in which the capacity parameter $g = \infty$, there exist algorithms to find an optimal solution for the MinTBT problem in polynomial time (Theorem 5).
- For a linear power model and a given set of VM requests in Cloud computing, the total energy consumption of all physical machines (PMs) is dominated by the total busy time of all PMs, i.e., a longer total busy time of all PMs for a scheduler leads to higher total energy consumption (Theorem 6).

The remaining content of this chapter is structured as follows: Section 7.2 presents our proposed approximation algorithm and its approximation bounds.

Section 7.3 discusses its application to VM scheduling in Cloud computing. Section 7.4 compares the performance of MFFDE with FFD and the theoretical optimal solution. Section 7.5 concludes and outlines the direction of future research in this area.

7.2   Approximation algorithm and its approximation ratio bound

For offline non-real-time scheduling, the longest processing time (LPT) is one of the best approximation algorithms. LPT is known to have the best possible upper bound for minimizing the maximum makespan for the case in which $g = 1$ in a traditional multiprocessor system [4]. In this chapter, the start-time and end-time of jobs are fixed, and the general case $g > 1$ is considered. We need to consider the fixed start-time and end-time of jobs with the capacity constraint of machines when allocating jobs. Our MFFDE algorithm, as shown in Algorithm 1, schedules jobs in the nonincreasing order of their process times and considers the earlier start-time first if two jobs have the same process time, or it breaks ties arbitrarily when two jobs have exactly the same start-time, end-time, and process time. Each job is scheduled to the first machine that has the capacity (so as to use as few machines as possible to minimize the total busy time).

MFFDE algorithm has the computational complexity $O(n \max(m, \log n))$, where n is the number of jobs and m is the number of machines used. It first sorts all jobs in the nonincreasing order of their process times, which takes $O(n \log n)$ time. Then it finds a machine for a request, which needs $O(m)$ steps, thus n jobs need $O(nm)$ steps. Therefore, the entire algorithm takes $O(n \max(m, \log n))$ time, where often $n > m$.

Input: (J, g) where J is set of jobs and g is maximum capacity of a machine

Output: Scheduled jobs, total busy time of all machines, and total number of machines used

Sort all jobs in non-increasing order of their process times, such that $p_1 \geq p_2 ... \geq p_n$ (Considers earlier start-time first if two jobs have the same process time. Breaks ties arbitrarily when two jobs have exactly the same start-time, end-time, and process time)
for $j = 1$ to n do

    Find first machine i with available capacity;

    Allocate job j to machine i and update its load;

Compute workload and busy time of all machines;

Algorithm 1 MFFDE Algorithm.

To see the hardness of the general problem:

Theorem 1 Minimizing the total busy time of multiple identical machines in offline scheduling without preemption and with a capacity constraint (MinTBT) is an NP-complete problem in the general case.

Proof This can be proved by reducing the well-known NP-complete set partitioning problem to the MinTBT problem in polynomial time as follows:

The K-partition problem is NP-complete [22] for a given arrangement S of positive numbers and an integer k; partition S into k ranges so that the sums of all of the ranges are close to each other. The K-partition problem can be reduced to the MinTBT problem as follows: For a set of jobs J where each job has capacity demand d_i (set as a positive number), partitioning J by capacity into K ranges is the same as allocating K ranges of jobs with the capacity constraint g (i.e., the sum of each range is at most g). On the other hand, if there is a solution to K-partition for a given set of intervals, there exists a schedule for the given set of intervals. Because K-partition is NP-hard in the strong sense, our problem is also NP-hard. In this way, we have shown that the MinTBT problem is an NP-complete problem.

Khandekar et al. [2] have shown by a simple reduction from the subset sum problem that it is already NP-hard to approximate our problem in the special case in which all jobs have the same (unit) process time and can be scheduled in one fixed time interval.

7.2.1 Bounds for approximation ratio when g is one unit and d_i is one unit

When g is one unit and d_i is one unit, our problem reduces to the traditional interval scheduling problem with the start-time and end-time constraints, where each job needs a one unit capacity and the total capacity of a machine is one unit.

Theorem 2 There exist algorithms to find an optimal solution for the MinTBT problem in polynomial time when the demand is one unit and the total capacity of each machine is also one unit, especially in the case of MFFDE(I) = OPT(I) = len(I).

Proof Because the capacity parameter g is one unit, let us set it to 1. As each job needs a capacity 1, each machine can only process one job at any time. In this case, using Definition 1 of interval length and Definition 2 of span, we have OPT(I) = len(I) no matter whether there are jobs that overlap or not. By allocating each interval to different machines for continuous working intervals, MFFDE(I) is also the sum of lengths of all intervals.

7.2.2 Bounds for the approximation ratio in the general case when g > 1

Observation 3 The case in which $d_i = 1$ as shown in Ref. [12], called the unit demand case, is a special case of $1 \leq d_i \leq g$ (let us call it a general demand case).

As for minimizing the total busy time, the unit demand case represents the worst-case scenario for FFD and MFFDE algorithms.

Proof Consider the general demand case, i.e., where $1 \le d_i \le g$. The adversary is generated as follows: All g groups of requests have the same start-time at $s_i = 0$, demand d_i (for $1 \le i \le h$, $\sum_{i=1}^{h} d_i = g$), and each has an end-time at $e_i = T/k^{g-i}$, where T is the length of time under consideration, k is a natural number, and $j = i \mod g$ if $i \mod g \ne 0$, else $j = g$. In this case, for the optimal solution, one can allocate all of the longest requests to a machine (m_1) for a busy time of $d_g T$, then allocate all of the second longest requests to another machine (m_2) for a busy time of $d_{g-1} T/k$, ... , and—finally—allocate all of the shortest requests to machine (m_g) with a busy time of $d_1 T/k^{g-1}$. Therefore, the total busy time of the optimal solution is

$$\text{OPT}(I) = T \sum_{i=1}^{g} \frac{d_i}{g k^{g-i}} = T \sum_{i=1}^{g} \frac{d_i}{k^{g-i}} \tag{7.1}$$

We consider the worst case (upper bound). For any offline algorithm, let us call it ALG_X, the upper bound will make ALG_X/OPT the largest while keeping other conditions unchanged. When k and T are given, Eq. (7.1) will have the smallest value if d_i has the smallest value, i.e., $d_i = 1$.

This means that the unit demand case represents the worst-case scenario.

Remark 1 We can easily check that Observation 3 is true for the worst-case scenario of FFD as shown in Figure 7.1. Because the unit demand case represents the worst-case scenario for the MinTBT problem, we only consider this case for the upper bound as follows.

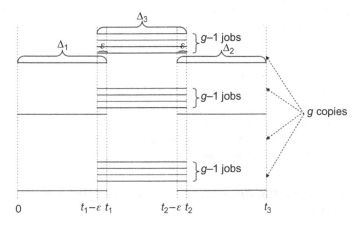

Figure 7.1 Generalized instance for the proof of the upper bound of FFD.

The following observation is given in Refs. [2,12]:

Observation 4 For any $1 \leq i \leq m - 1$, we have $\mathrm{span}(I_i + 1) \leq 3w(I_i)/g$, in the worst case for FFD algorithm, where m is the total number of machines used.

Remark 2   In Ref. [12], a result of $\mathrm{span}(I_i + 1) \leq 3w(I_i)/g$ is established and proved for the FFD algorithm. For a job i on machine M_i, p_i is its process time. Let i_L or i_R be the job with the earliest or latest completion times, respectively, in I_{i+1} on machine M_{i+1}. Because our proposed algorithm is also based on the FFD algorithm for process time and considers earlier start-times first when ties exist, we also have $\mathrm{span}(I_i + 1) \leq 3p_i = 3w(I_i)/g$.

Theorem 3 The approximation ratio of our proposed MFFDE algorithm for the MinTBT problem has an upper bound 3.

Proof Let us define that all of the jobs in J_{i+1} are assigned to machine M_{i+1}. For such a set, the total busy time of the assignment is exactly its span.

$$\sum_{i=1}^{m} \mathrm{MFFDE}(J_i) = \mathrm{MFFDE}(J_1) + \sum_{i=2}^{m} \mathrm{MFFDE}(J_i) \tag{7.2}$$

$$= \mathrm{MFFDE}(J_1) + \sum_{i=1}^{m-1} \mathrm{MFFDE}(J_{i+1}) \tag{7.3}$$

$$\leq \mathrm{MFFDE}(J_1) + \frac{3}{g}\sum_{i=1}^{m-1} w(J_i) \tag{7.4}$$

$$= \mathrm{MFFDE}(J_1) + \frac{3}{g}\sum_{i=1}^{m} w(J_i) - \frac{3}{g}w(J_m) \tag{7.5}$$

$$= \mathrm{MFFDE}(J_1) + \frac{3}{g}W(J) - \frac{3}{g}w(J_m) \tag{7.6}$$

$$\leq 3\,\mathrm{OPT}(J) + \mathrm{MFFDE}(J_1) - \frac{3}{g}w(J_m) \tag{7.7}$$

$$\leq 3\,\mathrm{OPT}(J) \tag{7.8}$$

Ideally, when $\mathrm{MFFDE}(J_1)$ has the largest value and $(3/g)w(J_m)$ has the smallest value at the same time, Eq. (7.6) will have the upper bound; but this generally is not true. The analysis is given as follows:

1. If $\mathrm{MFFDE}(J_1) = \mathrm{span}(J_1)$ has the upper bound $\mathrm{OPT}(J)$ when all long jobs are allocated on machine M_1, the optimal solution $\mathrm{OPT}(J)$ is dominated by $\mathrm{MFFDE}(J_1)$. In this case, allocations on other machines have little effect on $\mathrm{OPT}(J)$, then $(3/g)w(J_m)$ is very small

(which can be ignored as compared to span(J_1)), otherwiseMFFDE(J_1) = span(J_1) cannot reach the upper bound OPT(J). In this case, $\sum_{i=1}^{m}$ MFFDE(J_i) is dominated by span(J_1), which is very close or equal to OPT(J).

2. If MFFDE(J_1) = span(J_1) is small as compared to OPT(J) (i.e., OPT(J) is not dominated by MFFDE(J_1)), we consider the worst case since it is for the upper bound. In the worst case, span(I_{i+1}) $\leq 3w(I_i)/g$, thus we can easily check that MFFDE(J_1) $<(3/g)w(J_m)$ as shown in Figures 7.1 and 7.2. Set $\Delta_0 = \Delta_1 = \Delta_2 = \Delta_3$, Actually, MFFDE considers the earlier start-time first when jobs have the same process times, so MFFDE(J_1) = span(J_1) = $\Delta_0 - 2\varepsilon$, $(3/g)w(J_m) = (3/g)w(J_g) = (3/g)(g\Delta_0 + \Delta_0) = 3\Delta_0 + (3\Delta_0/g)$. In this case, OPT($J$) = $g\Delta_0 + \Delta_0$. Hence MFFDE(J_1) $- (3/g)w(J_m) = -2\Delta_0 - (3\Delta_0/g)$ is very small as compared to OPT(J) when g is large. From Eq. (7.7), we have MFFDE(J_1) $- (3/g)$ $w(J_m) + (3/g)w(J) \leq 3$ OPT(J), (i.e., MFFDE(J) ≤ 3 OPT(J)). In this case, a tight upper bound is proved using Figure 7.2 as the worst case (which is shown in the next proof).

3. For special cases, such as one-sided clique and clique cases [2,12], we can easily find that MFFDE(J) is very close to or equal to OPT(J).

By combining the aforementioned three analyses, we have proved Theorem 3.

Another simpler proof considers the worst case only because we are looking for the upper bound. As pointed out in Refs. [2,12], the worst case for the FFD algorithm is shown in Figure 7.1. Therefore, we can easily check that MFFDE(J) = OPT(J) because the MFFDE algorithm considers the earliest start-time first (ESTF) when two requests have the same length of process time. We further construct the worst case for the MFFDE algorithm and provide a proof as follows.

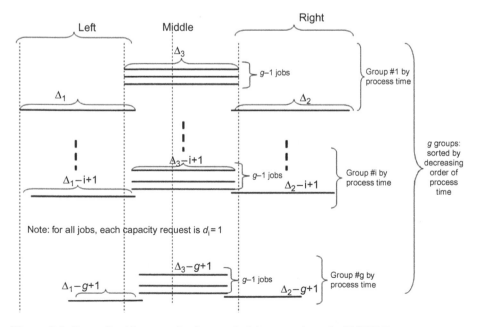

Figure 7.2 Generalized instance for the proof of the upper bound of MFFDE.

Proof The upper bound is tight: Consider the instance J as depicted in Figure 7.2. Assuming that $\Delta_1 = \Delta_2 = \Delta_3 = \Delta_0$, there are g groups of jobs sorted by the decreasing order of their process times. For group i, all jobs have the same process times: $\Delta_0 - i + 1, i \geq 1$. Notice that the left-side jobs have start-time, end-time $= [i - 1, \Delta_0]$; the right-side jobs have start-time, end-time $= [2\Delta_0 - 2i, 3\Delta_0 - 3i + 1]$, the middle-plane jobs have start-time, end-time $= [\Delta_0 - i, 2\Delta_0 - 2i + 1]$, where $\Delta_0 > 3g - 2$, so that the intervals intersect between different groups. In this case, the optimal solution uses one machine during $[0, \Delta_0]$, $(g - 1)$ machines with span $- \Delta_0 \mid 2$ $i, 1 \leq i \leq g$, and one during $[2\Delta_0 - 2g, 3\Delta_0 - 3g + 1]$, so OPT$(J) = (g + 1)\Delta_0 + 3(g - 1) - 0.5g(g - 1)$. In contrast, the MFFDE algorithm needs g machines with one machine for each group of jobs, whereby each machine has span $= 3\Delta_0 - 5i + 1$, $1 \leq i \leq g$. Hence MFFDE$(J) = \sum_{i=1}^{g} 3(\Delta_0 - 5i + 1) = 3g\Delta_0 - 2.5g^2 - 1.5g$. We now have the following:

$$\frac{\text{MFFDE}(J)}{\text{OPT}(J)} = \frac{3g\Delta_0 - 2.5g^2 - 1.5g}{(g + 1)\Delta_0 + 3(g - 1) - 0.5(g - 1)} = \frac{3 - (2.5g + 1.5)/\Delta_0}{1 + 1/g - (0.5g^2 - 3.5g + 3)/g\Delta_0}$$

which has an upper bound 3 when g is large since $\Delta_0 > 3g - 2$ by setting.

Remark 3 With comparison to the random capacity configuration case, there are many good features in the strongly divisible case [23]; thus it is possible to find an optimal number of machines for the MinTBT problem as follows.

Theorem 4 In the case in which the capacities of all requests form a strongly divisible sequence, there exists an algorithm to find an optimal solution of the minimum number of machines for the MinTBT problem in polynomial time.

Remark 4 In the strongly divisible capacity case, the total capacity of a machine and the capacities of all jobs form a strongly divisible sequence. Our scheduling problem therefore can be transformed into the classical one-dimensional interval (bin) packing problem, whereby the best-fit-decreasing algorithm produces the optimal result for offline scheduling [23]. Also in this case, the problem can be transformed into the interval scheduling problem, in which the minimum number of machines exist to host all requests [8]. Theorem 4 guides the design of the system to have the optimal number of machines used while minimizing the total busy time. In this way, the average utilization of all machines also improves. Notice that Theorem 4 is not true for the general capacity case where each job requests a random real number of capacity between 1 and g.

Example 2 Assuming that the total capacity of each machine is $g = 10$, there are four jobs in [StartTime, EndTime, RequestedCapacity] format: [0, 1, 9], [0, 1, 5], [0, 1, 3], and [0, 1, 3] with the capacity requirement of 9, 5, 3, and 3, respectively. In this case, the total requested capacity is 20, thus—ideally—two machines will be the optimal solution. But because of the randomness of each requested capacity, no subset sum of jobs has the total capacity exactly equal to 10. In fact, three machines are necessary regardless of what scheduling algorithms are used: one for [0, 1, 9]; one for [0, 1, 5] and [0, 1, 3]; and one for [0, 1, 3].

Theorem 5 For the case of the capacity parameter $g = \infty$, there exists an algorithm to find an optimal solution for the MinTBT problem in polynomial time.

Proof When $g = \infty$, one machine is sufficient for all jobs. Once all jobs J are given, their total span(J) is fixed by the definition and can be computed in polynomial time, which is linear to the number of total jobs. Let the intervals of all of the jobs be contained in $[0, T]$, assuming the time is in slotted window format and each slot has a unit time length. In addition, all start-times and end-times are integers. For example, a job J_j has requested $[t_j, e_j, d_j] = [2, 10, 1]$, which means it has a start-time at slot-2, an end-time at slot-10, and the required capacity of 1, respectively. One way to find the total busy time is to sum the lengths of all slots, which have at least one job spanning them. By Definition 2 of span(J), this is the total busy time.

In summary, the approximation ratio of the MFFDE algorithm for multiple machine scheduling has an upper bound 3, which is an improvement as compared to the 5-approximation algorithm proposed in Ref. [2].

7.3   Application to energy efficiency in Cloud computing

In this section, we introduce how our results are applied to Cloud computing. We consider VM allocation in Cloud data centers where PMs are major resources [4,10,17]. Each VM has a start-time s_i, an end-time e_i, and a capacity request d_i. The capacity request d_i of a VM is a natural number between 1 and the total capacity g of a PM. Our objective here is to minimize the total energy consumption of all PMs by minimizing the total busy time. This is exactly the same as the MinTBT problem.

7.3.1   Problem formulation

Theorem 6 For the abovementioned power model and a given set of VM requests in Cloud computing, the total energy consumption of all PMs is dominated by the total busy time of all PMs. That is, the longer the total busy time of all PMs for a scheduler, the higher the total energy consumption.

Proof By setting $\alpha = P_{\min}$ and $\beta = (P_{\max} - P_{\min})$, we have

$$
\begin{aligned}
\sum_{i=1}^{m} E_i &= \sum_{i=1}^{m} \left(E_{i_{\mathrm{on}}} + \sum_{j=1}^{k} E_{ij} \right) \\
&= \alpha \sum_{i=1}^{m} T_i + \beta \sum_{i=1}^{n} \sum_{j \in \mathrm{PM}_i} u_j t_j \\
&= \alpha T + \beta L
\end{aligned}
\tag{7.9}
$$

Where $T = \sum_{i=1}^{m} t_i$ is the total busy time of all PMs and L is the total workload of all VMs, which is fixed once the set of VM requests is given. From Eq. (7.9), we can see that the total energy consumption of all PMs is dominated by the total busy time (T) of all PMs, i.e., the longer the total busy time of all PMs for a scheduler, the higher the total energy consumption.

From Theorem 6, for energy efficiency, one should try to minimize the total busy time of all PMs. However, the general problem is an NP-complete problem as stated in Theorem 1.

Observation 5 For a given set of interval requests, the total busy time of all PMs depends on the scheduling algorithms (or schedulers). It is possible that different schedulers can have different total numbers of PMs used, but with the same total busy time of all PMs. In other words, a solution that minimizes the total busy time may not be optimal with respect to the number of PMs used, or a solution that minimizes the number of PMs used may not be optimal with respect to the total busy time.

Example 3 We assume that the total capacity of a PM is $g = 16$, and that each PM has a load threshold of 0.75. As given in Table 7.1, there are six VM requests in [StartTime, EndTime, RequestedCapacity] format: $v_1[1, 5, 4]$, $v_2[2, 4, 1]$, $v_3[4, 9, 8]$, $v_4[4, 6, 8]$, $v_5[4, 9, 8]$, $v_6[5, 9, 4]$. As shown in Figure 7.3, the VM allocations based on three scheduling approaches are as follows:

- Scheduler A (MFFDE) uses 3 PMs with a total busy time of 20 slots (PM_1 runs 9 slots for v_1, v_3; PM_2 runs 8 slots for v_2, v_5, v_6; PM_3 runs 3 slots for v_4).
- Scheduler B (earliest start-time first (ESTF)) uses 4 PMs with a total busy time of 20 slots (PM_1 runs 5 slots for v_1, v_2; PM_2 runs 6 slots for v_3; PM_3 runs 3 slots for v_4; PM_4 runs 6 slots for v_5, v_6).
- Scheduler C (shortest process time first (SPTF)) uses 3 PMs with a total busy time of 23 slots (PM_1 runs 8 slots for v_2, v_4, v_6; PM_2 runs 9 slots for v_1, v_3; PM_3 runs 6 slots for v_5).

Schedulers A and B show that two solutions can use different number of PMs but still have the same total busy time. Scheduler C uses 3 PMs (optimal) as scheduler A does but has longer total busy time.

Table 7.1 Six VM requests for Example 3

VM\slot	1	2	3	4	5	6	7	8	9
v_1	4	4	4	4	4				
v_2		1	1	1					
v_3				8	8	8	8	8	8
v_4				8	8	8			
v_5				8	8	8	8	8	8
v_6					4	4	4	4	4

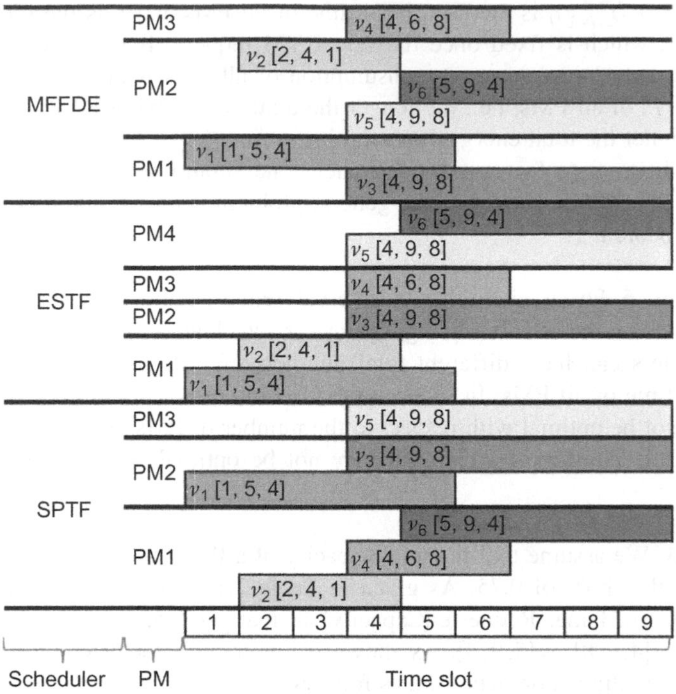

Figure 7.3 VM allocation based on the MFFDE algorithm, the ESTF, and the SPTF for Example 3.

From Theorem 6, we can induce the following two observations:

Observation 6 For a given set of VM requests, scheduler A uses the same number of PMs as scheduler B. Scheduler A has a total busy time T_A of all PMs, while scheduler B has total busy time T_B of all PMs. If $T_A > T_B$, then the total energy consumption of scheduler A is higher than scheduler B.

This means that the scheduler should attempt to minimize the total busy time of all PMs so as to reduce the total energy consumption when all other conditions are the same, which is one of main objectives of this chapter.

Observation 7 For the same set of VM requests, scheduler A uses more number of PMs than scheduler B. Scheduler A uses M_A number of PMs with a total busy time T_A, while scheduler B uses M_B number of PMs with a total busy time T_B. If $M_A > M_B$ but $T_A = T_B$, then the total energy consumption of scheduler A is the same as scheduler B.

Example 4 Let us consider a set of n VM requests, which are not overlapped and require unit demand. Then there are two ways to have optimal total busy time. The first way is to use one PM for all n requests. The second way is to use n PMs, respectively, for each job. It is obvious that these two ways result in the same total busy time.

This means that a solution that minimizes the total busy time may not be unique and may not be optimal in the number of PMs used. For practical consideration, one should attempt to minimize the total busy time and use the optimal number of PMs. Theorem 6 guides the design of the system to have the optimal number of PMs used while minimizing the total busy time. In this way, the average utilization of all PMs also improves.

Remark 5   Observations 6 and 7 also explain the feature of cost associativity in Cloud computing [24], i.e., 1000 computers used for 1 h costs the same as one computer used for 1000 h because the total busy time is 1000 h for the same given set of jobs in this case.

Observation 8   By applying our proposed MFFDE algorithm, the approximation ratio of minimizing the total energy consumption of Cloud data centers is 3 in the general case and can be near optimal in special cases such as one-sided clique and clique cases (special cases discussed in Refs. [2,12]).

7.3.2   Average case analysis

In the previous sections, we mainly focus on the worst-case analysis and provide the upper bound of approximation ratio for the worst case. For the average case, MFFDE algorithm accepts random inputs subject to some underlying random process (such as Poisson process). It is well known that the approximation ratio for the average case is below the upper bound for the worst case.

7.4   Performance evaluation

The open source private Cloud platform, Eucalyptus [25] provides two scheduling options: GREEDY and ROUNDROBIN. Both options do not shut down machines or put machines to sleep. GREEDY is similar to first-fit bin packing approximation by minimizing the total number of PMs used to save energy. ROUNDROBIN (also used in Amazon EC2 [6]) sets the order of PMs first and then allocates jobs (requests) to the PMs in that order. In this chapter, we discuss offline scheduling algorithms FFD [2,12] and MFFDE, which are known to have better approximation ratio than first-fit and ROUNDROBIN because preprocess sorting in the decreasing order of all process time are adopted. Therefore, for performance evaluation, we only compare the results of FFD, MFFDE, and the theoretical optimal solution (OPT).

7.4.1   Methodology

To evaluate performance, we use a Java discrete event simulator [26]. For incoming VM requests, we consider eight VM types in Amazon EC2 [6] as listed in Table 7.2. From these eight VM types, we derive three PM types as listed in Table 7.3. For example, PM type 1 is derived from the first three VM types 1-1, 1-2, and 1-3.

Table 7.2 **Eight VM types in Amazon EC2**

VM type	Compute units	Memory (GB)	Storage (GB)
1-1 (1)	1	1.875	211.25
1-2 (2)	4	7.5	845
1-3 (3)	8	15	1690
2-1 (4)	6.5	17.1	422.5
2-2 (5)	13	34.2	845
2-3 (6)	26	68.4	1690
3-1 (7)	5	1.7	422.5
3-2 (8)	20	6.8	1690

Table 7.3 **Three PM types for divisible configuration**

PM type	CPU	Memory (GB)	Storage (GB)	$P_{min}(W)$	$P_{max}(W)$
1	16	30	3380	210	300
2	52	136.8	3380	420	600
3	40	14	3380	350	500

7.4.2 Algorithms

We compare three algorithms as follows:

1. (FFD [2,12] first sorts all VM requests in the nonincreasing order of their process time and then allocates the requests to the first available PM;
2. MFFDE as proposed in this chapter;
3. Optimal solution (OPT) represents the theoretical lower bound, which is obtained by multiplying the sum of minimum number of machines needed in all slots and the time length of each slot.

We assume that all VMs occupy their requested capacity fully (the worst case). For each set of VM requests, simulations are run 10 times. All the results shown are the average of the 10 runs.

7.4.3 Simulation using real traces

Because of a lack of data from real Cloud data centers regarding the energy consumption of computing resources, we use the readily available Lawrence Livermore National Lab Thunder log from Parallel Workloads Archive [27] to model incoming VM requests. This log is collected by a large Linux cluster called Thunder installed at Lawrence Livermore National Lab. From the log, we can extract relevant data consistent with our problem model, which includes the request number, start-time, requested time, and requested number of processors. We convert the time unit from seconds—as in the log—to minutes because we set 1 min as the time slot length in our simulation. We also convert the requested number of processors to correspond

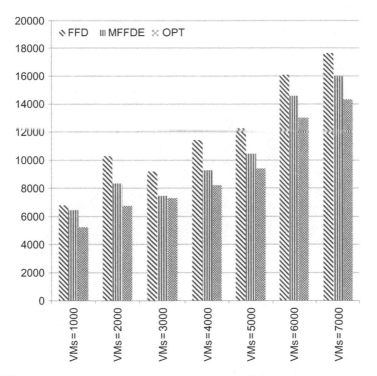

Figure 7.4 Total busy time (min) for increasing number of VM requests.

to the eight types of VM requests listed in Table 7.2. We run the simulations with sufficient number of PMs so that all VM requests can be allocated successfully without being rejected.

Figures 7.4–7.6 show the total busy time (in minutes), total energy consumption (in kilowatt hours), and total simulation time (in milliseconds), respectively, for the increasing number of VM requests (from 1000 to 7000).

7.4.4   Simulation using synthetic data

7.4.4.1   Data center energy consumption evaluation

All requests follow the Poisson arrival process and have exponential service times. The mean interarrival period is set as 5 slots, the maximum intermediate period between two arrivals is set as 50 slots, and the maximum duration of requests is set as 50, 100, 200, 400, and 800 slots, respectively. The total number of arrivals (VM requests) is 1000, each VM type has an equal number of 125 requests, and there are 60 PMs (20 for each PM type). Each slot is 5 min long. For example, if the requested duration (service time) of a VM is 20 slots, its actual time duration is $20 \times 5 = 100$ min.

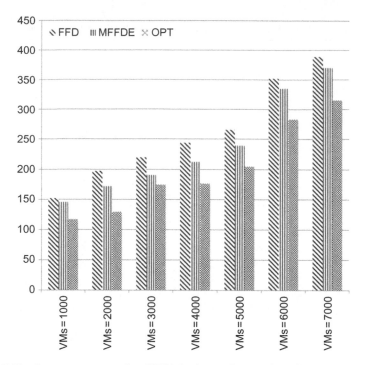

Figure 7.5 Total energy consumption (kWh) for increasing number of VM requests.

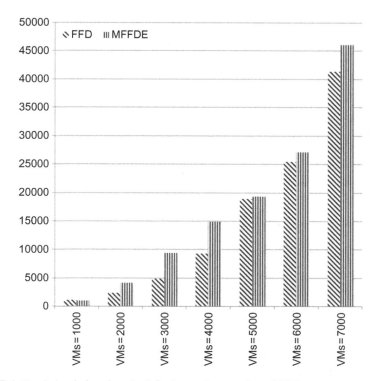

Figure 7.6 Total simulation time (ms) for increasing number of VM requests.

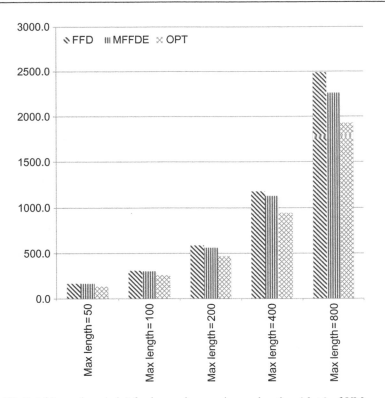

Figure 7.7 Total busy time (min) for increasing maximum duration (slots) of VM requests.

Figures 7.7 and 7.8 show the total busy time (in minutes) and total energy consumption (in kilowatt hours), respectively, for the increasing maximum duration (in slots) of VM requests (from 50 to 800). Results of the MFFDE are less than three times the results of the optimal solution (OPT). This validates our theoretical results and observations for total energy consumption.

7.4.4.2   Impact of total workload

Let us define the total workload $\rho = (\sum_{\forall j} d_j p_j)/mT_0$, where m is the total number of PMs, T_0 is the total time length under consideration, j is a VM request, and d_j is the capacity demand. By keeping the total number of VM requests fixed (e.g., VMs D 3000) and varying their durations, we can study the impact of total workload when p varies from 0.1 to 0.9.

Figures 7.9 and 7.10 show the total busy time (in minutes) and total energy consumption (in kilowatt hours), respectively, for the increasing total workload p (from 0.1 to 0.9). Both the FFD and the MFFDE have almost the same simulation times.

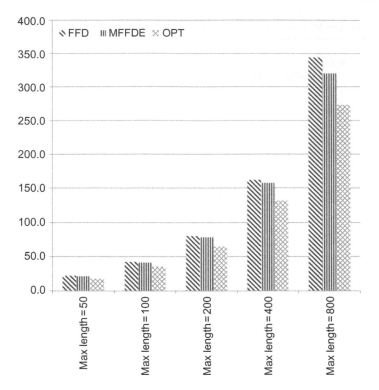

Figure 7.8 Total energy consumption (kWh) for increasing maximum duration (slots) of VM requests.

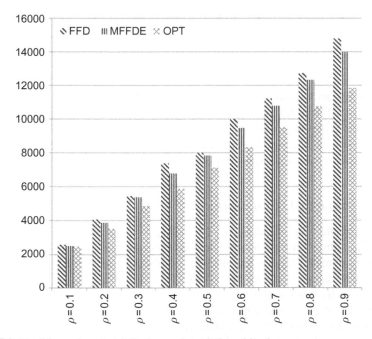

Figure 7.9 Total busy time (min) for increasing total workload p.

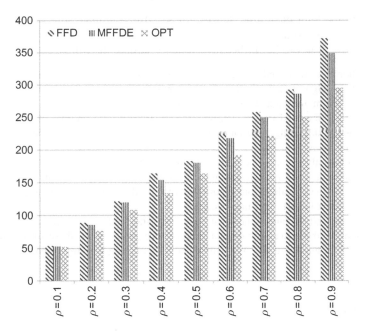

Figure 7.10 Total energy consumption (kWh) for increasing total workload p.

7.4.5   General observations

For both simulations using real traces and synthetic data, we observe that the total simulation times for the FFD and the MFFDE are in the same order, ranging from a few seconds to a few minutes. FFD > MFFDE > OPT for total busy time and total energy consumption; the results of the MFFDE are closer to the lower bound (OPT) and are about 2−10% more energy-saving than the FFD on the average. Hence, these simulation results validate our theoretical results and observations. Other similar results are not shown.

7.5   Conclusions

In this chapter, we improve the best-known bounds for multiple machine scheduling. As pointed out in [2,12], there is no existing polynomial time solution for the case of minimizing the total busy time of all machines to schedule all jobs nonpreemptively in their start-time−end-time windows, subject to the machine capacity constraint. We propose an approximation algorithm, the MFFDE, i.e., a 3-approximation in the general case and near optimal in the special and average cases. The MFFDE algorithm can be applied to Cloud computing and other related areas to improve energy efficiency. Because the MFFDE algorithm combines features of the FFD algorithm (largest process time first) and the ESTF algorithm, it also is a good approximation bound for minimizing the maximum makespan while minimizing the total busy time. It will not sacrifice the makespan in order to minimize the total busy time.

Some open issues to be further investigated include the following:

- Find better algorithms and bounds for general and special cases: We conjecture there are better offline algorithms for improving performance.
- Consider VM migration and energy consumption during migration transitions: It is possible to reduce the total energy consumption by limiting the number of VM migrations. As frequently migrating VMs can cause network congestion, the number of VM migrations should be minimized.
- Collect and analyze energy consumption data in real Cloud data centers: There is still a lack of data for real Cloud data centers regarding the energy consumption of computing resources. We can evaluate our algorithms in a medium-sized Cloud data center to analyze how they can be further improved.
- Considering start up time, shut down time, and other additional overheads in real implementation: In theoretical proofs and performance evaluations, these overheads are not considered for all algorithms. We will consider this during real implementation.

References

[1] Hoogeveen JA, van de Velde SL, Veltman B. Complexity of scheduling multiprocessor tasks with prespecified processor allocations. Discrete Appl Math 1994;55(3):259−72.
[2] Khandekar R, Schieber B, Shachnai H, Tamir T. Minimizing busy time in multiple machine real-time scheduling. Proceedings of IARCS annual conference on foundations of software technology and theoretical computer science (FSTTCS 2010), vol. 8. Chennai, India: LIPIcs, Schloss Dagstuhl—Leibniz-Zentrum fuer Informatik; 2010. p. 169−80.
[3] Brucker P. Scheduling algorithms. 5th ed. Berlin, Heidelberg, New York: Springer; 2007.
[4] Beloglazov A, Buyya R, Lee YC, Zomaya AY. A taxonomy and survey of energy-efficient data centers and Cloud computing systems. Adv Comput 2011;82:47−111.
[5] Jing SY, Ali S, She K, Zhong Y. State-of-the-art research study for green Cloud computing. J Supercomput 2011;1−24.
[6] Amazon EC2. Available from: <http://www.amazon.com/ec2>; 2013 [accessed 15.06.13].
[7] Graham RL. Bounds on multiprocessing timing anomalies. SIAM J Appl Math 1969;17 (2):416−29.
[8] Kleinberg JM, Tardos E. Algorithm design. Boston, MA: Addison-Wesley: Pearson Education, Inc.; 2006.
[9] Kovalyov MY, Ng CT, Cheng TCE. Fixed intervals scheduling: models, applications, computational complexity and algorithms. Eur J Oper Res 2007;178(2):331−42.
[10] Beloglazov A, Abawajy JH, Buyya R. Energy-aware resource allocation heuristics for efficient management of data centers for Cloud computing. Future Gen Comput Syst 2012;28(5):755−68.
[11] Winkler P, Zhang L. Wavelength assignment generalized interval graph coloring. Proceedings of fourteenth annual ACM-SIAM symposium on discrete algorithms (SODA 2003). Baltimore, MD: ACM/SIAM; 2003. p. 830−1.

[12] Flammini M, Monaco G, Moscardelli L, Shachnai H, Shalom M, Tamir T, et al. Minimizing total busy time in parallel scheduling with application to optical networks. Theor Comput Sci 2010;411(40−42):3553−62.

[13] Kolen AW, Lenstra JK, Papadimitriou CH, Spieksma FC. Interval scheduling: a survey. Nav Res Log 2007;54(5):530−43.

[14] Srikantaiah S, Kansal A, Zhao F. Energy aware consolidation for Cloud computing. Proceedings of USENIX workshop on power aware computing and systems (HotPower 2008). San Diego, CA: USENIX; 2008. p. 10−4.

[15] Lee YC, Zomaya AY. Energy efficient utilization of resources in Cloud computing systems. J Supercomput 2012;60(2):268−80.

[16] Liu H, Xu C, Jin H, Gong J, Liao X. Performance and energy modeling for live migration of virtual machines, the 20th international symposium on high performance distributed computing. 2011. p. 171−82.

[17] Kim KH, Beloglazov A, Buyya R. Power-aware provisioning of virtual machines for real-time Cloud services. Concurr Comput Pract Exp 2011;23(13):1491−505.

[18] Mathew V, Sitaraman RK, Shenoy PJ. Energy-aware load balancing in content delivery networks. Proceedings of IEEE INFOCOM. Orlando, FL: IEEE; 2012. p. 954−62.

[19] Rao L, Liu X, Xie L, Liu W. Minimizing electricity cost: optimization of distributed internet data centers in a multi-electricity-market environment. Proceedings of IEEE INFOCOM 2010. San Diego, CA: IEEE; 2010. p. 1145−53.

[20] Lin M, Wierman A, Andrew LLH, Thereska E. Dynamic right-sizing for power-proportional data centers. Proceedings of IEEE INFOCOM 2011. Shanghai, China: IEEE; 2011. p. 1098−106.

[21] Mertzios GB, Shalom M, Voloshin A, Wong PWH, Zaks S. Optimizing busy time on parallel machines. Proceedings of IPDPS. Shanghai, China: IEEE; 2012. p. 238−48.

[22] Garey MR, Johnson DS. Computers and intractability: a guide to the theory of NP-completeness. New York, NY: W. H. Freeman and Co.; 1979.

[23] Coffman EG, Garey MR, Johnson DS. Bin packing with divisible item sizes. J Complexity 1987;3(4):406−28.

[24] Armbrust M, Fox A, Griffith R, Joseph AD, Katz RH, Konwinski A, et al. A view of Cloud computing. Commun ACM 2010;53(4):50−8.

[25] Eucalyptus. Available from: <http://open.eucalyptus.com>; 2013 [accessed 15.06.13].

[26] Tian W, Zhao Y, Xu M, Zhong Y, Sun X. A toolkit for modeling and simulation of real-time virtual machine allocation in a Cloud data center. IEEE Transactions on Automation Science and Engineering 2013. Available from: http://dx.doi.org/10.1109/TASE.2013.2266338.

[27] Parallel Workloads Archive. Available from: <http://www.cs.huji.ac.il/labs/parallel/workload>; 2013 [accessed 10.07.13].

Comparative Study of Energy-efficient Scheduling in Cloud Data Centers

Main Contents of this Chapter:

- Background of energy-efficient scheduling
- Data center energy models
- MFFDE algorithm
- BFF algorithm
- GRID algorithm

8.1 Introduction

Today, the industry regards Cloud computing to be the fifth utility after water, electricity, gas, and oil resources. Cloud computing is a model of the business computing and information services, which allocate jobs to different data centers that consist of large numbers of physical or virtual servers, so applications can access computing power, storage space, and information services as needed.

Cloud computing is in an era of vigorous development, with new Cloud data centers becoming larger and larger. Additionally, energy consumption is gradually increasing. The current energy consumption in GDP in China is 11.5 times more than Japan, 8.7 times more than Germany and France, and 4.3 times more than the United States. In 2007, the total cost of energy consumption in China reached 13.68 billion yuan, which is equivalent to the amount of power generated by Gezhouba power station in 1 year. A data center with 500 servers will cost 1.8 million yuan in electricity bills each year. The power consumption used by server facilities—such as that for air-conditioning for cooling—is almost the same as that used by the server, itself. Once we spend 1 W of IT energy, we need more than 1 W of energy for cooling; but if we can save 1 W of IT energy, then we can also reduce the amount of energy used by the data center by at least as much. In order to avoid rising costs in terms of energy consumption, traditional data centers are struggling to find ways to enhance data center resource efficiency and reduce energy consumption.

According to statistics, a data center only uses about 20% of its computing power at any given time on average, therefore, 80% of its resources are idle or wasted. In addition, only about 3% of the power consumption in a data center is used to process the data. The huge waste of energy mainly stems from two separate sources: the need for redundant backup devices in order to ensure real-time system capabilities and a lack of efficient resource utilization.

With the development of Cloud computing, today's Cloud data centers must ensure critical business access capability, provide large-scale service scheduling ability or "transparent infinite capacity," ensure controllable bandwidth, and possess large-scale data center architecture. Well-designed energy-efficient scheduling algorithms can: centrally manage and dynamically use physical server and virtual resources in Cloud data centers, provide flexible and resilient services that help companies build dynamic, flexible infrastructure able to accommodate business growth; enable enterprises to provide high performance services; and achieve the goals of cost reduction and energy efficiency.

Power supply and air-conditioning needs currently make up the major costs of Cloud computing data centers. In order to measure the energy efficiency of Cloud data centers, the industry generally uses a data center energy consumption index. This index refers to the percentage of energy consumed by data center computing devices out of all of the energy consumed by the data center. Here the data center energy consumption includes the energy consumption of computing devices, as well as the energy used for temperature control, heating, ventilation, and lighting, among other things. The higher the energy consumption index, the better. In reality, the target value of the index should generally be between 0.8 and 0.9. Figure 8.1 shows 22 data center energy consumption indices, which indicate that the energy consumption in data centers has room for improvement. Energy-efficient scheduling algorithms for data centers are designed to target that need.

Scheduling algorithms for Cloud data centers need to dynamically allocate and integrate resources reasonably. Studies have shown that in the context of dealing with a fixed number of user requests, turning on fewer physical servers leads to less total energy consumption. However, what is the specific quantitative relationship between total data center energy consumption and the total number of physical machines being utilized? Is the total number of physical machine used directly

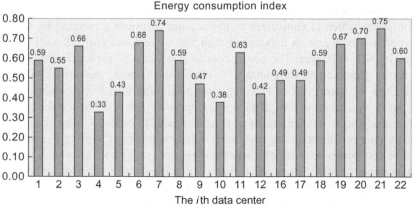

Figure 8.1 The comparison of 22 data centers' energy consumption [1] index.

related to the total energy consumption of a given total running time? Past studies have not engaged in an in-depth analysis of this relationship, so this chapter combines the energy consumption model with an in-depth study, and analyzes the results in details.

8.2 Related research

Kang and Wei-Min [2] introduce Cloud computing system instance and current status. Bing et al. [3] discuss green computing; Peng [4] introduces the research background and challenging Cloud computing and energy issues. Lin et al. [5] provide a detailed introduction to green power-saving mechanisms in networks, including the energy consumption model and evaluation methods. Ye et al. [6] analyze the current status and progress of research related to four aspects of energy management—energy measurement, energy modeling, management mechanisms, and management methods—and then presents ten further problems. Tan et al. [7] propose several optimal scheduling algorithms for Cloud platforms using the random task energy problem and an M/M/1 queuing model. Tian and Zhao [8] detail the basics of Cloud computing resource scheduling management. Lee and Zomaya [9] take the integration of real-time tasks into consideration for achieving the goal of maximum utilization: two real-time scheduling heuristic algorithms allocate real-time tasks to save energy by maximizing resource utilization. Eduardo et al. [10] propose to save energy through turning servers on or off according to system performance and current energy consumption. Energy-saving algorithms are implemented separately at the application level and at the operating system level. The scheduling algorithm considers energy consumption, performance, throughput, uptime, and other parameters to decide whether to add or remove nodes.

Flammini et al. [11] propose the minimization of the running time of all machines in order to save energy by designing a 4-approximation offline scheduling algorithm for task scheduling that considers the unit capacities and fixed process times of tasks. Khandekar et al. [12] provide a 5-approximation algorithm for general inputs and better bounds for some subclasses of inputs that relate to random request capacity. Shalom et al. [13] give an online scheduling algorithm with a competitive ratio of g (measuring physical server capacity) for general inputs and better bounds for some subclasses of inputs. Tan et al. [7] propose several optimal scheduling algorithms using the M/M/1 queuing model for Cloud platforms; Gandhia [14] discusses the physical server cluster, energy reduction, and performance (e.g., system response time) combining optimization and modeling methods to measure consumption and response times from different scheduling algorithms. Tian et al. [15] propose the implementation of a virtual computing platform as a service framework to facilitate user, resource, and access management—among other basic functions—through virtualization and 7×24 remote online services to improve resource sharing and utilization, and to provide more convenience to users. Tian [16] proposes different stochastic queuing models to meet quality of service requirements. Tian et al. [17] introduce several offline scheduling algorithms and their effects on energy consumption. Tian et al. [18] use parallel task scheduling to minimize the total running time of all physical servers: proposing a 3-approximation offline scheduling algorithm and applying related results to Cloud data center energy-efficient scheduling. Tian et al. [19] offer a dynamic dichotomy of online scheduling algorithms that provide better energy-saving results than the current online energy-saving algorithms.

8.3 Comparative study of offline scheduling algorithms

8.3.1 Energy models for data centers

8.3.1.1 Data center energy consumption evaluation

Data centers can be composed of a large number of servers. In the center, each row has rows of racks (cabinets) with multiple chassis on each shelf and each chassis containing multiple servers (blades). A server can be a single-core or a multi-core processor. All servers on a chassis share a power supply device. Data centers are now designed with hot and cold channel comprising intervals—a style shown in Figure 8.2—with each row of racks in a hot and a cold corridor of the middle [20]. The air-conditioning provides cold air, while the cold air passing through underfloor channels, and the gap to the ground.

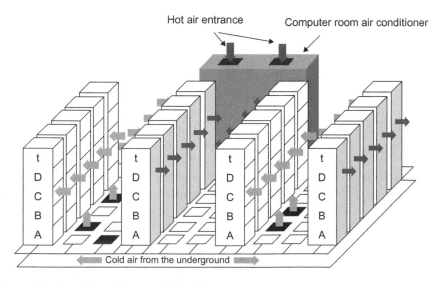

Figure 8.2 The airflow diagram of Cloud data centers.

Most of the power consumption in data centers is caused by computational processing, disk storage, networking, and cooling systems. The following is a formula

$$P_{\text{total}} = P_{\text{pm}} + P_{\text{AC}} + P_{\text{odditional}} \tag{8.1}$$

where P_{total} refers to the total energy consumption of the data center, P_{pm} refers to the total energy consumption of physical servers, P_{AC} refers to the energy consumption of the cooling system, and $P_{\text{odditional}}$ refers to other energy consumption (such as that from lighting and networking equipment).

The energy consumption of the refrigeration system can be represented by the following formula [4]:

$$P_{\text{AC}} = \frac{P_{\text{pm}}}{\text{CoP}(T_{\text{sup}})} \tag{8.2}$$

where T_{sup} is the temperature of the air entering the cooling system (air-conditioning) and $\text{CoP}(T_{\text{sup}})$ is the coefficient describing the performance of the cooling system (air-conditioning). This parameter presents the ratio of energy consumption by the refrigeration system compared to the energy consumption of the cooling system, itself. For example, the cooling system consumes 1000 W, itself consumes power is 500 W, the value of this coefficient is 2. This value is also related to the temperature of air entering the cooling system.

8.3.1.2 Server power consumption model

Combining with the existing research by other scholars, we can know that the utilization of a server is proportionate to the utilization of its CPUs. P_{min} is the power consumption when the server is idle; P_{max} is the maximum power consumed when the server is fully utilized. From this, we have the following formula:

$$P = P_{\text{min}} + (P_{\text{max}} - P_{\text{min}})u \tag{8.3}$$

where P refers to the power utilized by the physical servers and U refers to the CPU utilization of the physical servers.

In a real environment, the utilization of the CPU may change over time due to workload variability. Thus, CPU utilization is a function of time and is represented as $U_i(t)$. Therefore, the total energy consumption—E_i—by a physical machine can be defined as an integral of the power consumption function over a period of time as shown in the following:

$$E_i = \int_{t_0}^{t_1} P(U_i(t)) \mathrm{d}t \tag{8.4}$$

If $U_i(t)$ is constant over time (e.g., if average utilization is adopted, so $U_i(t) = U_i$), then

$$E_i = P(U_i)(t_1 - t_0) = P_{min}T_i + (P_{max} - P_{min})U_iT_i \qquad (8.5)$$

where T_i is the busy time of machine PM_i, $P_{min}T_i$ is the power consumed with a power-on time of PM_i, $P_{min}T_i = E_{pm_{on}}$, and $(P_{max} - P_{min})U_iT_i$ is the energy increase from hosting VMs. Assume that a VM increases the total utilization of a PM from U to U' and that $U - U' = \Delta U$, and that a VM is fully utilized in the worst case. Defining E_{vm_i} as the energy increase after running VM_i on PM_i from time t_0 to t_1, we obtain

$$\begin{aligned} E_{vm_i} &= (P_{min} + (P_{max} - P_{min})U' - (P_{min} + (P_{max} - P_{min})U))(t_1 - t_0) \\ &= (P_{max} - P_{min})(U' - U)(t_1 - t_0) \\ &= (P_{max} - P_{min})\Delta_u(t_1 - t_0) \end{aligned} \qquad (8.6)$$

To figure the real-time VM allocation, we can further show that the total energy consumption of PM_i is the sum of its idle energy consumption and the total energy increase from hosting all of the VMs allocated to it. The total energy consumption of the PM_i can be expressed as the sum of energy consumption when it is powered on and energy consumption by all VMs allocated to it. So, formally, the energy consumption of the PM_i is

$$\begin{aligned} E_i &= E_{i_{on}} + \sum_{j=1}^{k} E_{vm_j} \\ &= P_{min}T_i + (P_{max} - P_{min})\sum_{j=1}^{k} u_jt_j \end{aligned} \qquad (8.7)$$

where T_i is the total power-on time of machine PM_i, u_j is the utilization increase of VM_j allocated on PM_i, and t_j is the length of time that VM_j works on PM_i.

The total energy consumption of a Cloud data center is computed as

$$E_{cdc} = \sum_{i=1}^{n} E_i \qquad (8.8)$$

It is the sum of energy consumed by all PMs. Note that energy consumption of all VMs on PMs is included in the final figure.

8.3.2 FFD algorithm

FFD is short for the first-fit-decreasing algorithm. The main premise of the algorithm is that virtual requests are sorted in decreasing order of processing times first;

that is to say we first allocate a virtual request to a physical machine if its processing time is the longest out of all of the virtual requests. The algorithm allocates the virtual task to the first physical machine that can accommodate the virtual request.

8.3.3   MFFDE algorithm

For offline non-real-time scheduling, the longest processing time first (LPT) algorithm is one of the best approximation algorithms. The LPT is known to have the best possible upper bound for minimizing the maximum makespan in the case of $g = 1$ (where g is the capacity of a server as explained in Chapter 7) in a traditional multiprocessor system. In this paper, the start-times and end-times of jobs are fixed, and the general case $g > 1$ is considered. The fixed start-times and end-times of jobs and the capacity constraint of machines must be taken into account when allocating jobs. Our modified first-fit-decreasing-earliest (MFFDE) algorithm schedules jobs in the nonincreasing order of their process times and considers the earlier start-time first (STF) if two jobs have the same process times or breaks ties arbitrarily when two jobs have exactly the same start-times, end-times, and process times. Each job is scheduled to the first machine with the capacity to perform it (so as to use the fewest number of machines possible to minimize total busy time).

8.3.4   Other offline algorithms

In an offline situation, if we know all of the relevant information for requested VMs, the allocation of VMs and the energy consumption of the entire system can be calculated using the following algorithms.

8.3.4.1   The STF algorithm

The main idea behind the STF algorithm is that virtual machines are sorted in ascending order by start-times. The maximum load of overlapping time periods is used to determine the minimum number of physical machines needed (for the sake of energy efficiency and to maximize scheduling utilization). Then the virtual machines are allocated and, ultimately, the energy consumption of all of the pms can be determined.

The main pseudo-code of the STF algorithm is shown in Algorithm 1.

8.3.4.2   The earliest ending-time first algorithm

The main idea behind the ending-time first (ETF) algorithm is that, first, the virtual machines are sorted in ascending order by their end-times and based on the maximum load of overlapping time periods to find the minimum number of physical machines needed. Then virtual machines are allocated based on the physical machine load and, ultimately, the energy consumption of all the of the physical machines can be found (Algorithm 2).

Input: VM requests indicated by their (required VM type IDs, start-time, ending-time, requested capacity), the number of the request i is denoted as R_i.

Output: IDs of PMs for all VMs, the number of the needed PMs, the total energy consumption.

1.sort the virtual machine in ascending order of their start-time;

2.for $i =$ from 1 to n do

3. $d = 0$;

4.if they are not overlapped or overlapped but still can share resources of an PM do;

5.allocate i to the PM d ;

6.else;

7.start a new PM; $d = d + 1$; allocate i to PM d ;

8.end;

9.end for

Algorithm 1 The STF algorithm.

Input: VM requests indicated by their (required VM type IDs, start-time, ending-time, requested capacity), the number of the request i is denoted as R_i.

Output: IDs of PMs for all VMs, the number of the needed PMs, the total energy consumption.

Initialization: allocating an ID to each PM.

1. sort the virtual machine in ascending order of their end-time;

2. for $i =$ from1 to n do

3. $d = 0$;

4. if they are not overlapped or overlapped but still can share resources of an PM do;

5. allocate i to the PM d;

6. else;

7.start a new PM; $d = d + 1$; allocate i to PM d;

8. end;

9. end for

Algorithm 2 The earliest ETF algorithm.

Input: VM requests indicated by their (required VM type IDs, start-time, ending-time, requested capacity), the number of the request i is denoted as R_i.

Output: IDs of PMs for all VMs, the number of the needed PMs, the total energy consumption.

Initialization: allocating an ID to each PM.

1. calculate the approximate number of the $PM -d$ according to the load of each time slot;

2. for $i =$ from 1 to n do

3. select a PM randomly;

4. if the virtual machine can be allocated to the PM do;

5. allocate i to the PM d;

6. else;

7. loop 3–5 utill the VM has been allocated to a PM;

8. end;

9. end for

Algorithm 3 The random allocation algorithm.

8.3.4.3   Random allocation algorithm (Random)

The main idea underlying the random allocation algorithm is that a physical machine that can host the request is randomly selected, based on the number of virtual machines. The algorithm applies a random selection function; the core pseudocode is shown in Algorithm 3.

8.4   Online algorithms

The main idea behind this algorithm is that once a request is received, it must be allocated immediately; the scheduler must tell the user to which physical machine a request can be assigned (Algorithm 4).

8.4.1   BFF algorithm

The BFF (bipartition-first-fit) algorithm schedules the job on a first-come-first-service (FIFS) principle, dynamically partitioning the time plane into two sub windows (bipartitioning) and allocating the request to the first machine that can host it (first-fit). The BFF algorithm is described in more detail in Algorithm 5.

Input: a VM request indicates (required VM type IDs, start-time, ending-time, requested capacity), the number of the request i is denoted as R_i.

Output: IDs of PMs for all VMs, the number of the needed PMs, the total energy consumption.

Initialization: allocating an ID to each PM.

1. $d = 0$;

2. when there comes the request of the VM do;

3. if they are not overlapped or overlapped but still can share resources of an PM do;

4. allocate i to the PM d;

5. else;

6. start a new PM; $d = d + 1$; allocate i to PM d;

7. end;

8. end for

Algorithm 4 Online algorithm.

Input: g, the max capacity of a machine, and job I_i one by one.

Output: The scheduled jobs and total busy time of all machines and total number of machines used.

3. Allocates the first job to machine m_1;

4. **for** all job comes and time period in T **do**

5.   **IF** there is only one job, allocate it to the first machine;

4.   **ELSE** Computes the longest and the second longest interval of all current requests in

the system, set $k = \dfrac{span(the\ longest\ interval)}{span(the\ second\ longest\ interval)}$;

5.   **IF** $k > 1$, dynamically partitions the time plane into two sub windows LEFT and RIGHT using the median of all end-time of current requests as the partitioning point. The first job is counted as in LEFT window. Any job interval with end-time at left side of the partitioning point belongs to LEFT window, others belong to RIGHT;

6.   **Else** considers alljobs in LEFT window;

7.   allocate jobs to machines by First-fit for each time window;

8. **end**

9. Counts workload and busy time of all machines;

10. Returns the set of machines used and total busy time.

Algorithm 5 BFF algorithm.

This algorithm has computational complexity $O(nm)$, where n is the number of jobs and m is the number of machines used. The algorithm finds a machine for a request needing $O(m)$ steps, with n jobs needing $O(nm)$ steps. Therefore, the entire algorithm takes $O(nm)$ time, where $n > m$.

Theorem 1 describes the hardness of the general problem.

Theorem 1 Minimizing the total busy time of multiple, offline identical machines using real-time scheduling without preemption and with capacity constraints (MinTBT-ON) is—generally—an NP-complete problem.

One NP-hard proof of an offline version of this problem is provided in Ref. [15]. Peng [4] shows it is NP-hard to approximate the problem in the special case in which all jobs have the same (one unit) processing time and can be scheduled in one fixed time interval, with a simple reduction from the subset sum problem. This also can be proved by reducing a well-known NP-complete problem—a set partitioning problem—to an offline version of the MinTBT-ON problem in polynomial time.

In the following, we consider the unit demand case ($d_i = 1$) only for the competitive ratio analysis of the upper bound.

8.4.1.1 The bounds for the competitive ratio when g is one unit and d_i is one unit

When g is one unit and d_i is also one unit, our problem reduces to a traditional interval scheduling problem with the start-time and end-time constraint, where each job needs a one unit capacity and the total capacity of a machine is one unit.

Theorem 2 There exists an algorithm for the optimal solution in polynomial time for the MinTBT-ON problem when the demand is one unit and the total capacity of each machine is also one unit, especially $\mathrm{BFF}(I) = \mathrm{OPT}(I) = \mathrm{len}(I)$ in this case.

Proof Since the capacity parameter g is one unit, let us set it as 1. Each job needs a capacity of 1, and each machine can only process one job at any given time. In this case, using the definitions (Definition 1 and 2 given in Chapter 7) of interval length and span, we have $\mathrm{OPT}(I) = \mathrm{len}(I)$, whether there are overlapping jobs or not. By allocating each interval to a different machine for continuous working intervals, $\mathrm{BFF}(I)$ has a total busy time equal to the sum of the lengths of all of the intervals. This completes the proof.

8.4.1.2 The bounds for the competitive ratio in the general case when g > 1

Theorem 3 The competitive ratio of our proposed BFF algorithm for the MinTBT-ON problem has an upper bound of

$$\left(1 + \frac{g-2}{k} - \frac{g-1}{k^2}\right)$$

where $k =$ span(the longest interval)/span(the second longest interval).

Proof We use the adversary described in algorithm Adversary (r, t, d) [13]. The Adversary assigns a new machine to a job of length lk^j, for some job j, and recursively treats lk^j as t. The adversary is described by three parameters (r, t, d), where $1 \le d < g$ is the number of machines used by the Adversary. Initially, the parameters for Adversary is $(0, T, 1)$, where T can be set as a large number, set $T = glk^g$, so that $k = (T/gl)^{1/g}$.

The general example is shown in Figure 8.3. There are g groups of jobs, and each group has g columns of jobs from left to right, and each column of jobs has g requests with lengths $l, lk, \ldots, lk^g$. In this case, for the optimal solution, one can allocate all of the longest requests to a machine m_1 for a busy time of T, then allocate all of the second longest requests to another machine m_2 for a busy time of $T/k, \ldots$, etc., and then finally allocate all of the shortest requests to machine m_g with a busy time of T/k^{g-1}. The total busy time of the optimal solution, therefore, is

$$\sum_{i=0}^{g-1} \frac{T}{k^i} = \frac{T(1 - (1/k^g))}{1 - (1/k)}$$

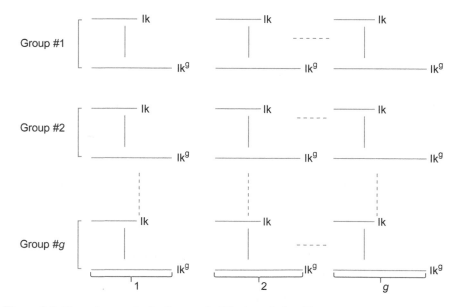

Figure 8.3 General example for the proof of the bound algorithm.

Adversary (r,t,d)
1:     WHILE $d \leq g$ DO
2:     $l = \dfrac{t}{k^g}$
3:     DO
4:     Release jobs with start-time r and length l, lk,
5:     WHILE (a new machine is used for a job of length lk^j)
6:     Adversary $(s, lk^j, d+1)$
7:     $s = s+lk^j$
8:     END WHILE

The BFF algorithm partitions the time plane into two parts, so that all of the longest jobs will be allocated to a single machine with a busy time of T, the remaining jobs will be allocated based on the first-fit principle, with a maximum possible busy time of T/k, therefore, the total busy time of BFF is expressed as $\mathrm{BFF}(I) = T + (g-1)(T/k)$. Therefore, the competitive ratio of BFF is

$$
\begin{aligned}
\frac{\mathrm{BFF}(I)}{\mathrm{OPT}(I)} &= \frac{T + (g-1)(T/k)}{T(1 - (1/k^g))/(1 - 1/k)} \\
&= \frac{k^g + (g-2)k^{g-1} - (g-1)k^{g-2}}{k^g - 1} \\
&\approx 1 + \frac{g-2}{k} + \frac{g-1}{k^2}, \quad k \geq 1
\end{aligned}
\tag{8.9}
$$

Note that the simple first-fit algorithm will have a total busy time of gT with the upper bound of g in this case; specifically, when $g = 1$, the above equation has a value of 1 for g, which validates our Theorem 2.

Theorem 4 For the case in which the capacity parameter $g = \infty$, there exists an algorithm in polynomial time to find an optimal solution for the MinTBT-ON problem.

Proof When $g = \infty$, one machine is enough for all of the jobs. In this case, the total busy time is determined by the span of all jobs. Any algorithm that solely allocates jobs based on their required start-times, end-times, and capacities, will have the same total busy times: Alg $x(I) = \mathrm{OPT}(I) = \mathrm{span}(I)$.

Before considering a few special cases, we have the following new observation:

Observation 1 In Ref. [13], $a(1 + \varphi)$-competitive for a one-sided clique instance where $\varphi = (1 + \sqrt{5})/2$, i.e., all job intervals have the same start-time, assuming

$\alpha^{i-1} < \text{len}(m_i) \le \alpha^i$, $\alpha = (3 + \sqrt{5})/2$. The assumption is that $\alpha = (3 + \sqrt{5})/2$ is too restrictive so that the result is only true for some specific examples.

Proof In Ref. [13], authors assume $\alpha^{i-1} < \text{len}(m_i) \le \alpha^i$, $\alpha = (3 + \sqrt{5})/2$ and obtain $a(1 + \varphi)$-competitive for one-sided clique instances where $\varphi = (1 + \sqrt{5})/2$. However, for the general one-sided case, this assumption is too restrictive (very unique). The GREEDYBUCKET algorithm in Ref. [13] assumes that a job j is categorized to a bucket according to len(j): the bucket of a job set J is the minimum value of i such that $\text{len}(j) \le \alpha^i$. For $i \ge 1$, the bucket i consists of a set of jobs J such that $\alpha^{i-1} < \text{len}(J) \le \alpha^i$. Considering the following adversary: job i has a start-time 0 and an end-time α^i. Using the definition of GREEDYBUCKET in Ref. [13], each job will be allocated to a different bucket (machine). If there are g^2 jobs, the GREEDYBUCKET algorithm needs g^2 machines with a total busy time of

$$\sum_{i=1}^{g^2} \alpha^i = \frac{\alpha^{g^2+1} - 1}{\alpha - 1} - 1, \quad \alpha > 1$$

The optimal solution in this case is to have g groups allocated to g machines, with a total busy time of

$$\sum_{i=1}^{g} \alpha^{gi} = \frac{\alpha^{g^2+g} - \alpha^g}{\alpha^g - 1}, \quad \alpha > 1$$

Therefore, we have

$$\frac{\text{GREEDYBUCKET}(I)}{\text{OPT}(I)} = \frac{((\alpha^{g^2+1} - 1)/(\alpha - 1)) - 1}{((\alpha^{g^2+g} - \alpha^g)/(\alpha^g - 1))}$$

$$= \frac{\alpha^{g+1} - \alpha}{\alpha^{g+1} - \alpha^g} = \frac{1 - (1/\alpha^g)}{1 - (1/\alpha)}, \quad \alpha > 1, g > 1$$

Therefore, in the worst case, the competitive ratio of the GREEDYBUCKET algorithm can be very large when α is close to 1 and g is large. This completes the proof.

Theorem 5 In the case in which all jobs form a one-sided clique [13] in which all jobs have the same start-time or end-time, the proposed algorithm has the competitive ratio $(1 + ((g - 2)/k) - ((g - 1)/k^2))$ in the worst case.

Proof We use the adversary described in the following. Consider the case in which all g^2 requests have the same start-time at $s_i = 0$, each has an end-time at $e_i = (T/k^{g-j})$, and where T is the time length under consideration, k is natural number, and if $(i \bmod g) \ne 0$, $j = (i \bmod g)$, else $j = g$. In this example, for the optimal solution, one can allocate all of the longest requests to a machine m_1 for a busy time of T, then allocate all of the second longest requests to another machine m_2 for a busy time of T/k, and, finally, allocate all of the shortest requests to a machine m_g with a busy time of T/k^{g-1}. The total busy time of the optimal solution therefore is

$$\sum_{i=0}^{g-1} \frac{T}{k^i} = \frac{T(1 - (1/k^g))}{1 - (1/k)}$$

The BFF algorithm partitions the time plane into two parts, so all of the longest jobs will be allocated to a single machine with a busy time T, the remaining jobs will be allocated based on the first-fit rule, with a busy time at most of T/k, therefore, the total busy time of BFF is $\text{BFF}(I) = T + (g - 1)(T/k)$.

So, the competitive ratio for the BFF algorithm is

$$\frac{\text{BFF}(I)}{\text{OPT}(I)} = \frac{T + (g - 1)(T/k)}{T(1 - (1/k^g))/(1 - 1/k)}$$

$$= \frac{k^g + (g - 2)k^{g-1} - (g - 1)k^{g-2}}{k^g - 1} \tag{8.10}$$

$$\approx 1 + \frac{g - 2}{k} + \frac{g - 1}{k^2}, \quad k \geq 1$$

In the specific case when $g = 1$, the above equation has a value of 1, which validates our Theorem 2. Note that if all job intervals have the same end-time, one can easily check that the same result is obtained.

8.4.2   GRID algorithm

8.4.2.1   GREEDYBUCKET is g-competitive in the worst-case scenario

Proof The adversary is as follows: there are α^{g-1} jobs with length α, which are consecutively in a line (i.e. the end-time of the previous job is the start-time of the next job); there are α^{g-2} jobs with length α^2 consecutively in a line; there are α^{g-i} jobs with length α^i consecutively in a line; and, finally, there is a job of length α^g. The GREEDYBUCKET algorithm in Ref. [21] will have a total busy time of $g\alpha^g$ with a competitive ratio g in this case, because different lengths of requests will be allocated to different buckets (machines). That is, jobs with the length of α are allocated to bucket 1 (machine M_1), jobs with the length of α^2 are allocated to bucket 2 (machine M_2),..., and, finally, the job with the length of α^g is allocated to bucket g (machine M_g). Therefore, the total busy time for GREEDYBUCKET is $g\alpha^g$, while the optimal solution uses just one machine for all jobs with a total busy time of α^g.

In this chapter, the start-times and end-times of jobs are fixed and the general case in which $g > 1$ is considered. We need to consider the fixed start-time and end-time of jobs and the capacity constraint of machines when allocating jobs. When considering online scheduling, we propose a new GRID algorithm. The GRID algorithm schedules the job on a FIFS principle, partitioning the time plane into sub grids and allocating the request to the first machine with the capacity to host (first-fit). The GRID depends on a parameter β, an integer, and $\beta \in (1, g)$. The GRID algorithm is described in detail in Algorithm 6 and an example is shown in Figure 8.4.

Definition 1 GRIDing rule: The absolute length of an interval is its process time. The relative length of an interval is the distance of its end-time from the origin point (start-point for the time plane). A job j_i is categorized to a grid according to the GRIDing rule: there are two types of grids: an absolute grid i contains jobs that have an absolute length between $(\beta^{i-1}, \beta^i]$; a relative grid i contains jobs that have a relative length between $(\beta^{i-1}, \beta^i]$.

This algorithm has a computational complexity of $O(nm)$, where n is the number of jobs and m is the number of machines used.

Theorem 6 The competitive ratio of the GRID algorithm for the MinTBT-ON problem has an upper bound of β in the worst case, where $1 < \beta < g$.

Proof The adversary is as follows: as shown in Figure 8.5, there are g groups of jobs in which each job has a length of $\beta^{g-1} + 1$. For group i, note that the left-side

---

Input: a job j_i comes one by one, and g, the max capacity of a machine

Output: The scheduled jobs and total busy time of all machines

6. Determine the GRID i of input job j according to the parameter β, a job j belongs to a relative or absolute GRID i if and only it satisfies GRIDing rule;

7. **if** GRID i has no machine allocated **then**

3.   open a new machine and make it the current machine;

4. **end**

5. **if** Current machine of GRID i can't host any more job because of capacity constraint **then**

6.   open a new machine;

7.   update load of current machine;

8. **end**

9. Find busy times of all machines;

10. Return the set of machines used, and the total busy time of all machines

Algorithm 6 GRID algorithm.

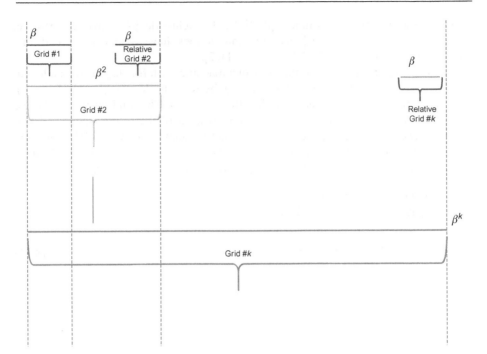

Figure 8.4 GRIDing rule for the GRID algorithm.

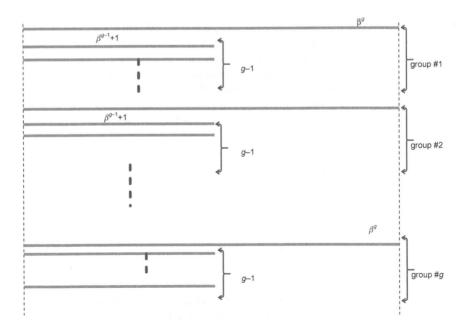

Figure 8.5 One worst-case example for the GRID algorithm.

jobs have a start-time, end-time $= [0, \beta^{g-1}]$, the right-side jobs have a start-time, end-time $= [\beta^g - \beta^{g-1} - 1, \beta^g]$, and the middle-jobs have a start-time, end-time between $[(\beta^g - \beta^{g-1} - 1)/2, (2\beta^g - \beta^{g-1} - 1)/2]$.

In this case, the optimal solution uses one machine for left-side jobs with a length of $(\beta^{g-1} + 1)$, $(g - 1)$ machines for middle-jobs with the length $(g - 1)(\beta^{g-1} + 1)$, one machine for right-side jobs with length $(\beta^{g-1} + 1)$. The total busy time for the optimal solution is $(g + 1)(\beta^{g-1} + 1)$. In contrast, all of these jobs have a relative length between $((\beta^{g-1}, \beta^g]]$ and will be put onto the same grid. The GRID algorithm needs g machines with one machine for each group of jobs, each group of jobs have a span length of $g\beta^g$. Hence $\text{GRID}(I) = g\beta^g$. We now have the following:

$$\frac{\text{GRID}(I)}{\text{OPT}(I)} = \frac{g\beta^g}{(g + 1)(\beta^{g-1} + 1)}$$

$$= \frac{g\beta^g}{(g + 1)\beta^{g-1} + g + 1} \tag{8.11}$$

$$\approx \frac{\beta}{1 + 1/g} \approx \beta, \quad 1 < \beta < g$$

This completes the proof.

Theorem 7 The GRID algorithm is $g/(1 + (g - 1)/\beta)$-competitive for a one-sided set of the MinTBT-ON problem, $1 < \beta < g$.

Proof The adversary is that there are g^2 jobs that all started at the same time (set all start-times as zero); there are g groups of jobs; all groups have a first job with length β^g, the others are $(g - 1)$ with length $(\beta^{g-1} + 1)$, in that order. In this case, GRID will allocate each group to a different Grid so that the total busy time for the GRID algorithm is $g\beta^g$; while the total busy time for the optimal solution is: $\beta^g + (g - 1)(\beta^{g-1} + 1)$, since all of the longest jobs can be allocated to a single machine and the others are allocated to $(g - 1)$ machines. Therefore, in this case:

$$\frac{\text{GRID}(I)}{\text{OPT}(I)} = \frac{g\beta^\alpha}{\alpha^g + (g - 1)(\alpha^{g-1} + 1)}$$

$$= \frac{g}{1 + ((g - 1)/\alpha) + ((g - 1)/\alpha^g)} \tag{8.12}$$

$$\approx \frac{g}{1 + ((g - 1)/\alpha)}, \quad 1 < \alpha < g$$

Remarks From Theorems 6 and 7, we should set β as small as possible to have the best performance in practice. For example, GRID is 2-competitive for a one-sided set when $\beta = 2$.

8.5 Summary

In this chapter, we have improved the best-known bounds for multiple machine real-time scheduling. As pointed out in Refs. [11,22], there is no existing polynomial time solution for an example that minimizes the total busy time of all machines to schedule all jobs non-preemptively in their start-time−end-time windows, subject to machine capacity constraints. Since the MFFDE algorithm combines features of the FFD algorithm (largest process time first) and the Earliest STF algorithm, it also has good approximation bounds for minimizing the maximum makespan while minimizing the total busy time. The design and analysis of approximation algorithms for other objectives—such as minimizing the total number of machines and minimizing the makespan—are currently under study.

There are still some research issues we can further investigate:

1. Finding better algorithms and bounds for general and special cases. We conjecture there are better bounds for online and offline algorithms and that this needs further investigation.
2. Considering arbitrary-sized jobs for online and offline scheduling. In this paper, we focus on unit-sized jobs. We believe these results can be extended for arbitrary-sized jobs and will provide further solid theoretical proofs.
3. Combining with load-balance and other related performance issues. Consideration of energy alone or load-balance alone is not enough for the whole system to perform efficiently in a real-world environment. We need to combine a few different objectives together to find a comprehensive way.

References

[1] Cloud-Standards. <http://cloud-standards.org/wiki/index.php?title=Main_Page#NIST _WorkingDefinition_of_Cloud_Computing>
[2] Kang C, Wei-Min Z. Cloud computing: system instance and current research. J Softw 2009;20(5):1339−48.
[3] Bing G, Yan S, Zi-Li S. The redefinition and some discussion about green computing. Chin J Comput 2009;32(12):2311−9.
[4] Liu P., Cloud computing, Publishing House of Electronics Industry, China, 2010.
[5] Lin C, Tian Y, Yao M. Green networks and green evaluation: the energy-saving mechanism, model and evaluation. Chin J Comput 2011;34(4):593−612.
[6] Ye K-J, Wu Z-H, Jiang X-H, He Q-M. Power management of virtualized Cloud computing platform. Chin J Comput 2012.
[7] Tan Y-M, Zeng G-S, Wang W. Policy of energy optimal management for Cloud computing platform with stochastic tasks. J Softw 2012;23(2):266−78.
[8] Tian W, Zhao Y. Cloud computing: resource scheduling and management. China: National Defense Industry Press; 2011.
[9] Lee YC, Zomaya AY. Energy efficient utilization of resource in Cloud computing systems. J Supercomput 2010; [Published online March 19, 2010].
[10] Pinheiro E, Bianchini R, Carrera EV, Heath T. Load balancing and unbalancing for power and performance in cluster-based systems, the workshop on compilers and operating systems for low power. 2001. p. 182−95.

[11] Flammini M, Monaco G, Moscardelli L, Shachnai H, Shalom M, Tamir T, et al. Minimizing total busy time in parallel scheduling with application to optical networks. Theor Comput Sci 2010;411(40−42):3553−62.

[12] Khandekar R, Schieber B, Shachnai H, Tamir T, Minimizing busy time in multiple machine real-time scheduling, IARCS annual conference on foundations of software technology and theoretical computer science, 2010, December 15−18. Chennai, India, 2010.

[13] Shalom M, Voloshin A, Wong PWH, Yung FCC, Zaks S. Online optimization of busy time on parallel machines, theory and applications of models of computation. Lect Notes Comput Sci 2012;7287:448−60.

[14] Gandhia A, Guptaa V, Harchol-Baltera M, Kozuchb MA. Optimality analysis of energy-performance trade-off for server farm management. Perform Eva 2010;1−23.

[15] Tian W, Su S, Lu G. A framework for implementing and managing platform as a service in a virtual Cloud computing lab, International workshop on education technology and computer science, 2010, 6−7 March. 2010. p. 273−76.

[16] Tian WH. Adaptive dimensioning of Cloud datacenters. In: Proceedings of the IEEE eighth international conference on dependable, autonomic and secure computing (DASC-09), Chengdu, China, December 12−14, 2009; 2009.

[17] Tian W-H, Yeo C-S, Xue R. Power-aware scheduling of real-time virtual machines in Cloud data centers considering fixed processing intervals. In: Proceedings of IEEE CCIS 2012, Hangzhou.

[18] Tian W-H, Yao CS. Minimizing total busy time of offline real-time parallel scheduling with application to energy efficiency in Cloud computing. Concurr Comput Pract Exp 2012;10.

[19] Tian W-H, et al. Energy-efficient online real-time parallel scheduling with application to Cloud computing. J Supercomput 2012;9.

[20] Moore J, Chase J, Ranganathan P. Making scheduling cool: temperature-aware workload placement in data centers. In: Proceedings of the annual conference on USENIX annual technical conference (ATC'05), 2005; 2005.

[21] Kovalyov MY, Ng CT, Cheng E. Fixed interval scheduling: models, applications, computational complexity and algorithms. Eur J Oper Res 2007;178(2):331−42.

[22] Foster I, et al. Cloud computing and grid computing 360-degree compared. IEEE international workshop on grid computing environments (GCE) 2008, co-located with IEEE/ACM Supercomputing 2008; 2008.

Energy Efficiency Scheduling in Hadoop

Main Contents of this Chapter:

- Hadoop introduction
- Scheduling algorithms
- Design and implementation of Hadoop energy control system
- Energy-efficient scheduling for multiple users
- Test and analysis of energy-efficient scheduling algorithms

9.1 Overview

9.1.1 Hadoop introduction

Hadoop is a distributed infrastructure system, developed by the Apache Foundation, in which users can develop distributed programs without first needing an understanding of the underlying details. Users can fully utilize the power of high-speed computing clusters and storage. Hadoop implements a distributed file system called the Hadoop Distributed File System (HDFS) that has high fault tolerance features and is designed to be deployed in low-cost hardware. Hadoop provides a high data transfer rate, making it suitable for applications that require large data to function. HDFS relaxes the requirements of the POSIX file system so data can be accessed in the form of streams. As a well-known open source project that focuses on distributed computing, Hadoop has received increasing amounts of attention. It has been used in many large companies, such as Amazon, Facebook, Yahoo!, and IBM, and is widely used in many fields, such as web search, log analysis, advertising computing, and data mining.

As a system with a large number of nodes, Hadoop has no dynamic node management in its early design. In a traditional Hadoop cluster, Hadoop determines the number of nodes once the system is open; therefore, the energy efficiency and resource utilization is not high. Thus, the study of Hadoop dynamic management can effectively improve its performance and efficiency. This improvement would be of great significance for improved energy conservation and large-scale applications of Hadoop.

9.1.2 Hadoop framework

Hadoop is a distributed process software framework that can be used for large data. It is reliable, efficient, and scalable. Hadoop is reliable because it assumes computing storage and facilities will fail; therefore, it maintains multiple working copies of data so that it can redistribute in case of node failure. It is efficient because it has a parallel design and by using parallel computing, it improves processing speed. Finally, Hadoop is scalable and can handle petabyte (PB)-level data. Moreover, because Hadoop relies on an ordinary server, it is relatively low cost. Hadoop has many modules, the most important of which are the HDFS and MapReduce modules. HDFS is the lowest level system in Hadoop; it stores all files on the storage node in the Hadoop cluster. MapReduce is the upper layer engine on HDFS and is composed of JobTrackers and TaskTrackers.

The core idea of MapReduce is to parallelly decompose the task and combine the results. HDFS provides the underlying storage support for distributed computing. MapReduce is a programming model for parallel computing of large data sets (typically greater than 1 terabyte (TB)). The program's main goal, to map and simplify (Map denotes mapping and Reduce denotes simplifying), is borrowed from other functional programming languages and takes some properties from vector programming languages. This model facilitates program function on a distributed system, requiring little distributed programming knowledge from the programmer. Current software implementation is to specify a mapping function for a group of key-value mapping into a new set of key-value pairs and run a Reduce (simplified) function to ensure all key mappings share the same key group. A simplified MapReduce task execution process is shown in Figure 9.1. The MapReduce framework consists of a single master node (JobTracker) and slave nodes (TaskTrackers). The master node is responsible for scheduling all tasks that constitute a job, distributing these tasks to slave nodes, and monitoring the task execution, which includes re-executing failed tasks. Slave nodes, however, are only responsible for the execution of the tasks assigned by the master node. A MapReduce job will usually divide the input data set into several separate blocks so the Map task can address them parallelly. Framework will sort the output of the Map first, then transfer them to the Reduce task. The input and output are stored in the HDFS. The framework is responsible for monitoring and re-executing the failed task.

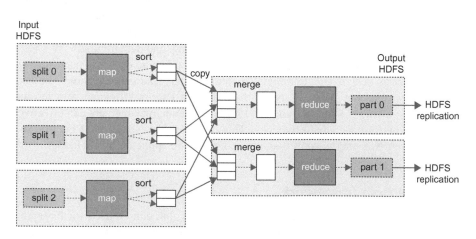

Figure 9.1 MapReduce flowchart.

HDFS is highly fault tolerant and designed to be deployed on cheap hardware. It provides high throughput to access application data and is suitable for applications with large data sets. HDFS usually has hundreds of server nodes, any one may fail; therefore, HDFS has the ability to automatically detect errors and rapidly recover. The usual HDFS file size ranges from gigabyte (GB) to TB, so HDFS is good to write, providing very high bandwidth data. Most data on HDFS only write once and read many times. Once a file is created, written, and closed, it has no need to modify. This simplifies the data consistency and high throughput data access problems. As a Master/Slave architecture, as shown in Figure 9.2, the HDFS cluster usually consists of a NameNode and multiple DataNodes. NameNode is the central server—it manages the file system namespace, as well as responds to the client. A DataNode is responsible for managing the data stored on that particular node. Users can store any data on the HDFS file system using namespace. In internal storage, a file is cut into one or more blocks. The NameNode performs file system namespace operations stored on a DataNode, such as open, close, and rename the file or directory. It also determines the mapping from the block to a specific DataNode. All data blocks on HDFS have copies. The number and size of the copied blocks are configurable. HDFS files are write once and have only one writer. The NameNode manages the process of data copy; it periodically receives DataNode block status report from heartbeat signals. Block status report contains a list of all of the data blocks on a DataNode.

9.1.3 Hadoop running processes

A complete Hadoop running process is based on the idea of "divide and conquer." The Map process is the "divide" step and the Reduce process is the "conquer" step. The entire process is shown in Figure 9.3.

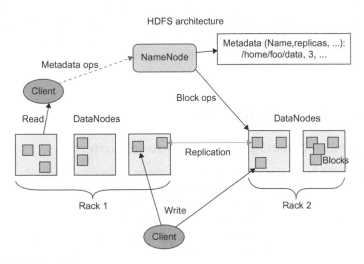

Figure 9.2 HDFS architecture.

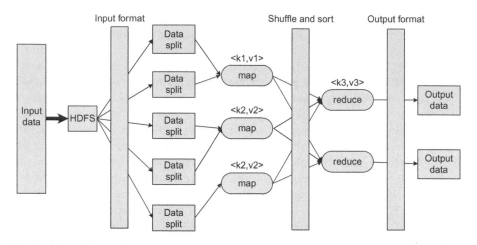

Figure 9.3 Hadoop run structure.

The Map process includes the following steps: (1) read data from the disk, (2) run Map task, and (3) write the results to disk.

The Reduce process includes the following steps: (1) Shuffle and sort, (2) run Reduce task, and (3) write the results to disk.

In the third phase of the Map step, the output of the Map task will be written to the output file by Partitioner class. If Combiner is provided, the Mapper output key will not be written to the output immediately; rather, it will be buffered in memory until it reaches a certain amount of data. Then, this part of the data will be merged in the Combiner and then transferred to the Partitioner. Through this stage, the data is written to disk to improve the reliability of the system though it decreases the performance. The Hadoop framework will transfer the Map key to the Reducer in the first Reduce stage. This step use remote transmission of the HTTP protocol. In the third Map phase, Hadoop Online Prototype lets the data between different tasks interact through a pipeline, on the premise that Hadoop's fault tolerance, which increases task concurrency and shorten the response time.

9.2 Scheduling algorithms

9.2.1 Dynamic management of Hadoop clusters

Research teams have already focused on Hadoop research extensively. A team in Stanford thinks there is a lot to do in Hadoop energy saving. They suggest using a new algorithm for node data placement [1]. U.C. Berkeley constructed a model, which they claimed achieved good results, based on node, working time, and power [2,3]. Further, they believe optimizing energy efficiency and performance have the same value [4]. Swiss scientists modified the block allocation algorithm to reduce the Hadoop energy consumption [5]. However, these research examples were all devoted to static data block allocation and could not be used in a dynamical situation. Researchers at Oben University [6] focused on optimizing the heterogeneous Hadoop cluster. Researchers at the Technical University of Catalonia [7] also studied MapReduce scheduling and performance management of Hadoop. Their research mostly focused on leveraging the adaptive MapReduce scheduler to meet user-defined high-level performance goals while transparently and efficiently exploiting the capabilities of hybrid systems. They described the changes introduced in the adaptive scheduler to enable it with hardware awareness and with the ability to co-schedule accelerable and nonaccelerable jobs on the same heterogeneous MapReduce cluster, making the most of the underlying hybrid systems. However, their research is more in line with the close integration of the hardware and scheduling efficiency, whereas energy consumption is not considered in the cluster. Additionally, dynamic voltage regulation is also widely used by researchers to reduce energy consumption in [8,9], but the disadvantage is that it requires special hardware environments.

Intel research shows energy consumption in the cluster has a positive correlation with average utilization. From the figure, we can determine that energy consumption increases as average utilization increases. This introduces a design can dynamic suspend and restart the nodes to decrease the average utilization, which leads to a decrease in energy consumption. This is completed using software and without using any specific hardware (Figure 9.4).

This section introduces a new Hadoop dynamic load balance method, Dynamic Adjusting and Negative Feedback (DANF), which has following features:

- Suspending and restarting the nodes according to the cluster load, thus decreasing the average utilization and reducing the node running time and energy consumption.
- Using feedback to increase the cluster stability.
- Using the jitter coefficient to avoid jitter, further reduce load variance, and increase load balance.
- This design is easy to implement and expand.

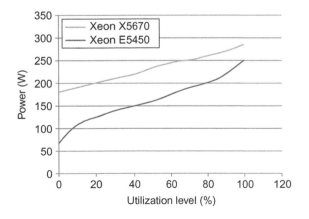

Figure 9.4 Power versus utilization.

9.2.2 Load modeling

To evaluate the load of a node, we must build a model. Research shows that the processor consumes the most energy in a system and occupies about 40% of the total energy consumption [10]. Therefore, we consider it as a factor in our model. Memory is another energy consumption module in the system.

9.2.2.1 Load information

Most existing load models only consider the CPU factor. We use a two-dimensional vector with a coefficient p. Let a node j have a load vector $L = <L_{cpu}, L_{mem}>$, we calculate its modulus, so the load is

$$L = \sqrt{p \times L_{cpu}^2 + (1 - p) \times L_{mem}^2} \tag{9.1}$$

Let us consider that a cluster has n nodes and the average load in t_i is

$$L_{avg} = \sum_{i=1}^{n} \frac{L_i}{n} \tag{9.2}$$

Therefore, the range of L_{avg} is $(0,1)$, and p can be assigned according to different tasks, meaning p can be larger, around 0.8, if the task, such as scientific calculation, requires a lot of CPU. Otherwise, if the task requires large memory consumption, we usually set a smaller p.

9.2.2.2 Period

This value is a variable and we must set an observation period to calculate it. If the period is too long, we cannot obtain the latest information. However, if the period is too short, the too frequent query will infect the result. Experiments show that the period relies on the task. Therefore, to consume less energy, an intensive computing application should use a long period and a data intensive application should use a short period.

9.2.2.3 Negative feedback mechanism

In a control system, there are many checks and balances. In a mathematical model, negative feedback means the feedback coefficient is negative. Negative feedback is added as portion of the input to offset the output changes:

$$x' = -k \times \Delta y \tag{9.3}$$

In the automatic control theory, the feedback method of root, derived from Newton's method, is widely used in automatically adjustment systems, such as combustion automatically adjustment, steam temperature automatically adjustment, transportation system automatically adjustment, and bypass system automatically adjustment. The main formula is as follows:

$$X^{n+1} = X^n + \sqrt[3]{\frac{X^{n+1}}{A} - X^n} \qquad (9.4)$$

where A is assigned closely to X^n. Here, we already know the initial value of X^n, so let the cluster in t_{i-1} have an average load $l^{t_{i-1}}_{\text{avg}}$, in t_i has average load $L^{t_i}_{\text{avg}}$, then we use Eq. (9.4) and in t_i, the DANF load is

$$L^{t_i}_{\text{DANF}} = L^{t_i}_{\text{avg}} + \sqrt[3]{L^{t_{i-1}}_{\text{avg}} - L^{t_i}_{\text{avg}}} \qquad (9.5)$$

9.2.3   Scheduling algorithm

9.2.3.1   Scheduling conditions

The load from Eq. (9.1) can use the default or user-defined threshold W_l and W_h. Here, W_l is the lower threshold and W_h is the upper threshold. When $W_l < L_{\text{DANF}} < W_h$, the system is in ideal status and no steps are required. When $L_{\text{DANF}} < W_l$, the system has a low load and we should suspend nodes one by one until they system is in ideal status. When $L_{\text{DANF}} > W_h$, the system has a high load and we must restart the suspended nodes.

9.2.3.2   Choosing a node to suspend

Selecting a node is one of the main purposes of DANF when used in a dynamic management system. Currently, there are several [11]:

a. **Random**
      This algorithm is simple and easy to understand. It randomly selects a node when the system reaches the threshold.
b. **Round-Robin**
      This algorithm assigns each node within a circular order and suspends according to this order.
c. **Minimum load**
      This algorithm sorts all node loads and selects the minimum load node to suspend.

Examining these algorithms, we find that when a system experiences a significant change, and if the suspend and restart operation occurred on the same node, this would create a large number I/O operations, which could seriously affect the performance. To reduce jitter in the DANF algorithm, we add a jitter coefficient to select the node.

Calculating each node load using Eq. (9.1), and to increase system stability, we introduce a jitter coefficient k:

$$k = \left| \frac{L^{t_i} - L^{t_{i-1}}}{\Delta t} \right| \qquad (9.6)$$

Here, Δt is a unit time period $\Delta t = t_i - t_{i-1}$ and k has a range greater than 0; considering k, the node load is

$$L^{t_i}_{\text{node}} = k \times L^{t_i} \tag{9.7}$$

At this time, the small load node with large change would not be selected due to the coefficient, thus greatly improving stability. The algorithm is effective in preventing frequent scheduling on the same node in the system.

9.2.3.3   Choosing a node to restart

When the system reaches W_h, we have to restart one or more nodes. Unlike with suspension, we remove the node from the queue using "first in, first out" (FIFO) in increasing order of their load.

9.2.3.4   Pseudocode

DANF algorithm is provided in Algorithm 1.

9.3   Energy control

9.3.1   System architecture

We implemented this DANF method using Java. The whole system includes resource collection, remote control, and node control modules.

```
Input: CPU and memory information of each node
Output: name and operation of a node
Initialization: allocating a name to each node
DO
calculate current load of Hadoop cluster, denote as c_l
  IF w_l< c_l<w_h
    continues;
  ELSE IF c_l<w_l
    FOR each node in active
      calculate load value of all current nodes and sort in increasing order
      sleep one or more of the lowest load nodes until w_l<c_l<w_h and
      put them in waiting queue
    END FOR
  ELSE
    open one or more nodes in the waiting queue until w_l< c_l<w_h
  ENDIF
ENDDO
```

Algorithm 1 DANF algorithm.

9.3.2   Detailed design

9.3.2.1   Resource collection

The resource collection module is implemented through reading Linux file system procfs. Procfs (or the proc filesystem) is a special file system in UNIX-like operating systems that presents information about processes and other system information. Therefore, we can use it to obtain CPU and memory information.

a. **Memory information**
   Total: The first line in /proc/meminfo;
   Available: The second line in /proc/stat;
   Mem = 1 - Available/Total.

b. **CPU**
   Total: The first line in /proc/stat;
   Each CPU: The second line /proc/stat;from CPU_0-CPU_n;
   user, nice, sys, idle: The following four column numbers;.
   We read these data twice, we present with "user_1 or user_2",user + sys is the used CPU.
   CPU = (int)rintf((((float)((user_2 + sys_2 + nice_2)-(user_1 + sys_1 + nice_1))/(float) (total_2 − total_1))*100).

9.3.2.2   Remote control

The remote control module is implemented using Security SHell (SSH). Here, we use the third-party lib Ganymed SSH-2 for Java, which can provide an SSH connection in Java.

a. **Create a connection using an IP**
   Connection conn = new Connection(hostname);
b. **Using username and password to log in**
   booleanisAuthenticated = conn.authenticateWithPassword(username,password);
c. **Begin a session and run the Linux shell**
   Session sess = conn.openSession();
   sess.execCommand("last");
d. **Receive the response from the console**
   InputStreamstdout = new StreamGobbler(sess.getStdout());
   BufferedReaderbr = new BufferedReader(new InputStreamReader(stdout));
e. **Get the status flag "0" success; "not 0" Failed**
   System.out.println("ExitCode: " + sess.getExitStatus());
f. **Close cession and connection**
   sess.close();
   conn.close();

9.3.2.3   Node control

Node control is implemented using the Hadoop configuration file and shell. The master can suspend and restart nodes by modifying them.

   Add node:
      ./hadoop-daemon.sh start datanode;
      ./hadoop-daemon.sh start tasktracker.

Delete node;
a. **Add the following in core-site.xml in master node**
   $<$ property $>$
   $<$ name $>$ dfs.hosts.exclude $<$ /name $>$
   $<$ value $>$ /data/hadoop-0.20.2/conf/excludes $<$ /value $>$
   $<$ /property $>$
   dfs.hosts.exclude: node to be deleted
   /data/hadoop-0.21.0/conf/excludes: The file and directory to be deleted.
b. **Using Java to write the node to be deleted in /data/hadoop-0.20.2/conf/excludes.**
c. **Refresh NameNode**
   Hadoopdfsadmin $-$refreshNodes
   The command can dynamic refresh dfs.hosts and dfs.hosts.exclude without restart NameNode.
d. **Using remote SSH**
   Stop datanode
   ./hadoop-daemon.sh stop datanode
   Stop Tasktracker
   ./hadoop-daemon.sh stop tasktracker

9.4   Energy-efficient scheduling for multiple users

9.4.1   Problem formulation

A MapReduce performance model is introduced in [12−14]. The model predict the completion time of the Map and Reduce stages as functions of the input data set size and allocated resources.

Definition 1 MapReduce slots. Depending on the configuration of a Hadoop cluster, each node in the cluster can proceed P Map and P Reduce tasks simultaneously. Thus, this Hadoop cluster has $P \times P$ MapReduce slots.

Definition 2 Execution waves. If the number of MapReduce tasks is greater than the number of MapReduce slots in the cluster, the task assignment proceeds in multiple rounds; each round is called an execution wave.

Figure 9.5 shows an example executed in two waves of 20×20 MapReduce slots.

Consider a job represented as a set of n tasks processed by $P \times P$ MapReduce slots (workers) in Hadoop environments. Each MapReduce job consists of a specified number of Map and Reduce tasks. The job execution time and the specifics of the execution depend on the amount of resources (Map and Reduce slots) allocated for the job. A simple abstraction is adopted [12], where each MapReduce job, J_i, is defined by the durations of its Map and Reduce stages, m_i and r_i, i.e., $J_i = (m_i, r_i)$. Let us consider the execution of two independent MapReduce jobs, J_1 and J_2, in a Hadoop cluster with a FIFO scheduler. There are no data dependencies between these jobs. Therefore, once the first job completes its Map stage and begins

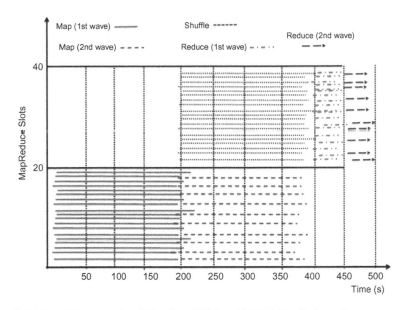

Figure 9.5 Execution example of TeraSort [15] in a 20 × 20 MapReduce slot.

processing its Reduce stage, the next job can start its Map stage execution with the released Map resources in a pipelined fashion. There may be "overlap" in the executions of the Map stage of the next job and the Reduce stage of the previous one. We further consider the following problem. Let $J = \{J_1, J_2, \ldots, J_n\}$ be a set of n MapReduce jobs with no data dependencies between them. Here, J_i requests $R_i \times R_i$ MapReduce slots and has Map and Reduce phase durations (m_i, r_i), respectively.

The system scheduler can change a job's MapReduce slots allocation depending on available resources. Let T be the makespan of all n jobs. We aim to determine an order (a schedule) of execution of jobs $J_i \in J$ such that the makespan of all jobs is minimized. Let us set the end-time of the Map stage and start-time of the Reduce stage of job J_i as (t_m^i, t_r^i), respectively. Thus, the actually allocated MapReduce slots for job J_i are $P_i \times P_i$, the max available MapReduce slots in the Hadoop cluster is $P \times P$. Formally, the problem of minimizing the makespan, T, can therefore be formulated as

Min T (9.8)

subject to

1.

$$\forall J_i, P_i \leq P \tag{9.9}$$

2.

$$\forall J_i, t_r^i \leq t_m^i \tag{9.10}$$

where Eq. (9.9) is the available capacity constraint, i.e., actually allocated MapReduce slots, P_i, to any job are not more than the number of available MapReduce slots in the system, P. Equation (9.10) is the time nonoverlapping constraint of the Map and Reduce stages for a single job—meaning that for the same job, the end-time of its Map stage should not be less than the start-time of its Reduce stage.

Based on the problem formulation, we propose a new approach to minimize the makespan of a set of given MapReduce jobs.

9.4.2   Revised Johnson's algorithm and HScheduler

Before introducing the new algorithm, let us revisit the classical Johnson's algorithm [16] to determine if it can be applied to the MapReduce scheduling directly.

9.4.2.1   Johnson's algorithm revisited

The original Johnson's algorithm [16] considers that "there are n items which must go through one production stage or machine and then a second one. There is only one machine for each stage. At most one item can be on a machine at a given time." To adapt the MapReduce model, we treat the Map and Reduce stage resources as a whole (like a single machine), i.e., to represent the resources as MapReduce slots, then we can apply Johnson's algorithm. Using a similar notation to the one found in [12], let us consider a collection of n jobs, where each job, J_i, is represented by the pair, m_i, r_i, of Map and Reduce stage durations, respectively. Each job $J_i = (m_i, r_i)$ with an attribute D_i is defined as follows:

$$D_i = \begin{cases} (m_i, m), \text{if } \min(m_i, r_i) = m_i; \\ \quad (r_i, r), \text{ otherwise} \end{cases} \tag{9.11}$$

The first argument in D_i is called the stage duration and denoted as D_i^1. The second argument is called the stage type (Map or Reduce) and denoted as D_i^2. Notice that when $r_i = 0$, Johnson's algorithm reduces to the shortest process time first algorithm, which is known to be optimal for minimizing total finish (flow) time of all jobs. Algorithm 2 presents the pseudocode of the Revised Johnson's algorithm for MapReduce. First, it sorts all n jobs from the original set J in the ordered list L in such a way that job J_i precedes job J_{i+1} if and only if $\min(m_i, r_i) \leq \min(m_{i+1}, r_{i+1})$. It finds the smallest value among all durations, if the stage type in D_i is m (i.e., it represents the Map stage), then the job J_i is placed at the head of the schedule. Otherwise, J_i is placed at the tail. Then, the allocated job is removed and other jobs are considered in the same fashion. The complexity of Johnson's algorithm is dominated by the sorting operation and thus is $O(n \log n)$.

Theorem 1   Johnson's algorithm obtains the theoretical lower bound of total elapsed time (makespan) for a two-stage production system when all jobs go through the same two stages and each job utilizes all resource of each stage.

> **Input**: All Jobs' Map and Reduce durations, number of machines for the Hadoop cluster
> **Output:** Scheduled jobs, makespan
> 1   List the Map and Reduce durations in two vertical columns (implemented in a list);
> 2   **for** *all entries* **do**
> 3 | Find the shortest one among all durations;
> 4 | In case of ties, for the sake of simplicity order the item with the smallest subscript first. In case of a tie between Map and Reduce, order the item according to the Map;
> 5 | IF it is for the Map, place the corresponding item at the first place;
> 6 | ELSE it is for the Reduce, place the corresponding item at the last place ;
> 7 | Remove both time durations for that task;
> 8 | Repeat the steps on the remaining set of items;
> 9   **end**
> 10 Compute makespan;

Algorithm 2 Revised Johnson's algorithm for MapReduce.

The detailed proof for Theorem 1 is provided in Johnson [16]. From Johnson's algorithm, we can obtain the ideal makespan (theoretical lower bound) as follows:

1. Considering there are n tasks for Map and Reduce stages. Let m_i denote the work time of the ith task for the Map phase and r_i denote the corresponding time on the Reduce phase for a given Hadoop cluster with P machines (slots).
2. Then, the optimal total elapsed time (makespan) is as follows:

$$T = \sum_{i=1}^{n} r_i + \max_{u=1}^{n} K_u \tag{9.12}$$

$$K_u = \sum_{i=1}^{u} m_i - \sum_{i=1}^{u-1} r_i \tag{9.13}$$

Observation 1 If each job utilizes either all Map or all Reduce slots during its processing, there is a perfect match between the assumptions of the classic Johnson's algorithm for a two-stage production system and MapReduce job processing. Then Johnson's algorithm can be applied to find the theoretical lower bound of minimizing the makespan of all MapReduce jobs.

Example 1 We reproduce the five MapReduce jobs given in [12] in Figures 9.6(a) and (b), respectively, where Figure 9.6A shows the durations of the Map and Reduce stages of each job and Figure 9.6B provides an ordered list of the five jobs by applying Johnson's algorithm. According to Johnson's algorithm, the optimal

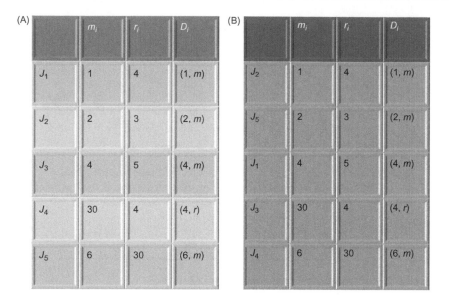

Figure 9.6 Five MapReduce jobs examples by one cluster. (A) Before applying the algorithm; (B) After applying the algorithm.

sequence is $\delta = (2, 5, 1, 3, 4)$. The total delay time for this sequence can be computed using Eq. (9.13), i.e., 4 units, and the total elapsed time (makespan) is 47 units (using Eqs. (9.12) and (9.13)). If one reverses the order of the jobs, then the worst-case result can be obtained (as the upper bound), i.e., 78 units.

Observation 2 For multiple MapReduce jobs, besides Map and Reduce phases, there are additional process times, such as job setting up, migration, and dispatch, which also should be included in the actual makespan. Based on Eqs. (9.12) and (9.13), the actual makespan is adjusted to $\hat{T} = (1 + c_0)T$, where c_0 is a weight factor that depends on the job types.

We will validate Observation 2 in the performance evaluation section.

Observation 3 The job stage duration closely depends on the amount of allocated resources (Map and Reduce slots). If the system scheduler allocates more or less MapReduce slots than their required slots, the jobs' appearance can be changed.

Example 2 Consider Scenario 2 in [12]: For Example 1, now let jobs J_1, J_2, and J_5 be comprised of 30 Map and 30 Reduce tasks, and jobs J_3 and J_4 be comprised of 20 Map and 20 Reduce tasks, while all other parameters are the same as in Example 1. We reproduce results in Figure 9.7 that visualize the execution of these five MapReduce jobs according to the generated Johnson's schedule, $\delta = (J_2, J_5, J_1, J_4, J_3)$. For jobs J_3 and J_4, [12] assumes that they only use 20×20 MapReduce slots, even if the system has 30×30 MapReduce slots available. However, if we allow that any job can use all available MapReduce slots in the system during execution, which can be implemented easily in Hadoop (e.g., by splitting the large input files based on available number of MapReduce slots), the result is very different from [12]. For the same example in Scenario 2 [12], now jobs J_3 and J_4 can use all available 30×30 MapReduce slots. Here, J_3 will have Map and Reduce durations of $(20, (8/3))$, respectively, and J_4 will have Map and Reduce durations of $(4, 20)$, respectively. Both are shorter than only using 20×20 MapReduce

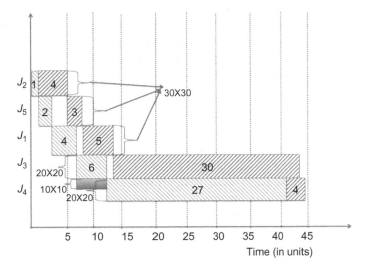

Figure 9.7 Five MapReduce jobs executions in one cluster.

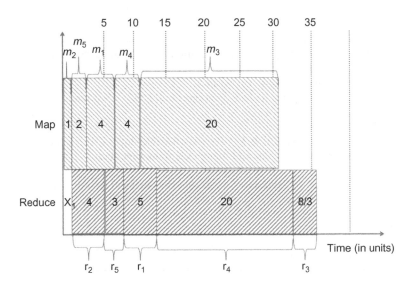

Figure 9.8 New result of five MapReduce jobs execution.

slots. Therefore, the makespan will be $35(2/3)$, as shown in Figure 9.8, where $X_1 = 1$. This result is 12% smaller than the result obtained by the two pools approach [12]. Therefore, the following principle is the key strategy for our results.

Claim 1 The system scheduler can decrease or increase the allocated number of MapReduce slots for a job if the job's requested number of MapReduce slots is larger than or less than the available MapReduce slots in the system.

Assuming that there are $P \times P$ MapReduce slots in the given Hadoop cluster, then there are two Jobs A and B and each has requested MapReduce slots, R, and time duration, T_A, T_B, respectively. Note their theoretical makespan, T_1, can be easily computed using Eqs. (9.12) and (9.13) directly. Then, the actual makespan of job A and B using all available slots (P) is (T_A):

$$T_A = \frac{R}{P} T_1 \qquad (9.14)$$

Based on Observations 1–3 and Claim 1, we design a new approach called HScheduler to efficiently schedule MapReduce jobs to minimize makespan. Algorithm 3 presents the pseudocode of the HScheduler algorithm for MapReduce. First, it allocates all available MapReduce slots to a given set of jobs by recomputing their actual durations based on available slots. This changes their Map and Reduce durations by taking more or less execution waves based on available slots. Then it used the Revised Johnson's algorithm to schedule all updated jobs. The complexity of HScheduler is dominated by Johnson's algorithm and thus is $O(n \log n)$.

Input: All Jobs' Map and Reduce durations, number of machines for the Hadoop cluster
Output: Scheduled jobs, makespan
1 Compute the Map and Reduce durations of all jobs by their required slots and Equations (11–14);
2 **for** all jobs **do**
3   IF a job's required slots $R_i \geq P$ (total available slots), THEN allocates all available slots to it and adds more execution waves based on tasks' splitting;
4   ELSE IF $R_i < P$, allocates all available slots to it and records actual execution waves;
5   End;
6 **end**
7 Call Revised Johnson's Algorithm;
8 Compute makespan;

Algorithm 3 HScheduler.

9.5 Performance evaluation

9.5.1 Evaluation platform

We build a 16-node Hadoop cluster and each node has the same dual-core Pentium CPU, 512 M memory. Each node was installed with CentOS 6.3, Hadoop 0.21.

9.5.2 Evaluation design

a. Energy control system

We use the Hadoop WordCount as a large memory task example and TeraSort as an intense calculation task example. The WordCount data are from Wiki, whereas TeraSort data are generated by TeraGen. For both tasks, the data sizes are 500 megabytes (M), 1G, 2G, 4G, and 8G. We set the time period to 10 s and use the threshold 0.2 as the lower threshold and use 0.8 as the upper threshold. In WordCount, we set p to 0.5, whereas in TeraSort, we set p to 0.8. Each test is repeated five times and we record the mean result.

b. Energy-efficient scheduling

We use similar workloads to those found in [12] for our experiments:

This workload represents a mixed number of MapReduce jobs based on the analysis performed on the Yahoo! M45 cluster [12]. The number of Map and Reduce tasks is generated by Normal distribution and the durations of the Map and Reduce phases are obtained from real data of WordCount [17] and TeraSort [15].

- Unimodel: where a set of 50 WordCount [17] (with mean Map duration 65 s and mean Reduce duration 57 s, uniformly distributed) and 50 TeraSort jobs [15] (with mean Map duration 73 s and Reduce duration 58 s, uniformly distributed) are tested, it uses a single scale factor for the overall workload, i.e., the scale factor for each job is drawn uniformly from [1,10], and Normal distribution with parameter round(N(154, 558)0.1) for the number of Map tasks and round(N(19,145)0.1) for Reduce tasks.

- Bimodal: where a subset of 20 WordCount from [17] (with mean Map duration 448 s and mean Reduce duration 413 s, uniformly distributed) and 20 TeraSort jobs from [15] (with mean Map duration 287 s and Reduce duration 306 s, uniformly distributed). In this case, 80% of the jobs are scaled using a factor uniformly distributed between [1,2] and the remaining jobs (20%) are scaled using [8,10] and Normal distribution with parameter round(N(154, 558)_0.3) for the number of Map tasks and round (N(19,145)_0.3) for Reduce tasks. This mimics workloads that have a large fraction of short jobs and a small subset of long jobs.

All results are obtained by the average of six runs.

9.5.3 Results analysis

9.5.3.1 Energy control system

a. Load balance test

To evaluate the node chosen algorithm, we can compare the load balance. Here, the variance is calculated in following formula.

$$\sigma^2 = (L_{\mathrm{avg}} - L)^2 \tag{9.15}$$

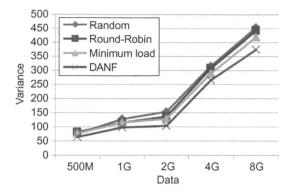

Figure 9.9 WordCount variance comparisons.

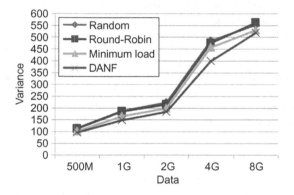

Figure 9.10 TeraSort variance comparisons.

Figures 9.9 and 9.10 show the WordCount and TeraSort results, respectively, for the Random, Round-Robin, Minimum load, and DANF tests.

From the result, we can see that TeraSort has a larger variance than WordCount. Compared to others, the DANF has smaller variance for both results, which proves our algorithm is efficient and has an improved load balance [18].

b. Energy test

$$E = P(u) \times T_{all} = [P_{min} + (P_{max} - P_{min}) \times u] \times T_{all} \qquad (9.16)$$

Here, P_{min} is the system's idle energy consumption, P_{max} is the system's full load energy consumption, u is the average utilization in T_{all}, and T_{all} is the system's boot time. Further, T_r is the node working time and T_s is the node idle time. For $T_{all} = T_r + T_s$, the total node idle time is the sum of the idle time for all nodes (Tables 9.1–9.3).

Table 9.1 WordCount total working time

	500 MB	1G	2G	4G	8G
Without dynamic Management systems	111	153	250	430	836

Table 9.2 WordCount idle nodes

	500 MB	1G	2G	4G	8G
Idle nodes	1	1	2	3	4

Table 9.3 WordCount total idle time

	500 MB	1G	2G	4G	8G
Without DANF dynamic management system (s)	32	96	208	448	928
With DANF dynamic management system (s)	40	120	250	570	1140

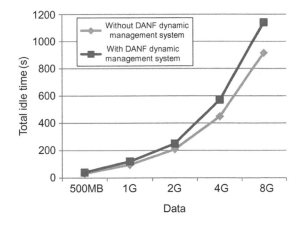

Figure 9.11 WordCount total idle time comparison.

Figure 9.11 is the comparison (Tables 9.4−9.6).

Figure 9.12 is the comparison.

From Figures 9.11 and 9.12, we observe that DANF increases the idle time in both tests. It is clear that in TeraSort and WordCount, tests show the advantage of DANF.

Table 9.4 TeraSort total working time

	500 MB	1G	2G	4G	8G
Without DANF dynamic management systems	64	130	279	664	1384

Table 9.5 TeraSort idle nodes

	500 MB	1G	2G	4G	8G
Idle nodes	1	1	2	4	4

Table 9.6 TeraSort total idle time comparison

	500 MB	1G	2G	4G	8G
Without DANF dynamic management systems	32	112	224	560	1184
With DANF dynamic management systems	40	140	270	680	1490

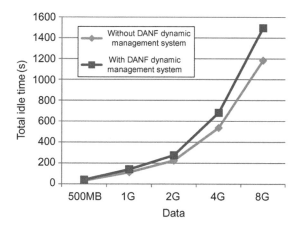

Figure 9.12 TeraSort total idle time comparison.

In Eq. (9.14), u is the average utilization of system boot time, we use Ganglia to record: (Figures 9.13 and 9.14).

From Eq. (9.14), because T_{all} is the same, P_{min}, P_{max} are constants. Therefore, the energy consumption and average utilization are proportional. In our experiment environment, we measured $P_{min} = 50$ W, $P_{max} = 300$ W. The energy consumption comparison figures are Figures 9.15 and 9.16:

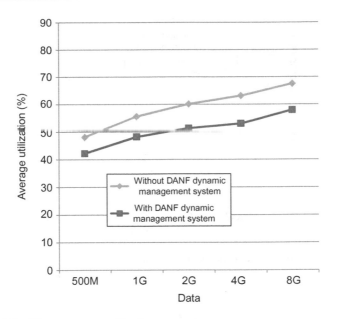

Figure 9.13 WordCount average utilization comparison.

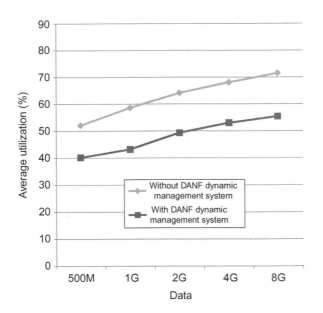

Figure 9.14 TeraSort average utilization comparison.

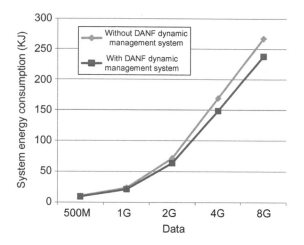

Figure 9.15 WordCount system energy consumption comparisons.

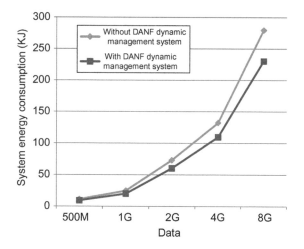

Figure 9.16 TeraSort system energy consumption comparisons.

From the figure, we observe that the system's energy consumption was reduced with DANF, compared to the original system. All DANF test examples have an average energy reduction of 14%.

9.5.3.2 Energy-efficient scheduling

We compare the following algorithms:

- Random Order (Rand): this algorithm schedules all jobs in a random order based on their job IDs.

- Reversed Order of Johnson's Algorithm (R_Johnson): this algorithm schedules all jobs in reverse order of Revised Johnson's algorithm. It is the worst case regarding makespan of all jobs and is proved in [16].
- HScheduler: this is our proposed algorithm.
- Johnson's Algorithm (Johnson T): this is the classical Johnson's algorithm, which works as a theoretical lower bound because it does not consider additional process time caused by jobs setting up, dispatch, and migration, etc. in the real Hadoop cluster.
- BalancedPools (BP) is another way to minimize makespan proposed in [12]. It partitions the Hadoop cluster into two balanced pools and then allocates each job to a suitable pool to minimize the makespan.

In all tests, 18 data nodes each with two MapReduce slots are set, two pools each with 12 and 24 MapReduce slots are set respectively for the BalancedPools algorithm.

Figures 9.17 and 9.18 present the makespan comparison of four algorithms. R_Johnson is the worst case, working as the upper bound of makespan, whereas results obtained from Johnson's algorithm are the theoretical lower bounds. Rand and R_Johnson have higher makespans than HScheduler. HScheduler has 8−10% less makespan on the average than BP. HScheduler is 15% and 13% larger on average than theoretical lower bound in Unimodel and Bimodel, respectively. This is because HScheduler has additional process times, such as job setting up, dispatch, and migration, in a real Hadoop environment. In Figure 9.19, we conducted tests with 50 TeraSort data (with mean Map duration 73 s and Reduce duration 58 s, uniformly distributed) without considering Bimodel or Unimodel. From extensive real experiments, similar results are observed and omitted because of the page limit.

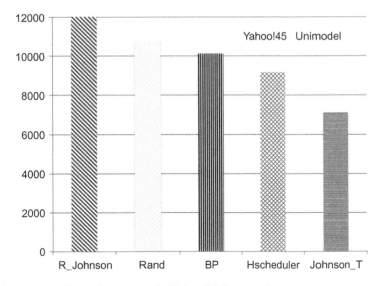

Figure 9.17 Comparison of makespan in Unimodel (in seconds).

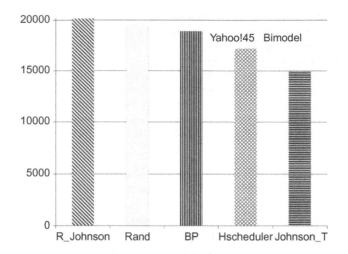

Figure 9.18 Comparison of makespan in Bimodel (in seconds).

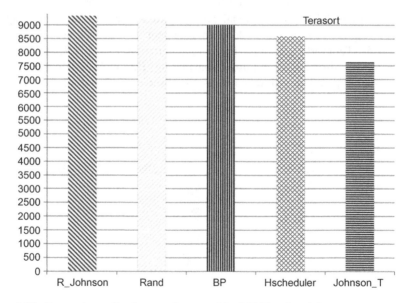

Figure 9.19 Comparison of makespan (in seconds) of 50 TeraSort jobs.

9.6 Summary

This chapter described the basic principles and architecture of Hadoop, the MapReduce mechanism, and the HDFS file system and presented previous Hadoop research. The core of DANF, an approach to combine dynamically the load balance and energy efficiency of Hadoop, was implemented and tested. Further, an energy-efficient scheduler was introduced and compared to several existing algorithms. It was found that these two methods not only improve efficiency in the Hadoop cluster, but also reduce energy consumption.

Questions

1. What is Hadoop? Which parts make up its basic frames?
2. How does Hadoop work?
3. List the usual energy algorithms and try to improve them.
4. What should one consider when designing an energy control system?
5. Design an online energy-efficient schedule for multiple users.
6. Add an energy control system in a Hadoop kernel.

References

[1] Leverich J, Kozyrakis C. On the energy (in)efficiency of Hadoop clusters. SIGOPS Oper Syst Rev 2010;44(1):61−5.

[2] Chen Y, Ganapathi AS, Fox A, Katz RH, Patterson DA. Statistical workloads for energy efficient MapReduce : Technical Report. Berkeley: UCB/EECS; 2010.

[3] Chen Y, Keys L, Katz. RH. Towards energy efficient MapReduce: Technical Report. Berkeley: UCB/EECS; 2009.

[4] Nedevschi S, Popa L, Iannaccone G, et al. Reducing network energy consumption via rate-adaption and sleeping: Technical Report. Berkeley: UCB/EECS; 2007.

[5] Polo J, Carrera D, Becerra Y, Beltran V, Torres J, Ayguad E. Performance management of accelerated MapReduce workloads in heterogeneous clusters. ICPP2010 2010:653−62.

[6] Xie J, Yin S, Ruan X, Ding Z, Tian Y, Majors J, et al. Improving MapReduce performance through data placement in heterogeneous Hadoop clusters. IPDPSW 2010:1−9.

[7] Polo J, Carrera D, Becerra Y, Beltran V, Torres J, Ayguadé E. Performance management of accelerated MapReduce workloads in heterogeneous clusters. Proceedings of the ICPP. San Diego, CA: IEEE Press; 2010. p. 653−62.

[8] Kim KH, Buyya R, Kim J. Power aware scheduling of bag-of-tasks applications with deadline constraints on DVS-enabled clusters. CCGRID 2007;85(10):541−8.

[9] Lee YC, Zomaya AY. Minimizing energy consumption for precedence-constrained applications using dynamic voltage scaling. CCGRID 2009;9:92−9.

[10] Cooper BF, Sillberstein A, Tam E, et al. Benchmarking cloud serving systems with YCSB, SoCC'10 2010;10:143−54

[11] Bryhni H, Klovning E, Kurc O. A comparison of load balancing techniques for scalable web server. IEEE Netw 2000;7/8:58−63.

[12] Verma A, Cherkasova L, Campbell RH. Orchestrating an ensemble of MapReduce jobs for minimizing their makespan. IEEE Trans Dependable Sec Comput 2013;April: [online version].

[13] Verma A, Cherkasova L, Campbell RH. Two sides of a coin: optimizing the schedule of MapReduce jobs to minimize their makespan and improve cluster performance p. 11−18. MASCOTS. Washington, DC: IEEE Computer Society; 2012.
[14] Verma A, Cherkasova L, Campbell RH. ARIA: automatic resource inference and allocation for MapReduce environments. In: Proc. of ICAC; 2011.
[15] <http://sortbenchmark.org/YahooHadoop.pdf>.
[16] Johnson S. Optimal two-and three-stage production schedules with setup times included. Naval Res Log Quart 1954;1(1):61−8.
[17] WordCount, <http://www.cs.cornell.edu/home/llee/data/simple/>.
[18] Beloglazov A, Abawajy J, Buyya R. Energy-aware resource allocation heuristics for efficient management of data centers for cloud computing. Future Generation Comput Syst 2012;28(5):755−68.

Maximizing Total Weights in Virtual Machines Allocation

Main Contents of this Chapter

- Background of maximizing total weights
- Problem formulation
- Exact approach
- Applications discussion
- Related work and conclusions

10.1 Introduction

Cloud computing is developing based on various recent advancements in virtualization, grid computing, web computing, utility computing, and related technologies. Cloud computing provides both platforms and applications on demand through the internet or intranet. Cloud computing allows the sharing, allocation, and aggregation of software, computational, and storage network resources on demand. Some key benefits of cloud computing include the hiding and abstraction of complexity, virtualized resources, and efficient use of distributed resources. Cloud computing is still considered in its infancy, as there are many challenging issues to be resolved. In this chapter, we focus on infrastructure as a service in cloud data centers. Using a large-scale application of cloud computing, maximizing profits becomes one of key factors for many service providers to be considered. We consider maximizing profits (weights) of virtual machines (VMs) allocation in cloud data centers. For example, Amazon offers two different purchase types: on-demand and spot instances. On-demand instances are more expensive, but have a fixed price. Spot instances are usually cheaper than on-demand instances. However, because the spot instance price varies and customers specify a maximum price they are willing to pay, the provider may terminate the instance prematurely depending on how the spot price changes. A third pricing option, called timed instances, is proposed by Knauth and Fetzer [1]. Timed instances have an *a priori* specified fixed length reservation time. The scheduling algorithm uses the reservation time to colocate instances with similar expiration times. We based our maximizing weights scheduler on these timed instances in the following discussion. This problem can be modeled using our proposed new model, the capacity sharing interval scheduling (IS).

Interval scheduling problems (ISPs) have been studied extensively for a long time [2]. Traditionally, scheduling problems are stated in terms of machines and jobs. The machines represent resources and the jobs (requests) represent tasks that need to be carried out using these resources. The IS with fixed processing time is that each request has a fixed start- and end-time [3]. Similar to Ref. [2], a basic ISP can be stated as follows. Given n intervals of the form $[s_j, f_j]$ with start-time $s_j < f_j$ (end-time), for $j = 1, \ldots, n$. These intervals are the jobs that require uninterrupted processing during that interval, and assume that:

1. Each machine can process, at most, one job at a time and is always available, i.e., each machine is continuously available in $[0, \infty)$.
2. Without loss of generality, i.e., s_j and f_j are nonnegative integers.
3. Two intervals (or jobs) are said to overlap if their intersection is nonempty; otherwise, they are called compatible or disjoint.
4. Machines are identical.

The objective of basic ISP is to process all jobs using a minimum number of machines. In other words, finding an assignment of jobs to machines such that no two jobs assigned to the same machine overlap while using a minimum number of machines.

Definition 1: IS An assignment of (a subset of) the jobs to the machines is called IS, which requires that all intervals assigned to the same machine are compatible.

The maximum of overlapped intervals is called the depth of all intervals. It has been proven that this number of machines actually suffices to process all jobs [4].

The weighted interval scheduling problem (WISP) is that each request is associated with a weight, with the goal to find a subset of mutually compatible intervals with maximal total weight.

In this chapter, we consider the scheduling algorithm for WISWCS (SAWISWCS). The difference of SAWISWCS from WISP is that all intervals may require part of the total capacity of a single resource so they can share that capacity if their total required capacity at any time does not surpass the total capacity a machine can provide. To the best of our knowledge, this problem is not studied in the open literature. The major contributions of this chapter are:

1. Formulating a model for the Weighted Interval Scheduling with Capacity Sharing (WISWCS) for the first time. Providing an exact scheduling algorithm and its complexity analysis for a WISWCS problem.
2. The remaining content of this chapter is structured as follows: Section 10.2 provides formulation of and complexity analysis of the WISWCS problem. Section 10.3 shows some possible applications. Section 10.4 concludes the chapter.

10.2   Problem formulation: WISWCS

10.2.1   Traditional WISP

A set of requests $\{1,2,\ldots,n\}$ where the ith request corresponds to an interval of time starting at s_i and finishing at f_i, where each request is associated with a weight w_i. The goal is to find a subset of mutually compatible intervals, so to maximize the sum of the values of the selected intervals. There are the following assumptions:

1. All data are deterministic and unless otherwise specified, the time is formatted in slotted windows, as shown in Figure 10.1. We partition total time period $[0,T]$ into slots with

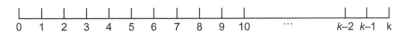

Figure 10.1 Time in slotted format.

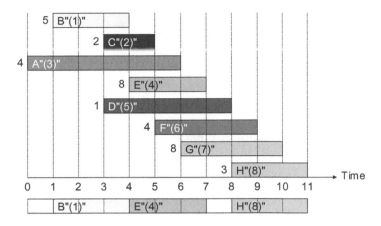

Figure 10.2 Example of WIS.

equal length s_0, the total slots is $k = T/s_0$, all are integer numbers. The starting time s_i and finishing time f_i are integer numbers of one slot. Then the interval of a request can be represented in slot format with start-time, end-time. For example, if $s_0 = 5$ min, an interval [4,5] means that it has start-time and end-time, respectively, at the third slot and tenth slot, making the actual duration of this request $(10 - 3)*5 = 35$ min.

2. All tasks are independent. There are no precedence constraints other than those implied by the start- and end-time.
3. The required capacity of each request is a positive real number between [0,1]. Note that the capacity of a single machine is normalized to be 1.
4. Assuming that, when processed, each job is assigned to a single machine, thus, interrupting a job and resuming it on another machine is not allowed, unless explicitly stated otherwise.
5. Machines are identical; each machine can process, at most, one job at a time.

Definition 2 Compatible intervals for WISP A subset of intervals is compatible if no two of them overlap in time, i.e., either request i is for an earlier time interval than request j ($f_i < s_j$), or request i is for a later time than request j ($f_j < s_i$). More generally, a subset A of requested intervals is compatible if all pairs of requests (i, j in A, $i \neq j$) are compatible.

Definition 3 WISP In the WISP, we want to find the maximum weight subset of nonoverlapping jobs, given a set J of jobs that have weights associated with them. Job i in J has a start-time s_i, a finish time f_i, and a weight w_i. Suppose we have a set of weighted intervals $J = \{I_1, I_2, I_3, \ldots, I_n\}$ and w_j is the weight of interval I_j. We seek to find an optimal schedule—a subset O of nonoverlapping jobs in J with the maximum possible sum of weights. In other words, the goal is to choose intervals from J that don't overlap in time that gives the highest possible total weight. Figure 10.2 shows an example of WIS.

Opt_Weight_Com()

1.   If j=0 then
2.   Return 0
3.   Else if M[j] is not empty then
4.   Return M[j]
5.   Else
6.   M[j]=max(wj+Opt_Weight_Com(p(j)),Opt_w
     eight_Com(j-1))
7.   return M[j]
8.   Endif

Figure 10.3 Algorithm for computing the optimal total weight in DP.

Opt_Solution_Find()

1.   If j=0 then
2.   Output nothing
3.   Else if (wj+M[p(j)]>M[j-1] then
4.   Output j together with the result of
     Opt_Solution_Find(p(j))
5.   Else
6.   Output the result of Opt_Solution_Find(j-1)
7.   Endif
8.   Endif

Figure 10.4 Algorithm for the find optimal solution in DP.

Note that when the weights are all 1, this problem is identical to basic ISP, and for that, we know that a greedy algorithm that chooses jobs in order of earliest finish time first gives an optimal schedule [4].

For a traditional WISP, the classic dynamic programming (DP) approach provides an efficient solution to find both the optimal total weight and the subset of intervals that are compatible, see Ref. [4].

The basic optimization model in DP is as follows. After sorting all intervals in the nondecreasing finish time, consider the optimal total weight using the following recursive formula for the jth interval:

$$\text{OPT}(j) = \max(w_j + \text{OPT}(p(j)), \text{OPT}(j - 1)) \tag{10.1}$$

where $p(j)$ is the largest index $i < j$, such that intervals i and j are disjoint for an interval j, $\text{OPT}(j)$ is the optimal total weight for j intervals. Figure 10.3 shows the algorithm to find an optimal total weight using a recursive formula, as shown in Eq. (10.1), where $M[j]$ is defined as the optimal total weight for all j intervals [4]. Figure 10.4 presents an algorithm to find the optimal solutions (subset of intervals) using a recursive method.

In Figure 10.2, there are eight interval requests (jobs) in (start-time, end-time, weight) format, respectively: A(0,6,4),B(1,4,5),C(3,5,2),D(3,8,1), E(4,7,8), F(5,9,4), G(6,10,8), and H(8,11,3). By applying the DP algorithm, it can be easily shown that the optimal total weight is 16 and optimal subset is {B,E,H}.

10.3 WISWCS

Definition 4 WISWCS The only difference for WISWCS from traditional weighted interval scheduling (WIS) is that a resource (to be concrete, a machine or a processor or a circuit) can be shared by different jobs if the total capacity of all jobs allocated on the single source at any time does not surpass the total capacity of a resource can provides. A request can be represented in a victor [ID, s_i, f_i, c_i, w_i], where ID denotes the ID number, s_i denotes the start-time, f_i denotes the end-time, c_i denotes the capacity request, and w_i denotes the weight of the request. The objective of WISWCS is to maximize the total weight by accepting a subset of requests for a given number of machines.

Definition 5 Sharing-compatible intervals for WISWCS A subset of intervals that have the total required capacity does not surpass the total capacity of a machine at any time.

Definition 6 Divisible capacity for WISWCS The capacity of different requests (jobs) have follows feature:

$$c_1 > c_2 > \ldots > c_i > c_{i+1} > \ldots$$

Such that for all $i >= 1$, c_{i+1} exactly divides c_i. There is a list L of requests (each can have arbitrary number), the capacity of requests in L form a divisible capacity. If L is a list of requests and C is the total capacity of a machine (considering homogeneous case here), we say that the pair (L,C) is strongly divisible if, in addition, the largest item capacity c_1 in L exactly divides the total capacity C.

See Ref. [6] for a more detailed discussion about divisible size bin-packing. We observe that popular providers, such as Amazon and Google, have a small and finite set of instance sizes following the divisible capacity pattern in [7]. Similarly, Knauth and Fetzer [1] also introduce a similar idea. In [1], VMs, as rented out to customers, have fractional sizes of the original hardware, e.g., 1/8, 1/4, 1/2, or 1/1. Individual resources of a VM, such as CPU, RAM, and local disk, double between VM sizes. For example, a small instance may have one CPU, 1 GB RAM, and 100 GB local disk. The next instance size has 2 CPUs, 2 GB RAM, and 200 GB local disk. This abstractly quantifying a server's compute power with resources is justified by real providers such as Amazon and Google.

Definition 7 Capacity-length proportional weight for WISWCS We assume that the weight of a request is proportional to the product of its capacity and length.

Definition 7 is a reasonable assumption found in the literature and is important assumption for our primary results. For WISWCS with divisible capacity and capacity proportional profit, we seek to find an optimal schedule—a subset O of sharing-compatible intervals (jobs) with the maximum possible sum of weights. Note that WIS is the special case of WISWCS when all weights are equal to 1. Therefore, the WISWCS problem is more difficult.

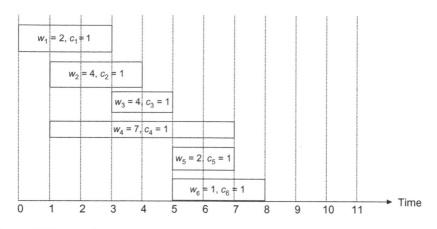

Figure 10.5 Example of WIS.

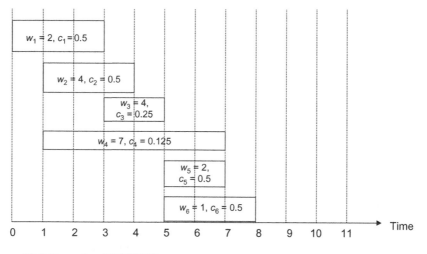

Figure 10.6 Example of WISWCS.

For comparison, we show two examples, one for WIS in Figure 10.5 and another for WISWCS in Figure 10.6. The only difference between these two examples is the required capacity of each job.

In Figure 10.5, an example of WIS is shown. The $n = 6$ requests (jobs), in (start-time, end-time, request capacity, weight) format, respectively, are #1(0,3,1,2), #2(1,4,1,4), #3(3,5,1,4), #4(1,7,1,7), #5(5,7,1,2), and #6(5,8,1,1).

Applying DP, we can easily obtain optimal total weight = 8 for Figure 10.5 and optimal subset is {#1,#3,#5}.

In Figure 10.6, there are $n = 6$ requests and their start-time, end-time, and weights are same as the example given in Figure 10.5. However, their required capacities are different. Unfortunately, in this case of WISWCS, we cannot use the DP technique any longer for the traditional WIS problem. The reason is that the situation of sharing-compatible intervals makes WISWCS different from WIS, meaning we cannot use compatible intervals defined by WIS to recursively apply the memorization technique in DP to find an optimal solution. For example, using the example in Figure 10.6, if we still apply DP technique, the result will be that the optimal subset is $\{I_1, I_3, I_5\}$, with an optimal total weight of 8. However, this is far from optimal because of the sharing-compatible intervals in WISWCS. We will show that the results for WISWCS are different from WIS in the following section.

10.4   An exact SAWISWCS

In the following, we introduce an exact SAWISWCS. The algorithm is shown in Figure 10.7.

<u>**SAWISWCS()**</u>
Input: requests indicated by their (start times, finish-times, requested capacity, weight), the request i is denoted as I_i .
Assuming that the weight of a request is proportional to the product of its capacity and length
<u>**Output:**</u> finding sets of sharing compatible intervals which have maximum total weights for each of the given number of machines.

1. Sort all requests in non-increasing order of their weights, if two requests have same weights, the one with shorter duration is considered first, otherwise breaking ties arbitrarily; w_i denotes as the weight of interval I_i
2. d=1;
3. **for** j = from 1 to n **do**
4.   **if** I_j can share capacity of k-th machine (start from lowest index machine to d-th machine)
5.   Assign I_j to machine k;   W[k]=W[k]+w(I_j); S(k)=S(k)U I_j
6.   else
7.   allocate a new machine d+1
8.   assign I_j to d+1;d=d+1
9.   W[d]=W[d]+w(I_j); S(d)=S(d)U I_j
10.   endif
11.   endfor
12.   sort W by non-increasing order of their values and record corresponding subsets S. The largest value of W (W[1]) and corresponding subsets S (S(1)) are optimal solutions for the first machine, the second largest value of W (W[2] and corresponding subsets S (S(2)) are optimal solutions for the second machine, so on until the last one for the d-th machine.

Figure 10.7 SAWISWCS.

For better understanding, let us take the example shown in Figure 10.6 to show how algorithm for WISWCS works:

1. Sorting all requests in nonincreasing order of their weights, we have $I_4(w_4 = 7)$, $I_3(w_3 = 4)$, $I_2(w_2 = 4)$, $I_1(w_1 = 2)$, $I_5(w_5 = 2)$, $I_6(w_6 = 1)$;
2. $j = 1$, I_4 with weight $w_4 = 7$ and capacity $c_4 = 0.125$ is considered, it is allocated to the first ($d = 1$) machine; $W[1] = w_4 = 7$, $S(1) = \{I_4\}$;
3. $j = 2$, I_3 with $w_3 = 4$ (shorter duration than I_2) and capacity $c_3 = 0.25$ is selected, it is allocated to the first machine because it is sharable compatible with I_4, $W[1] = w_4 + w_3 = 11$, $S(1) = \{I_4, I_3\}$;
4. $j = 3$, I_2 with $w_2 = 4$ and capacity $c_2 = 0.5$ is selected, it is allocated to the first machine since it can share the capacity, so $W[1] = w_3 + w_4 + w_2 = 15$, $S(1) = \{I_3, I_4, I_2\}$;
5. $j = 5$, I_5 with $w_5 = 2$ (shorter duration than I_1) and capacity $c_5 = 0.5$ is selected, it can share the capacity of machine 1 with existing intervals, so it is allocated to machine 1, $W[1] = w_3 + w_4 + w_2 + w_5 = 17$, $S(1) = \{I_3, I_4, I_2, I_5\}$;
6. $j = 4$, I_1 with $w_1 = 2$ and capacity $c_1 = 0.5$ is selected, it cannot share the capacity of machine 1 with other existing intervals, so $d = 1 + 1 = 2$ is allocated for it, $W[2] = w_1 = 2$, $S(2) = \{I_1\}$;
7. $j = 6$, I_6 with $w_1 = 1$ and capacity $c_6 = 0.5$ is selected, it cannot share capacity with machine 1 but can share capacity of machine 2, so it is allocated to machine 2, $W[2] = w_1 + w_6 = 3$, $S(2) = \{I_1, I_6\}$.

From preceding steps, it is shown that the optimal subset is $\{I_3, I_4, I_2, I_5\}$, with total weight 17. Obviously, these results are different from the WIS case.

Lemma 1 The SAWISWCS correctly finds the optimal solution for a subset of sharing-compatible intervals (jobs) with the maximum possible sum of weights.

Proof The SAWISWCS, as shown in Figure 10.7, first sorts all requests by nonincreasing order of their weights—this guarantees that requests with larger weights are considered first—then the algorithm applies the sharing-compatible rule (Definition 6) for all requests, as shown in line 1 of Figure 10.7. This ensures all possible requests are included in the optimal solution if they are sharing-compatible, as shown in line 2−11. Finally, the algorithm finds optimal results by comparing total weights of each machine, as shown in line 12. By the definition of the objective of WISWCS, the algorithm finds the optimal solution for a subset of sharing-compatible intervals (jobs) with the maximum possible sum of weights.

Remarks for Lemma 1: We conducted many examples using the proposed algorithm, both for WISP and WISWCS problems. In all cases, it finds optimal solutions.

Lemma 2 The time complexity of the SAWISWCS, as shown in Figure 10.7, is O $(n\ d)$, where n is the number of requests (jobs) and d is the number of machines.

Proof As shown in Figure 10.7, the algorithm first sorts all intervals in nonincreasing order of their weights (if two requests have same weights, the one with the shorter duration is considered first, otherwise breaking ties arbitrarily). This takes O

($n \log n$) time, where n is the number of intervals (requests). Then, the algorithm finds sharing-compatible intervals for all intervals, as shown in lines 6 to 12. This takes $O(n \ d)$ steps in worst case. The worst case is that all intervals have large capacity (e.g., 1), and the same start-time and end-time. So that all intervals are not sharing-compatible, therefore finding a machine for a job to allocate needs $O(d)$ steps, n intervals need $O(nd)$ steps. Finally, the algorithm finds optimal solutions using a simple comparison with costs $O(nd \log n)$ time. So all together, the algorithm for WISWCS takes $O(nd)$ time, where normally $n > m$

For implementation of SAWISWCS, interval tree data structure can be used. An interval tree is an ordered tree data structure used to hold intervals. It allows one to efficiently find all intervals that overlap with any given interval or point. The trivial or traditional solution (e.g., using arrays) is to visit each interval and test whether it intersects the given point or interval, which requires $\Theta(n^2)$ times or higher, where n is the number of intervals in the collection. Interval trees are dynamic, i.e., they allow insertion and deletion of intervals. They obtain a query time of $\Theta(\log n)$, whereas the preprocessing time to construct the data structure has tight bound $\Theta(n \log n)$, see Ref. [8].

Lemma 3 The maximum number of machines needed for WISWCS is the depth of all intervals that are overlap. This is the optimal number of resources needed.

Proof Suppose a set of intervals has depth d in the WISWCS problem. If $J = \{I_1,\ldots,I_k\}$ is the set, we know that d is the maximal value (round in integer) of the required capacity in which all intervals overlap. That is, d is the ceiling (in integer) of the sum of all requested capacities by intervals in J. These intervals all pass over a common point on the time line. Then, these intervals must be scheduled on d resources so that the capacity constraint is satisfied.

From remarks of SAWISWCS, Lemmas 1 and 3, we know that:

1. If there are d resources, the SAWISWCS can find optimal solutions for all requests using d resources.
2. If there are $m < d$ resources, the SAWISWCS also can find optimal solutions for all requests. It sorts W by nonincreasing order of their values and records corresponding subsets S. The largest value of W and corresponding subsets S are optimal solutions for the first machine, the second largest value of W and corresponding subsets S are optimal solutions for the second machine, so on until the last one for the dth machine.
3. If there is only a single resource, the SAWISWCS in the line 12 of Figure 10.7 uses a simple comparison to find the largest value of W and corresponding subsets S, which are optimal solutions for the single resource (machine).

10.5 Applications of WISWCS

In this section, we list a few typical applications, but it is not meant to be an exhaustive list.

10.5.1 *Virtual machine scheduling in cloud computing*

Let us consider a physical machine (PM) with 2×68.4 GB memory, 16 cores $\times$ 3.25 units, 2×1690 GB storage. There are three types of VMs with capacities 1/8, 1/4, and 1/2 of the total capacity of the given PM. As an example, a set of six VM requests are considered: vm1(0, 6, 1, 0.25), vm2(1, 4, 2, 0.125), vm3(3, 6, 3,0.25), vm4(3, 8, 4, 0.5), vm5(4, 8, 5, 0.25), and vm6(5, 9, 6, 0.25). Here, vm1 (0, 6, 1, 0.25) means vm1 starts at time 0, ends at time slot 6, has weight 1, and capacity requirement of 0.25 of the given PM's total capacity. Others are similar. We can use our proposed algorithm for WISWCS to find the optimal solution.

10.5.2 *Performance evaluation*

In this section, we provide numerical results for our proposed algorithm. We note that in some special cases, such as all requests have the same start-time and end-time, the Knapsack algorithm (KA) [4] can be applied to our problem repeatedly to obtain optimal results. Once one "sack" is packed with the max weight, it loops for the next sack until all requests are packed. In this section, we provide numerical results comparison between the KA and the SAWISWCS. Because the KA does not work for real-time ISP, in this section, we consider special cases, i.e., all requests have the same start-time (zero) and end-time (one), so that KA can be applied. Also, assuming there are three types of requests that occupy ¼, ½, and 1 of the total capacity of a machine, the weight of a request is three times of the product of its capacity and length. In Table 10.1, we provide the total number of machines used (# machines) and running time (run time) results for both KA and the SAWISWCS when the total number of intervals is varied from 10 to 100,000. One can observe that the SAWISWCS takes much less time to obtain the same result than KA, especially when the total number of intervals is larger.

Table 10.1 **Performance comparison between KA and SAWISWCS**

# Intervals	#PMs by (KA)	Run time (KA)	#PMs (WISCS)	Run time (WISCS)
10	4	15 ms	4	15 ms
100	30	16 ms	30	16 ms
500	147	32 ms	147	32 ms
1000	291	62 ms	291	32 ms
5000	1457	1016 ms	1457	250 ms
10000	2896	9951 ms	2896	922 ms
50000	14527	3 min 10 s	14527	1 min 1 s
100000	29164	16 min 58 s	29164	3 min 26 s

10.6   Related work

There is a long research history for ISPs, which can be traced back to the 1950s when Dantzig and Fulkerson [9] studied a tanker scheduling problem. Kolen et al. [2] provide a comprehensive survey for ISPs. Ford and Fulkerson [10] solved a basic ISP and specified the staircase rule, which is based on Dilworth's theorem and involves $O(n^2)$ operations. Gupta et al. [11] propose another procedure that runs in $O(n \log n)$ time and they show to be the best possible procedure for partitioning a set of n intervals into a minimal subsets that do not overlap with each other. If each job can only be carried out by a given subset of the machines, the problem is proved to be NP-hard [12]. Heuristics and exact algorithms are proposed by Kroon et al. [5]. WISP for single machine can be solved using DP [4]. WIS for multiple machines can be solved using a min-cost flow formulation with computational complexity $O(n^2 \log n)$, where n is the number of jobs (see Arkin and Silverberg [3], Bouzina and Emmons [13], and Orlin [14]). Bar-Noy et al. [15] introduced IS applications in bandwidth allocation. Bhowmik et al. [16] discussed the principles, strengths, and limitations of DP.

To the best of our knowledge, WISWCS is not studied in the open literature.

10.7   Conclusions

In this chapter, a new algorithm for WISWCS is proposed by considering divisible capacity and capacity-length proportional weight. It is interesting to note that the proposed algorithm works for both single machine and multiple machines cases. Our future work will investigate scheduling problems in which a certain time of delay is allowed for a number of requests. Cases other than divisible capacity capacity-length proportional weight will be extended.

References

[1] Knauth T, Fetzer C. Energy-aware scheduling for infrastructure clouds. In: Proceedings of CloudCom; 2012.

[2] Kolen AWJ, Lenstra JK, Papadimitriou CH, Spieksma FCR. Interval scheduling: a survey. Published online March 16, 2007 in Wiley InterScience, <www.interscience.wiley.com>.

[3] Arkin EM, Silverberg EB. Scheduling with fixed start and end times. Discrete Appl Math 1987;18:1−8.

[4] Kleinberg J, Tardos E. Algorithm design. Edinburgh Gate, UK: Pearson Education Inc; 2005.

[5] Kroon LG, Salomon M, van Wassenhove L. Exact and approximation algorithms for the operational fixed interval scheduling problem. Eur J Oper Res 1995;82:190−205.

[6] Coffman Jr. EG, Grarey MR, Johnson DS. Bin-packing with divisible item sizes. J Complexity 1987;3:406−28.

[7] Tian W, Yeo CS, Xue R, Zhong Y. Power-aware scheduling of real-time virtual machines in cloud data centers considering fixed processing intervals. In: Proceedings of IEEE CCIS 2012. October 30−November 1, Hangzhou, China; 2012. p. 337−41.

[8] Cormen TH, Leiserson CE, Rivest RL, Stein C. Introduction to algorithms. 2nd ed. MIT Press and McGraw-Hill; 2001. ISBN 0-262-03293-7.

[9] Dantzig GB, Fulkerson DR. Minimizing the number of tankers to meet a fixed schedule. Nav Res Logist Q 1954;1:217−22.

[10] Ford Jr. LR, Fulkerson DR. Flows in networks. Princeton, NJ: Princeton University Press; 1962.

[11] Gupta UI, Lee DT, Leung JY-T. An optimal solution for the channel—assignment problem. IEEE Trans Comput 1979;C-28:807−10.

[12] Bellman RE. Dynamic programming. Princeton, NJ: Princeton University Press; 1957.

[13] Bouzina KI, Emmons H. Interval scheduling on identical machines. J Global Optim 1996;9:379−93.

[14] Orlin JB. A Faster strongly polynomial minimum cost flow algorithm. In: Proceedings of the 20th ACM symposium on the theory of computing; 1988. p. 377−87.

[15] Bar-Noy A, Canetti R, Kutten S, Mansour Y, Schieber B. Bandwidth allocation with preemption. SIAM J Comput 2005;28:1806−28.

[16] Bhowmik B. Dynamic programming—its principles, applications, strengths, and limitations. Int J Eng Sci Technol 2010;2(9):4822−6.

A Toolkit for Modeling and Simulation of Real-time Virtual Machine Allocation in a Cloud Data Center

Main Contents of this Chapter

- CloudSched architecture and main features
- Performance metrics for different scheduling algorithms Status and trends of cloud computing
- Design and implementation of CloudSched
- Performance evaluation

11.1 Introduction of the cloud data center

Cloud computing is developing based on various recent advancements in virtualization, grid computing, web computing, utility computing, and related technologies. Cloud computing provides both platforms and applications on demand through the internet or intranet [1]. Some key benefits of cloud computing include the hiding and abstraction of complexity, virtualized resources, and efficient use of distributed resources. Some examples of emerging cloud computing platforms are the Google App Engine [2], the IBM blue cloud [3], Amazon EC2 [4], and Microsoft Azure [5]. Cloud computing allows the sharing, allocation, and aggregation of software, computational, and storage network resources on demand. Cloud computing is still considered in its infancy, as there are many challenging issues to be resolved [1,6,7,8]. Youseff et al. [9] established a detailed ontology of dissecting the cloud into five main layers from top to down, as shown in Figure 11.1:

1. cloud application (SaaS)
2. cloud software environment (PaaS)
3. cloud software infrastructure (IaaS)
4. software kernel
5. hardware (HaaS)

Figure 11.1 also illustrates the interrelations, as well as the interdependency, on preceding technologies. In this chapter, we focus on infrastructure as a service (IaaS) in cloud data centers (CDCs).

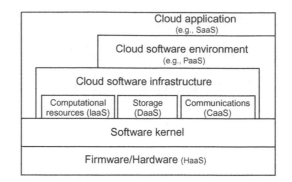

Figure 11.1 Layered architecture of cloud computing [9].

A CDC can be a distributed network in structure, which is composed of many computing nodes (such as servers), storage nodes, and network devices. Each node is formed using a series of resources such as CPU, memory, network bandwidth, etc. Each resource has its own corresponding properties. There are many different types of resources for cloud providers. This chapter focuses on IaaS. The definition and model defined in this chapter are aimed to be general enough to be used by a variety of cloud providers. In a traditional data center, applications are tied to specific physical servers that are often over-provisioned to deal with workload surges and unexpected failures. Such configuration rigidity makes data centers expensive to maintain because of wasted energy and floor space, low resource utilization, and significant management overhead.

Using virtualization technology, current CDCs become more flexible, secure, and allow on-demand allocating. With virtualization, CDCs should have the ability to migrate an application from one set of resources to another in a nondisruptive manner. Such agility becomes important in modern cloud computing infrastructures that aim to efficiently share and manage extremely large data centers. A technology plays an important role in CDCs is resource scheduling.

Much research has been conducted in scheduling algorithms. Most of them are for the load balancing of traditional web servers or server farms. One of the challenging scheduling problems in CDCs is to consider allocation and migration of reconfigurable virtual machines (VMs) and integrated features of hosting physical machines (PMs). Unlike traditional load balancing scheduling algorithms, which consider only physical servers with one factor (such as CPU), new algorithms treat CPU, memory, and network bandwidth integrated for both PMs and VMs. In addition, real-time VM allocation for multiple parallel jobs and PMs is considered.

With the development of cloud computing, the size and density of the CDC became large and problems that need to be solved therewith. Examples of these problems include: how to intensively manage physical resources and virtual resources and dynamically use them, how to improve elasticity and flexibility (which can improve service and reduce cost and risk management), and how to help customers build flexible, dynamic, and adaptive infrastructure that allows enterprises to ensure sustainable future development without an increase in spending. It is extremely difficult to research widely for all these problems in real internet platforms because the application developers cannot control and process the network environment. What's more, the network conditions cannot be predicted or controlled, but they still affect the quality evaluation of the strategies. The research of dynamic and large-scale distributed environments can be achieved by building a data center simulation system, which supports visualized modeling and simulation in large-scale applications in cloud infrastructure. A data center simulation system can describe the application workload statement, which includes user information, data center position, the amount of users and data centers, and the amount of resources in each data center. Using this information, the data center simulation system generates response requests and allocates these requests to VMs. By using a data center simulation system, application developers can evaluate suitable strategies, such as distributing reasonable data center resources, selecting a data center to match special requirements, reducing costs, etc.

Buyya et al. [7] introduced the GridSim toolkit for the modeling and simulation of distributed resource management for grid computing. Dumitrescu and Foster [8] introduced the GangSim tool for grid scheduling. Buyya et al. [7] introduced the modeling and simulation of cloud computing environments at the application level, in which simple scheduling algorithms, such as time-shared and space-shared, are discussed and compared. CloudSim [7] is a cloud computing simulator, which has the following functions:

1. supporting modeling of large-scale cloud computing infrastructure, both in a single physical computing node and a Java VM data center
2. modeling of the data center, service agency, and scheduling and distributing strategies
3. providing virtual engines, which is helpful for creating and managing several independent and collaborative virtual services in a data center node
4. be able to switch flexibly between processing cores with space-sharing and time-sharing

CloudAnalyst [12] aims to achieve the optimal scheduling among user groups and data centers based on the current configuration.

Both CloudSim and CloudAnalyst are based on SimJava [11] and GridSim [10], which makes them complicated. In addition, CloudSim and CloudAnalyst treat a CDC as a large resource pool and consider only application-level workloads. Therefore, they may not suitable for an IaaS simulation where each VM as resource is considered requested and allocated.

Wood et al. [13] introduced techniques for VM migration and proposed migration algorithms. Zhang [15] compared major load balance scheduling algorithms for traditional web servers. Singh et al. [14] proposed a novel load balancing algorithm called Vector Dot to handle the hierarchical and multidimensional resource constraints by considering both servers and storage in cloud computing.

There is a lack of tools that enable developers to evaluate the requirements of large-scale cloud applications in terms of comparing different resource scheduling algorithms regarding the geographic distribution of both computing servers and user workloads. To fill this gap in tools for evaluation and modeling of cloud environments and applications, in this chapter we propose CloudSched to be used for dynamic resource scheduling in a CDC. CloudSched supports multiple scheduling algorithms and it is suitable for the use and comparison of different scheduling algorithms. Unlike traditional scheduling algorithms that consider only one factor (such as CPU), which can cause hotspots or bottlenecks in many cases, CloudSched treats multidimensional resources (such as CPU, memory, and network bandwidth integrated for both PMs and VMs). Real-time constraint of both VMs and PMs, which is often neglected in the literature, is considered in this chapter. The main contributions of this chapter are:

1. proposing a simulation system for modeling cloud computing environments and performance evaluation of different resource scheduling policies and algorithms;
2. focusing on the simulation of scheduling in an IaaS layer where related tools are still lacking;
3. designing and implementing a lightweight simulator combining real-time multidimensional resource information.

CloudSched offers the following novel features:

1. Modeling and simulation of large-scale cloud computing environments, including data centers, VMs, and PMs
2. Providing a platform for modeling different resource scheduling policies and algorithms at the IaaS layer for clouds
3. Both graphical and textual outputs are supported

The organization of remaining parts of this chapter is as follows: Section 11.2 introduces the CloudSched architecture and its main features. Section 11.3 discusses performance measurements of different scheduling algorithms. Section 11.4 presents the design and implementation of CloudSched. Section 11.5 discusses the simulation results by comparing a few different scheduling algorithms. Finally, conclusions are provided in Section 11.6.

11.2 The architecture and main features of CloudSched

The simplified layered architecture is shown in Figure 11.2:

1. Web portal. At the top layer is a web portal for users to select resources and send requests; essentially, a few types of VMs are preconfigured for users to choose.
2. Core layer of scheduling. Once user requests are initiated, they go to next level CloudSched scheduling, which is for selecting appropriate data centers and PMs based on user requests. CloudSched provides support for modeling and simulation of CDCs, especially allocating VMs (consisting of CPU, memory, storage, bandwidth, etc.) to suitable PMs. This layer can manage a large scale of CDCs consisting of thousands of PMs. Different scheduling algorithms can be applied in different data centers based on customers' characteristics.
3. Cloud resource. At the lowest layer are cloud resources that include PMs and VMs, both consisting of certain amounts of CPU, memory, storage, and bandwidth.

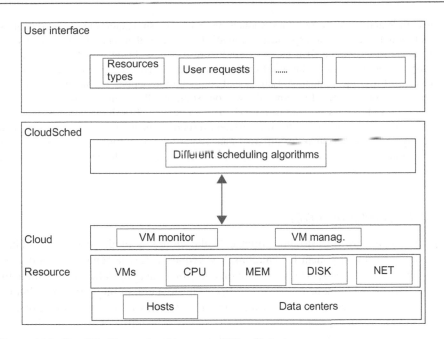

Figure 11.2 Simplified layered architecture of CloudSched.

Some other tools, such as CloudSim and CloudAnalyst, are based on existing simulation tools such as JavaSim and GridSim, which makes the simulation system very large and complicated. Considering these, CloudSched uses a lightweight design and is focused on resource scheduling algorithms.

The main features of CloudSched are the following:

1. Focus on the IaaS layer. Unlike existing tools that focus on the application (task) level, such as CloudSim and CloudAnalyst, CloudSched focuses on scheduling VMs at the IaaS layer, i.e., each request needs one or more VMs, whereas each request only occupies a portion of the total capacity of a VM in CloudSim and CloudAnalyst.
2. Providing a uniform view of all resources. Similar to Amazon EC2 real applications, CloudSched provides a uniform view of all physical and virtual resources so that both system management and user selections are simplified. We will explain this in detail in the following section.
3. Lightweight design and scalability. Compared to other existing simulation tools, such as CloudSim and CloudAnalyst, which are built on GridSim (may cause complications), CloudSched focuses on resource scheduling polices and algorithms. CloudSched can simulate tens of thousands of requests in a few minutes.
4. High extensibility. Modular design is applied in CloudSched. Different resource scheduling policies and algorithms can be plugged into and compared with each other for performance evaluation. In addition, multiple CDCs are modeled and can be extended to a very large distributed architecture.
5. Easy to use and repeatable. CloudSched enables users to set up simulations easily and quickly with easy-to-use graphical user interfaces and outputs. It can accept inputs from

text files and output to text files. CloudSched can save simulation inputs and outputs so that modelers can repeat experiments. CloudSched ensures that repeated simulation yields identical results. Some GUIs are shown in Figure 11.3 and illustrated in Figure 11.4.

6. Easy to configure and evaluate different algorithms. CloudSched provides a high degree of control over the simulation. Entities and configuration options are modeled with major features: CDC is defined in terms of PMs consisting of CPU, memory, and bandwidth (or storage); VM is defined in terms of CPU, memory, and bandwidth (or storage), a few typical types of VMs are preconfigured; different resource scheduling policies and algorithms are dynamically selectable for different data centers. Using identical inputs for different scheduling policies and algorithms, CloudSched can collect results and automatically plot different outputs to compare performance indices.

11.2.1 Modeling CDCs

The core hardware infrastructure related to the clouds is modeled in the simulator by a data center component for handling VM requests. A data center is mainly composed by a set of hosts, which are responsible for managing VMs during their life cycles. Host is a component that represents a physical computing node in a cloud: it is assigned a preconfigured processing capability (expressed in computing power in CPU units), memory, bandwidth, storage, and a scheduling policy for allocating processing cores to VMs. A VM can be represented in a similar way.

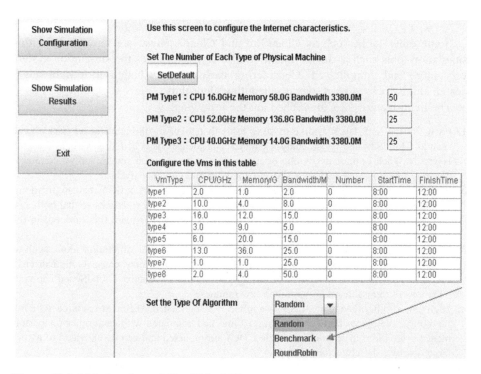

Figure 11.3 Main interface of CloudSched [1].

11.2.2   Modeling VM allocation

With virtualization technologies, cloud computing provides flexibility in resource allocation. For example, a PM with two processing cores can host two or more VMs on each core concurrently. VMs can only be allocated if the total used amount of processing power by all VMs on a host is not more than the one available in that host.

Taking the widely used example of Amazon EC2, we show that a uniform view of different types of VMs is possible. Table 11 1 provides eight types of VMs from Amazon FC2 online information. Amazon EC2 does not provide information on its hardware configuration. However, we can therefore form three types of different PMs (or PM pools) based on compute units. In a real CDC, for example, a PM with 2×68.4 GB memory, 16 cores $\times 3.25$ units, and 2×1690 GB storage can be provided. In this way, a uniform view of different types of VMs is possibly formed. This kind of classification provides uniform view of virtualized resources for heterogeneous virtualization platforms, e.g., Xen, KVM, VMWare, and brings great benefits for VM management and allocation. Customers only need to select suitable types of VMs based on their requirements. There are eight types of VMs in

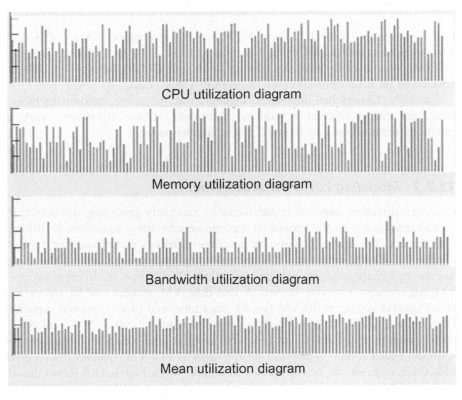

Figure 11.4 Main interface of CloudSched [2].

Table 11.1 **Eight types of VMS in Amazon EC2**

MEM	CPU (units)	BW(or Sto)	VM
1.7	1 (1 cores × 1 units)	160	1-1(1)
7.5	4 (2 cores × 2 units)	850	1-2(2)
15.0	8 (4 cores × 2 units)	1690	1-3(3)
17.1	6.5 (2 cores × 3.25 units)	420	2-1(4)
34.2	13 (4 cores × 3.25 units)	850	2-2(5)
68.4	26 (8 cores × 3.25 units)	1690	2-3(6)
1.7	5 (2 cores × 2.5 units)	350	3-1(7)
7.0	20 (8 cores × 2.5 units)	1690	3-2(8)

Table 11.2 **Three types of PMs suggested**

PM	CPU (units)	MEM	BW (or Sto)
1	16 (4 cores × 4 units)	160	1-1(1)
2	52 (16 cores × 3.25 units)	850	1-2(2)
3	40 (16 cores × 2.5 units)	1690	1-3(3)

EC2, as given in Table 11.1, where MEM stands for memory with unit GB, CPU is normalized to unit (each CPU unit is equal to 1 Ghz 2007 Intel Pentium processor [4]) and Sto stands for hard disk storage with unit GB. Three types of PMs are considered for heterogeneous cases, as given in Table 11.2.

Currently, CloudSched implements dynamic load balancing, maximizing utilization, and energy-efficient scheduling algorithms. Other algorithms, such as reliability-oriented and cost-oriented, can be applied as well.

11.2.3 Modeling customer requirements

CloudSched models customer requirements by randomly generating different types of VMs and allocating VMs based on appropriate scheduling algorithms in different data centers. The arrival process, service time distribution, and required capacity distribution of requests can be generated according to random processes. The arrival rate of customers' requests can be controlled. Distribution of different types of VM requirements can also be set. A real-time VM request can be represented in an interval vector: vmID(VM typeID, start-time, end-time, requested capacity). For example, vm1(1, 0, 6, 0.25) shows that the request ID is 1, VM is of type 1 (corresponding to integer 1), start-time is 0, and end-time is 6 (here, 6 can mean the sixth slot ended at time 6) and 0.25 for the capacity of a VM occupies from a given PM. Other requests can be represented in similar ways. Figure 11.5 shows the life cycles of VM allocation in a slotted time window using two PMs, where PM1 hosts vm4, vm5, and vm6, whereas PM2 hosts vm1, vm2, and vm3.

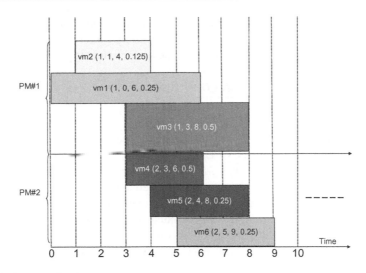

Figure 11.5 Example of user requests.

11.3   Performance metrics for different scheduling algorithms

Unlike traditional scheduling algorithms that consider only one aspect, which can cause hotspots or bottlenecks in many cases, CloudSched treats multidimensional resources, such as CPU, memory, and network bandwidth integrated for both PMs and VMs. There is lack of related metrics for scheduling algorithms considering multidimensional resources. For different scheduling objectives, there are different metrics. In the following, we consider metrics for load balancing, energy efficiency, and maximizing utilization. Other metrics for different objectives can be extended easily.

11.3.1   Metrics for multidimensional load balancing

In the following, we review some existing metrics and then develop an integrated measurement for the total imbalance level of the CDC, as well as the average imbalance level of each server. Wood et al. [13] introduced a few VM migration techniques. One integrated load balance metric is applied as follows:

$$V = \frac{1}{(1 - \mathrm{CPU}_u)(1 - \mathrm{MEN}_u)(1 - \mathrm{NET}_u)} \tag{11.1}$$

where CPU_u, MEN_u, and NET_u are the average utilization of CPU, memory, and network bandwidth, respectively, during each observed period. The large value V is, the higher of integrated utilization. Migration algorithms can therefore be based on this measurement. This actually is a strategy of minimizing integrated resource utilization by converting three-dimensional (3D) resource information into a one-dimensional (1D) value. This conversion may cause multidimensional information loss.

Zheng et al. [16] proposed another integrated load balancing metric as follows:

$$B = \frac{aN1_iC_i}{N1_mC_m} + \frac{bN2_iM_i}{N2_mM_m} + \frac{cN3_iD_i}{N3_mD_m} + \frac{dNet_i}{Net_m} \tag{11.2}$$

The referred physical server m is selected first. Then, other physical servers i are compared to server m. $N1_i$ is the CPU capability, $N2_i$ is the memory capability, and $N3_i$ is the hard disk. Here, C_i and M_i denote the average utilization of CPU and memory, respectively. D_i represents the transferring rate of hard disk and Net_i represents the network throughput. Here, a, b, c, and d denote the weighting factors for CPU, memory, hard disk, and network bandwidth, respectively. The major idea of this algorithm is to select the smallest value B among all physical servers to allocate VMs. This technique is also converting 3D resource information into a 1D value.

Singh et al. [14] introduced a novel Vector Dot algorithm to consider integrating factors of load balance for flow paths in data centers. For a server node, the node fraction vector $<$(CPUU/CPUCap), (memU/memCap), (netU/netCap)$>$ is defined, where CPUU, memU, and netU denote the average utilization of CPU, memory, and network bandwidth of a server, respectively. CPUCap, memCap, and netCap denote the total capacity of CPU, memory, and network bandwidth of a server, respectively. And the node utilization threshold vector is given by $<$CPUT, memT, netT, ioT$>$, where CPUT, memT, netT, and ioT represent the utilization threshold of CPU, memory, network bandwidth, and IO, respectively. To measure the degree of overload in a node and the system, the notion of an imbalance score is used. The imbalance score for a node is given by:

$$\text{IBscore}(f, T) = \begin{cases} 0, & \text{if} \quad f < T \\ e^{(f-T)/T}, & \text{otherwise} \end{cases} \tag{11.3}$$

By summing imbalance scores of all nodes, the total imbalance score of the system is obtained. This nonlinear measurement has the advantage of distinguishing between a pair of nodes at 3T and T and a pair of nodes both at 2T. The imbalance score is a good measurement for comparing average utilization to its threshold. Considering the advantages and disadvantages of existing metrics for resource scheduling, an integrated measurement for the total imbalance level of a CDC, as well as the average imbalance level of each server, has been developed for load balancing strategy. Other metrics for different scheduling strategies can be developed as well. The following parameters are considered:

1. Average CPU utilization CPU_i^u of a single server i. This is defined as the averaged CPU utilization during an observed period. For example, if the observing period is 1 min and the CPU utilization is recorded every 10 s, then CPU_i^u is the average of six recorded values of server i.

2. Average utilization of all CPUs in a CDC. Let CPU_i^n be the total number of CPUs of server i,

$$CPU_u^A = \frac{\sum_i^N CPU_i^U CPU_i^n}{\sum_i^N CPU_i^n} \tag{11.4}$$

where N is the total number of physical servers in a CDC. Similarly, the average utilization of memory, network bandwidth of server i, all memories, and all network bandwidth in a CDC can be defined as MEM_i^U, NET_i^U, MEM_u^A, and NET_u^A, respectively.

3. Integrated load imbalance value (ILB_i) of server i. Variance is widely used as a measure of how far a set of numbers are spread out from each other in statistics. Using variance, an integrated load imbalance value (ILB_i) of server i is defined:

$$\frac{(Avg_i - CPU_u^A)^2 + (Avg_i - MEM_u^A)^2 + (Avg_i - NET_u^A)^2}{3} \tag{11.5}$$

where

$$Avg_i = \frac{(CPU_i^U + MEM_i^U + NET_i^U)}{3} \tag{11.6}$$

(ILB_i) is applied to indicate load imbalance level comparing utilization of CPU, memory, and network bandwidth of a single server itself.

4. The imbalance value of all CPUs, memories, and network bandwidth. Using variance, the imbalance value of all CPUs in a data center is defined as

$$IBL_{cpu} = \sum_i^N (CPU_i^U - CPU_u^A)^2 \tag{11.7}$$

Similarly, imbalance values of memory and network bandwidth can be calculated. Then total imbalance values of all servers in a CDC is given by

$$IBL_{tot} = \sum_i^N ILB_i \tag{11.8}$$

5. Average imbalance value of a physical server i. The average imbalance value of a physical server i is defined as

$$IBL_{avg}^{PM} = \frac{IBL_{tot}}{N} \tag{11.9}$$

where N is the total number of servers. As its name suggests, this value is used to measure imbalance level of all physical servers.

6. Average imbalance value of a CDC. The average imbalance value of a CDC is defined as

$$IBL_{avg}^{CDC} = \frac{IBL_{cpu} + IBL_{mem} + IBL_{net}}{N} \tag{11.10}$$

7. Average running times. Average running time of the proceeding same amount of tasks can be compared for different scheduling algorithms.

8. Makespan. This is defined as the maximum load (or average utilization) on any PM.

9. Utilization efficiency. In this case, this is defined as the minimum load on any PM divided by the maximum load on any PM.

11.3.2   Metrics for energy efficiency

11.3.2.1   Power consumption model

1. The power consumption model of a server. Most power consumption in data centers comes from computation processing, disk storage, network, and cooling systems. In Ref. [17], the authors proposed a power consumption model for blade server, where P is defined as

$$14.5 + 0.2U_{cpu} + (4.5E - 8)U_{men} + 0.003U_{disk} + (3.1E - 8)U_{net} \tag{11.11}$$

where U_{CPU}, U_{mem}, U_{disk}, and U_{net} are the utilization of CPU, memory, hard disk, and network interface, respectively. It can be seen that other factors such as memory, hard disk, and network interface have a very small impact on the total power consumption. In Ref. [3], the authors found that CPU utilization is typically proportional to the overall system load, and proposed the following power model:

$$P(U) = kP_{max} + (1 - k)P_{max}U \tag{11.12}$$

where P_{max} is the maximum power consumed when the server is fully utilized, k is the fraction of power consumed by the idle server (studies show that on average it is about 0.7), and U is the CPU utilization. This chapter focuses on CPU power consumption, which accounts for the main part of energy compared to other resources such as memory, disk storage, and network devices.

In the real environment, CPU utilization may change over time due to the workload variability. Thus, the CPU utilization is a function of time and is represented as $u(t)$. Therefore, the total energy consumption by a PM (E_i) can be defined as an integral of the power consumption function over a period of time as:

$$E_i = \int_{t_0}^{t_1} P(u(t))dt \tag{11.13}$$

If $u(t)$ is constant over time (e.g., average utilization is adopted, $u(t) = u$), then $E_i = P(u)(t_1 - t_0)$.

2. The total energy consumption of a CDC is computed as

$$E_{cdc} = \sum_{i=1}^{n} E_i \tag{11.14}$$

It is the sum of all energy consumed by all PMs. Note that energy consumption of all VMs on PMs is included.

3. The total number of PMs used. This is the total number of PMs used for the given set of VM requests. It is important for energy efficiency.

4. The total power-on time of all PMs used. Based on the energy consumption equation of each PM, the total power-on time is the key factor.

11.3.3   Metric for maximizing resource utilization

1. Average resource utilization. Average utilization of CPU, memory, hard disk, and network bandwidth can be computed and an integration utilization of all these resources can also be used.

2. The total number of PMs used. It is closely related to the average and entire utilization of a CDC.

11.4 Design and implementation of CloudSched

In this section, we provide details related to the design and implementation of CloudSched. A Java discrete simulator is implemented. In the following, major building blocks of the CloudSched are described briefly.

11.4.1 IaaS resources considered

IaaS resources considered in this chapter include:

1. PMs: Physical computing devices that form data centers. Each PM can provide multiple VMs and each PM can have a multiple composition of CPU, memory, hard drives, network cards, and related components.
2. Physical clusters: These consist of a number of PMs, necessary network, and storage infrastructure.
3. VM: A virtual computing platform on the PM that uses virtualization software. It has a number of virtual CPUs, memory, storage, network cards, and related components.
4. Virtual cluster: consists of a number of VMs and necessary network and storage infrastructure.

11.4.2 Scheduling process in CDC

Figure 11.6 provides a referred architecture of CDCs and major operations of resource scheduling:

1. User requests: The user initiates the request through the internet (such as login cloud service provider's web portal).
2. Scheduling management: Scheduler Center makes decisions based on the user's identity (geographic location, etc.) and the operational characteristics of the request (quantity and quality requirements). The request is submitted to the appropriate data center and then the data center management program submits it to Scheduler Center. The Scheduler Center allocates the request based on scheduling algorithms applied in CDCs.
3. Feedback: The scheduling algorithm provides available resources to the user.
4. Execute scheduling: The scheduling results (such as deploying steps) are sent to the next stage.
5. Updating and optimization: Scheduler updates resource information and optimizes resources among different data centers according to the optimizing objective functions.

Figures 11.7 and 11.8 show general and detailed UML diagrams of the main resources in CDCs, respectively. Figure 11.7 shows the major resources and their relationships in CDCs and Figure 11.8 shows the properties of each major resource (classes).

11.4.3 Scheduling algorithms: taking the LIF algorithm as an example

Figure 11.9 shows the pseudocodes of least imbalance level first (LIF) algorithm for dynamic load balance of a CDC. Inputs to the algorithm include current

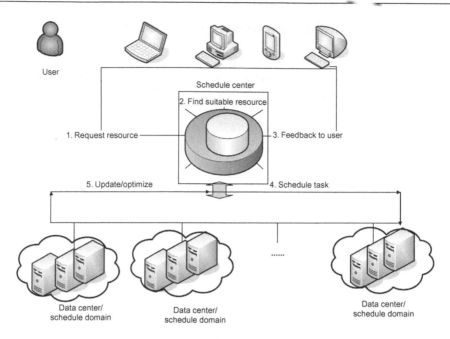

Figure 11.6 Referred architecture of CDCs.

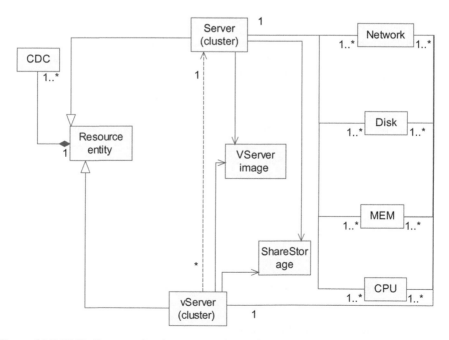

Figure 11.7 UML diagram of main resources in CDCs.

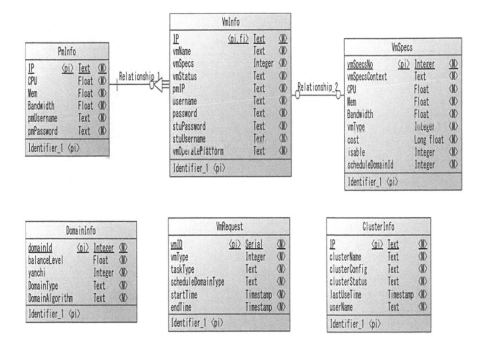

Figure 11.8 Detailed UML diagram of main resources in CDCs.

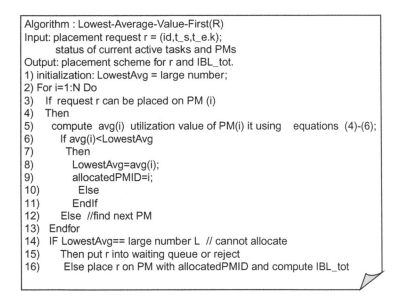

Figure 11.9 LIF algorithm.

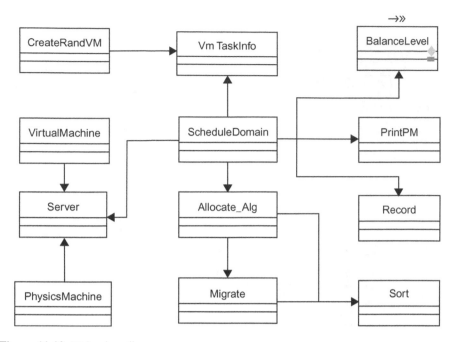

Figure 11.10 Main class diagram.

VM request r, status of current active tasks, and PMs. For dynamic scheduling, the output is placement scheme for request r. Basically, the algorithm dynamically finds the lowest total imbalance value of the data center when placing a new VM request by comparing different imbalance values if the request is allocated to different PMs. The algorithm finds a PM with the lowest integrated load. This will make the total imbalance value of all servers in a CDC the lowest.

Figures 11.10 and 11.11 show the main class diagram and sequence diagram, respectively, of the LIF algorithm. Class ScheduleDomain consists of main methods and handles tasks in each queue by calling other classes. Class CreateRandVM and VmTaskInfo generate task requests. Class Allocate and Sort allocate the requests of VMs. Class Migrate and Allocate-Alg can migrate VMs. Record, PrintPM, and BalanceLevel are responsible for printing and output functions. Server, PM, and VM accomplish functions of physical servers and VMs.

Sequence diagram shows the following sequences of the algorithm:

1. Initialize the system
2. Obtain task requests
3. Allocate VM requests in the waiting queue
4. Operate migrating queues
5. Operate requesting queues
6. Operate deleting queues

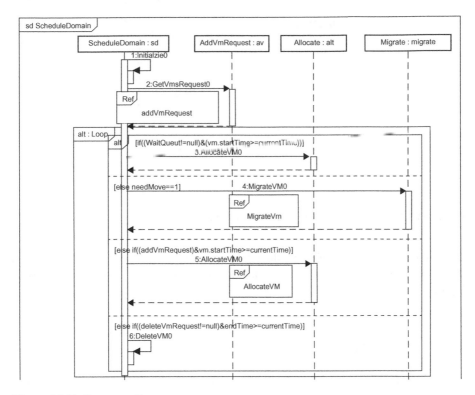

Figure 11.11 Sequence diagram.

Figure 11.12 One interface of configuring CDCs.

Figure 11.12 shows one of the interfaces of configuring CDCs in CloudSched. First, a data center is selected (by the manager) using different IDs, then the number of and types of PMs are set up. Manager can also add/delete data centers. Figure 11.13 shows one of the interfaces of configuring user requests. Probability

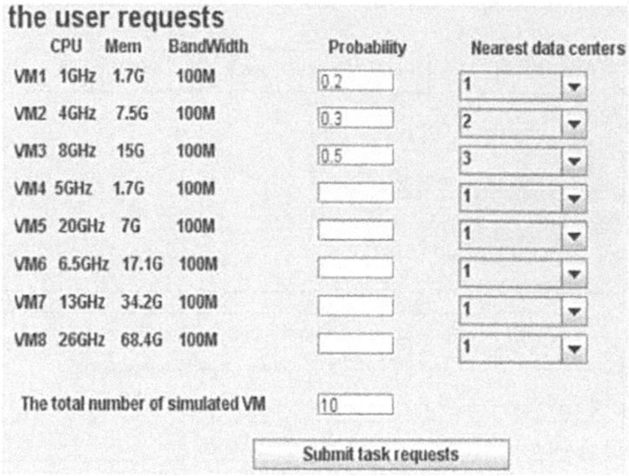

the user requests

	CPU	Mem	BandWidth	Probability	Nearest data centers
VM1	1GHz	1.7G	100M	0.2	1
VM2	4GHz	7.5G	100M	0.3	2
VM3	8GHz	15G	100M	0.5	3
VM4	5GHz	1.7G	100M		1
VM5	20GHz	7G	100M		1
VM6	6.5GHz	17.1G	100M		1
VM7	13GHz	34.2G	100M		1
VM8	26GHz	68.4G	100M		1

The total number of simulated VM 10

Submit task requests

Figure 11.13 One interface of configuring user requests.

distribution of each type of VMs, the total number of simulated VMs, and preferred data centers can be set up. The design diagram of main classes is depicted in Figure 11.10.

11.5 Performance evaluation

We use regular Pentium PC with CPU 2 Ghz and 2 GB of memory for the simulation.

11.5.1 Random configuration of VMs and PMs

In this section, we provide simulation results for comparing four different scheduling algorithms for load balance. For convenience, short name is given for each algorithm as follows:

1. ZHCJ algorithm: As introduced in Ref. [16], the algorithm always chooses PMs with the lowest V value (as defined in Eq. (11.1)) and available resources to allocate VMs (Figure 11.14).
2. ZHJZ algorithm: Selects a referring PM [16], calculates the value, and chooses PMs with lowest B value (as defined in Eq. (11.2)) and available resources to allocate VMs.
3. LIF algorithm: Based on demands characteristics (e.g., CPU intensive, high memory, high bandwidth requirements etc.), always selects PMs with lowest integrated imbalance value (as defined in Eq. (11.5)) and available resource to allocate VMs.
4. Rand algorithm: randomly assigns requests (VMs) to PMs that have available resources.
5. Round-Robin algorithm: One of the simplest scheduling algorithms, it assigns tasks to each physical server in equal portions and in circular order, handling all tasks without priority (also known as cyclic executive).

For the simulation, three types of heterogeneous PMs are considered, each PM pool consists of some amount of PMs (can be dynamically configured and extended). For the simulation of a large number of VM requests,

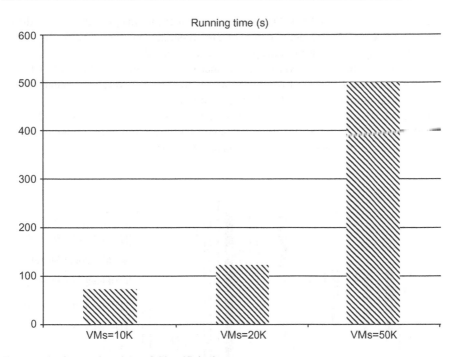

Figure 11.14 Running time of CloudSched.

both CPU and memory are configured with a large size, which can be set dynamically:

PM type 1: CPU = 6 GHz, memory = 8 G, and bandwidth = 1000 M
PM type 2: CPU = 12 GHz, memory = 16 G, and bandwidth = 1000 M
PM type 3 CPU = 18 GHz, memory = 32 G, and bandwidth = 1000 M.

Similar to eight Amazon EC2 instances with high CPU, high memory, and standard configurations (but not exactly the same), eight types of VMs with equal probability of requests are generated randomly as follows (can be dynamic configured):

Type 1: CPU = 1.0 GHz, memory = 1.7 G, bandwidth = 100 M
Type 2: CPU = 4.0 GHz, memory = 7.5 G, bandwidth = 100 M
Type 3: CPU = 8.0 GHz, memory = 15.0 G, bandwidth = 100 M
Type 4: CPU = 5.0 GHz, memory = 1.7 G, bandwidth = 100 M
Type 5: CPU = 20.0 GHz, memory = 7.0 G, bandwidth = 100 M
Type 6: CPU = 6.5 GHz, memory = 17.1 G, bandwidth = 100 M
Type 7: CPU = 13.0 GHz, memory = 34.2 G, bandwidth = 100 M
Type 8: CPU = 26.0 GHz, memory = 68.4 G, and bandwidth = 100 M.

For all simulations, the number of PMs ranges from 100 to 600, the number of requests of VMs varies from 1000 to 6000, a Pentium PC with CPU 2 Ghz and 2 GB of memory is used for all simulations. The input data of user requests is generated using a program by considering equal probabilities of the previously mentioned eight types of VMs. Of course, different (random) probabilities of different types of VMs can be generated. For steady-state analysis, a warm-up period (initial 2000 requests) is used to drop the transient period.

Figure 11.15 shows the average imbalance level, defined in Eq. (11.10), of a CDC. It can be seen that the LIF algorithm has the lowest average imbalance level when the total number of VMs and PMs are varied.

Figure 11.16 shows the average imbalance level of the entire physical server defined in Eq. (11.5). The LIF algorithm again has lowest average imbalance level for all PMs when the total number of VMs and PMs are varied.

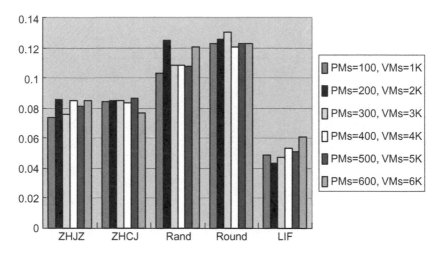

Figure 11.15 Average imbalance values of a CDC.

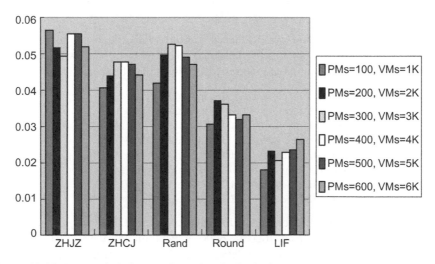

Figure 11.16 Average imbalance values of each physical server.

Figure 11.17 shows the average imbalance level, defined in Eq. (11.10), of a CDC when the total number of physical servers is fixed but the number of VMs is varied.

Figure 11.18 shows the average imbalance level of the entire physical server, defined in Eq. (11.5), when the total number of physical servers is fixed but the number of VMs is varied. Through extensive simulation, similar results are observed.

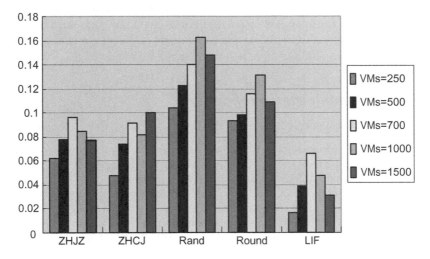

Figure 11.17 Average imbalance values of a CDC when PMs = 100.

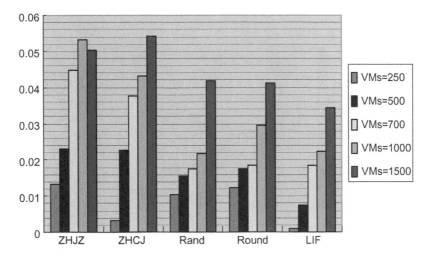

Figure 11.18 Average imbalance values of each physical server when PMs = 100.

11.5.2   Divisible size configuration of PMs and VMs

The configuration of VMs and PMs are explained in section 11.2.2. In Figures 11.19–11.21, we show the average utilization of CPU, memory, bandwidth, and the average of these three utilizations. We also show the imbalance value (IBL, as in Eq. (11.10)) of the entire data centers by running five different algorithms: Rand, Round-Robin, ZHJZ, ZHCJ, and LIF. It can be seen that in all the cases (when the total number of VMs and PMs are varying), that LIF has highest average utilization of CPU, memory, and bandwidth but has the lowest imbalance value. These results demonstrate that metrics obtained in divisible cases are much better than random configuration cases. Therefore, cloud providers such as Amazon can adopt these configurations to provide better quality of service regarding load balancing, energy efficiency, and other performance related requirements.

11.5.3   Comparing energy efficiency

We considered four algorithms here:

1. **Round-Robin:** The Round-Robin is the most commonly used scheduling algorithm (e.g., by Eucalyptus and Amazon EC2 [18]), which allocates VM requests in turn to each PM. The advantage of this algorithm is that it is simple to implement.
2. **Modified Best Fit Decreasing (MBFD):** MBFD is a bin-packing algorithm. Best Fit Decreasing is shown to use no more than 11/9 optimal solution (OPT)+1 bins (where OPT is the number of bins given by the optimal solution) [6]. The MBFD algorithm [6] first sorts all VMs in decreasing order of their current CPU utilizations and allocates each VM to a host that provides the least increase of power consumption due to this allocation. This allows leveraging the heterogeneity of resources by choosing the most power-efficient nodes first. For homogenous resources (PM), the VM can be allocated to any running PM that can still host because the power increasing is the same for homogenous

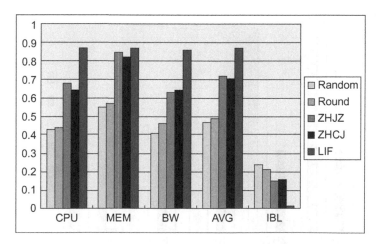

Figure 11.19 Utilization and imbalance value of the entire data center when PMs = 100 and VMs = 1000.

resources. The complexity of the allocation part of the algorithm is *nm*, where *n* is the number of VMs that must be allocated and *m* is the number of hosts. MBFD needs sorting requests so that it is only suitable for offline (or semi-offline) scheduling.

3. Offline Without Delay (OFWID): OFWID knows all requests in advance and follows the requests exactly without delay. It firstly sorts requests in increasing order of their start-times and allocates requests to PMs in increasing order of their IDs. If all running PMs cannot host the request, then a new PM is turned on.

4. Online Without Delay (ONWID): ONWID knows one request each time. It allocates requests to PMs in increasing order of their IDs. If all running PMs cannot host the

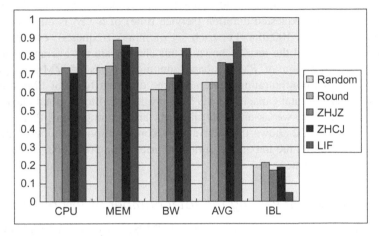

Figure 11.20 Utilization and imbalance value of the entire data center when PMs = 200 and VMs = 4000.

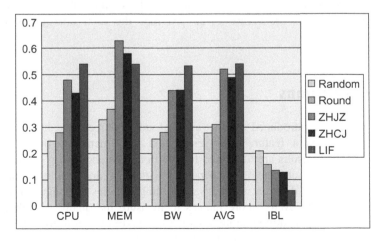

Figure 11.21 Utilization and imbalance value of the entire data center when PMs = 500 and VMs = 5000.

request, a new PM is powered on. When the total number of PMs is fixed, if all PMs still cannot host the request, then the request is blocked.

11.5.3.1 Impact of varying maximum duration of VM requests

In this case, eight types of VMs are considered, as given in Table 11.1, which is based on Amazon EC2. The total number of arrivals (requests) is 1000 and each type of VMs has an equal number, i.e., 125. All requests follow the Poisson arrival process and have exponential service time, the mean interarrival period is set as 5, the maximum intermediate period is set as 50, and the maximum duration of requests are set as 50, 100, 200, 400, and 800 slots, respectively. Each slot is 5 min. For example, if the requested duration (service time) of a VM is 20 slots, actually its duration is 20*5 = 100 min. For each set of inputs (requests), experiments are run three times and all the results shown in this chapter are the average of the three runs. The configuration of PMs is based on eight types of VMs, as given in Table 11.2. In this configuration, there are three different types of PMs (heterogeneous case) and the total capacity of a VM is proportional to the total capacity of a PM. For comparison, we assume that all VMs are running using their requested capacity. Figure 11.22 shows the total energy consumption (in kilowatt hours) of the four algorithms as the maximum duration varies from 50 to 800, while all other parameters are the same.

11.5.3.2 Impact of varying the total number of VM requests

Next, we fix the total number of each type of PM but vary the total number of VM requests. The system load is defined as the average arrival rate (λ) divided by the average service rate (u). The arrival process follows the Poisson distribution and service time follows uniform distribution. To increase the system load, we vary the maximum duration of each request, whereas the total number of PMs remains fixed as 15 (each type has 5). Figure 11.23 provides the total energy consumption comparison.

11.6 Conclusions

In this chapter, we introduced a lightweight cloud resources scheduling emulator, CloudSched. Its major features and design and implementation details are presented. Simulation results are discussed for load balance and energy-efficient algorithms. CloudSched can help developers to identify and explore appropriate solutions considering different resource scheduling policies and algorithms. In the near future, we will develop more indices to measure the quality of related algorithms for different scheduling strategies such as maximization utilization of multidimensional resource. In addition, more simulation results, such as varying the

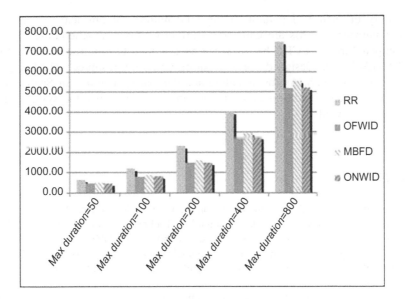

Figure 11.22 Total energy consumption (in kilowatt hours) by varying maximum duration of VM requests.

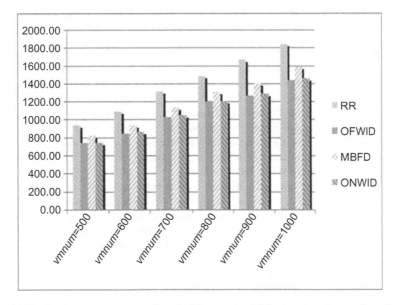

Figure 11.23 Total energy consumption (in kilowatt hours) by varying the number of VM requests.

probability of each VM request, fixing total number of physical servers, with a varying number of VMs are collected. Currently, different scheduling algorithms are compared inside a CDC but they can be extended to multiple data centers easily. CloudSched is designed for comparing different resource scheduling algorithms regarding IaaS. As for modeling and comparing features in SaaS (software as a service), PaaS (platform as a service), and other domains, the system needs to be extended as well.

References

[1] Armbrust M, Fox A, Griffith R, Joseph A, Katz R, Konwinski A, et al. Above the clouds: a Berkeley view of cloud computing. Technical Report No. UCB/EECS-2009-28. University of California at Berkley, CA; February 10, 2009.

[2] Google App Engine, <https://appengine.google.com/> [last accessed 25.03.14].

[3] IBM blue cloud, <http://www.ibm.com/grid/> [last accessed 26.03.14].

[4] Amazon EC2, <http://aws.amazon.com/ec2/> [last accessed 25.03.14].

[5] MicrosoftWindows Azure, <http://www.microsoft.com/windowsazure> [last accessed 26.03.14].

[6] Beloglazov A, Abawajy J, Buyya R. Energy-aware resource allocation heuristics for efficient management of data centers for cloud computing accepted by future generation computer systems; 2012.

[7] Buyya R, Ranjan R, Calheiros RN. Modeling and simulation of scalable cloud computing environments and the CloudSim toolkit: challenges and opportunities. In: Proceedings of the seventh high performance computing and simulation conference (HPCS 2009, ISBN: 978-1-4244-4907-1, IEEE Press, New York, NY), Leipzig, Germany; June 21−24, 2009.

[8] Dumitrescu CL, Foster I. GangSim: a simulator for grid scheduling studies. In: Proceedings of the IEEE international symposium on Cluster Computing and the Grid (CCGrid 2005), Cardiff, UK; 2005.

[9] Youseff L, Butrico M, Da Silva D. Toward a unified ontology of cloud computing. In: Proceedings of the grid computing environments workshop, GCE'08; 2008.

[10] Buyya R, Murshed M. GridSim: a toolkit for the modeling and simulation of distributed resource management and scheduling for grid computing. J Concurrency Comput Pract Exp 2002;14(13−15): Wiley Press, Nov.-Dec.

[11] Howell F, Mcnab R. SimJava: a discrete event simulation library for java. In: Proceedings of the first international conference on web-based modeling and simulation; 1998.

[12] Wickremasinghe B, Calheiros RN, Buyya R. CloudAnalyst: a CloudSim-based tool for modelling and analysis of large scale cloud computing environments. In: Proceedings of the 24th IEEE international conference on advanced information networking and applications (AINA 2010), Perth, Australia; April 20−23, 2010.

[13] Wood T, Shenoy P, Venkataramani A, Yousif M. Black-box and gray-box strategies for virtual machine migration. In: Proceedings of the symposium on networked systems design and implementation (NSDI); 2007.

[14] Singh A, Korupolu M, Mohapatra D. Server-storage virtualization: integration and load balancing in data centers. In: Proceedings of the 2008 ACM/IEEE conference on super-computing; 2008, p. 1−12.

[15] Zhang W. Research and implementation of elastic network service [PhD dissertation]. National University of Defense Technology, China (in Chinese) 2000102353.

[16] Zheng H, Zhou L, Wu J. Design and implementation of load balancing in web server cluster system. J Nanjing University Aeronaut Astronaut 2006;38(3).

[17] Economou D, Rivoire S, Kozyrakis C, Ranganathan P. Full-System power analysis and modeling for server environments. Stanford University; 2006, [HP Labs Workshop on Modeling, Benchmarking, and Simulation (MoBS) June 18]. Full-System power analysis and modeling for server environments. Stanford University; 2006

Toward Running Scientific Workflows in the Cloud

Main Contents of this Chapter

- Towards running scientific workflows in the cloud
- Experiment procedure
- Experiment on Amazon EC2

12.1 Introduction

Scientific workflow management systems (SWFMSs) have proven essential to scientific computing because they provide functionalities such as workflow specification, process coordination, job scheduling and execution, provenance tracking, and fault tolerance. Systems such as Taverna [1], Kepler [2], Vistrails [3], Pegasus [4], Swift [5], and VIEW [6] have seen wide adoption in various disciplines such as physics, astronomy, bioinformatics, neuroscience, earth science, and social science. Nevertheless, advances in science instrumentation and network technologies are posing new challenges to our workflow systems in both data scale and application complexity.

We are entering into a big data era. The amount of data created in the world is growing explosively. According to recent International Data Corporation (IDC) research, the total amount of digital information in the world reached 1 zettabyte in 2010. Popular search engines such as Google and Bing can generate multiple terabytes of search logs every day. Social network data is also tremendous: each month, the Facebook community creates more than 30 billion pieces of content ranging from web links, news, stories, blog posts, and notes to videos and photos [7]. The scientific community is also facing a data deluge [8] coming experiments, simulations, sensors, and satellites. The Large Hadron Collider [9] at CERN can generate more than 100 terabytes of collision data per second. GenBank [10], one of the largest DNA databases, already hosts over 120 billion bases and the number is expected to double every 9–12 months. Data volumes are also increasing dramatically in physics, earth science, medicine, and many other disciplines. As for application complexity, a protein simulation problem [11] involves running many instances of a structure prediction simulation, each with different random initial conditions, performs multiple rounds, and can run up to tens of CPU years.

As an emerging computing paradigm, cloud computing [12] is gaining tremendous momentum in both academia and industry: not long after Amazon opened its Elastic Computing Cloud (EC2) to the public, Google, IBM, and Microsoft all released their cloud platforms. Meanwhile, several open source cloud platforms, such as Hadoop [13], OpenNebula [14], Eucalyptus [15], Nimbus [16], and OpenStack [17], became available because of the fast growth within their respective communities.

There are major benefits and advantages that are driving the widespread adoption of the cloud computing paradigm:

1. Easy access to resources: resources are offered as services and can be accessed over the internet. For instance, with a credit card, you can get access to Amazon EC2 virtual machines (VMs) immediately.
2. Scalability on demand: once an application is deployed onto the cloud, the application can automatically be made scalable by provisioning the resources in the cloud on demand. The cloud takes care of scaling out and in and load balancing.
3. Better resource utilization: cloud platforms can coordinate resource utilization according to resource demand of the applications hosted in the cloud.
4. Cost saving: cloud users are charged based on their resource usage in the cloud, meaning they only pay for what they use, and if their applications are optimized, that will immediately be reflected into a lowered cost.

Scientific workflow systems have been formerly applied over a number of execution environments, such as workstations, clusters/grids, and supercomputers. The new cloud computing paradigm, with an unprecedented size of datacenter-level resource pools and on-demand resource provisioning, can offer much more to such systems, enabling scientific workflow solutions capable of addressing peta-scale scientific problems. The benefit of running scientific workflows on top of a cloud can be multifold:

1. The scale of scientific problems that can be addressed using scientific workflows can be greatly increased compared to cluster/grid environments, which was previously upbounded by the size of a dedicated resource pool with limited resource sharing extension in the form of virtual organizations. Cloud platforms can offer a vast amount of computing resources, as well as storage space for such applications, allowing scientific discoveries to be carried out on a much larger scale.
2. Application deployment can be made flexible and convenient. With bare-metal physical servers, it is not easy to change the application **deployed**and the underlying supporting platform. However, with virtualization technology in a cloud platform, different application environments can either be preloaded in VM images or deployed dynamically onto VM instances.
3. The on-demand resource allocation mechanism in the cloud can improve resource utilization and change the experience of end users for improved responsiveness. Cloud-based workflow applications can allocate resources accordingly with the number of nodes at each workflow stage instead of reserving a fixed number of resources upfront. Cloud workflows can scale out and in dynamically, resulting in a fast turnaround time for end users.
4. Cloud computing provides a much larger room for the trade-off between performance and cost. The spectrum of resource investment now ranges from dedicated private resources, a hybrid resource pool combining local resource and remote clouds, and a full outsourcing of computing and storage to public clouds. Cloud computing not only provides the potential to solve larger-scale scientific problems, but also presents the opportunity to improve the performance/cost ratio.

In an earlier paper [18], we identified various challenges associated with migrating and adapting an SWFMS in the cloud. In this chapter, we present an end-to-end approach that addresses the integration of Swift, an SWFMS that has a broad application in grids and supercomputers, with the OpenNebula cloud platform. The integration covers all major aspects of workflow management in the cloud, from client-side workflow submission to the underlying cloud resource management, thus providing scientific-workflow-management-as-a-service in the cloud.

12.2 Related work

There have been a couple of early explorers that tried to evaluate the feasibility, performance, and adaptation of running data-intensive and HPC applications on clouds or hybrid grid/cloud environments. Palankar et al. [19] evaluated the feasibility, cost, availability, and performance of using Amazon's S3 service to provide storage support to data-intensive applications and identified a set of additional functionalities that storage services targeting data-intensive scientific applications should support. Oliveira et al. [20] evaluated the performance of X-ray crystallography workflow using SciCumulus middleware with Amazon EC2. These studies provide a good source of information about cloud platform support for scientific applications. Other studies investigated the execution of real science applications on commercial clouds [21,22], mostly High Performance Computing (HPC) applications, and compared the performance and cost against grid environments. Although such applications indeed can be ported to a cloud environment, cloud execution doesn't show a significant benefit, because of the applications' tightly coupled nature.

There are also endeavors to run workflow applications on top of clouds. This research [23,24] focused on running scientific workflows composed of loosely coupled parallel applications on various clouds. The study conducted on an experimental Nimbus Cloud test bed [25] dedicated to scientific applications involved a nontrivial amount of computation performed over many days, which allowed the evaluation of the scalability, as well as the performance and stability of the cloud over time. Their studies demonstrated that multisite cloud computing is a viable and effective solution for some scientific workflows, the networking and management overhead across different cloud infrastructures do not have a major effect on the overall user experience, and the convenience of being able to scale resources at runtime outweighs such overhead.

With VGrADS [26], not only did the virtual grid abstraction enable a more sophisticated and effective scheduling of workflow sets, unifying workflow execution over batch queue systems and cloud computing sites (including Amazon EC2 and Eucalyptus), but the Virtual Grid Execution System also provided a uniform interface for provisioning, querying, and controlling the resources. Its workflow planner could interact with a DAG scheduler, an Amazon EC2 planner, and fault tolerance subcomponents to trade-off various system parameters—performance, reliability, and cost.

Approaches for automated provisioning include the Context Broker [16] from the Nimbus project, which supported the concept of a one-click virtual cluster that allowed clients to coordinate large virtual cluster launches in simple steps. The Wrangler system [27] was a similar implementation that allowed users to describe a desired virtual cluster in XML format and send to a web service, which managed the provisioning of VMs and the deployment of software and services. It was also capable of interfacing with many different cloud resource providers.

Bresnahan et al. [28] introduced Cloudinit.d, a tool for launching, configuring, monitoring, and repairing a set of interdependent VMs in one or a set of infrastructure-as-a-service (IaaS) clouds. In addition, as its name suggested, Cloudinit.d could launch groups of interdependent VMs and optimize the launch by allowing independent VMs to launch at the same time.

12.3 Integration

In this section, we discuss our end-to-end approach for integrating Swift with the OpenNebula cloud platform. Before we go into further details of the integration, we will discuss some background information with regard to workflow systems and cloud integration options.

12.3.1 Integration options

In our earlier paper [18], we described a reference architecture of SWFMSs and identified four integration approaches for the deployment of SWFMSs in a cloud computing environment according to the reference architecture. The reference architecture for SWFMSs [29] is proposed as an endeavor to standardize SWFMS research and development efforts, and an Service Oriented Architecture (SOA)-based instantiation is first implemented in the VIEW system. As shown in Figure 12.1, the reference architecture consists of four logical layers, seven major functional subsystems, and six interfaces. The first layer is the Operational Layer, which consists of a wide range of heterogeneous and distributed data sources, software tools, services, and their operational environments, including high-end computing environments. The second layer is the Task Management Layer, which consists of three subsystems: Data Product Management, Provenance Management, and Task Management. The third layer, the Workflow Management Layer, consists of Workflow Engine and Workflow Monitoring. Finally, the fourth layer, the Presentation Layer, consists of the Workflow Design subsystem and the Presentation and Visualization subsystem. The reference architecture would allow the scientific workflow community to focus on different layers and subsystems of SWFMSs, and enable such systems to interact and interoperate with each other based on the interface definitions.

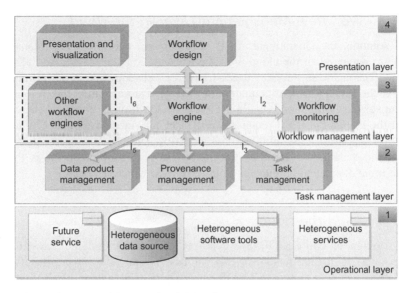

Figure 12.1 Reference architecture for SWFMSs.

The four deployment options, accordingly, correspond to deploying different layers of the reference architecture into the cloud:

12.3.1.1 Operational-Layer-in-the-cloud

In this solution, only the Operational Layer lies in the cloud with an SWFMS running out of the cloud. An SWFMS can now leverage cloud applications as another type of task component. Cloud-based applications can take advantage of the high scalability provided by the cloud and large resource capacity provisioned by the data centers. This solution also relieves a user from the concern of vendor lock-in due to the relative ease of using alternative cloud platforms for running cloud applications. However, the SWFMS itself cannot benefit from the scalability offered by the cloud.

12.3.1.2 Task-Management-Layer-in-the-cloud

Both the Operational and Task Management Layers will be deployed in the cloud. The Data Product Management, Provenance Management, and Task Management components can now leverage the high scalability provided by the cloud. For Task Management, rather than accommodating the user's request based on a batch-based scheduling system, all or most tasks with a ready state can now be immediately deployed over cloud computing nodes and executed instead of waiting in a job queue for the availability of resources. One limitation of this solution is the economic cost associated with the storage of provenance and data products in the cloud. Moreover, although task scheduling and management can benefit from the scalability offered by the cloud, workflow scheduling and management do not benefit because the workflow engine runs outside of the cloud.

12.3.1.3   Workflow-Management-Layer-in-the-cloud

In this solution, the Operational, Task Management, and Workflow Management Layers are deployed in the cloud with the Presentation Layer deployed at a client machine. This solution provides a good balance between system performance and usability: the management of computation, data, and storage and other resources are all encapsulated in the cloud, while the Presentation Layer remains at the client to support the key architectural requirement of user interface customizability and user interaction support. In this solution, both workflow and task management can benefit from the scalability offered by the cloud. However, the downside is that they become more dependent on the cloud platform over which they run.

12.3.1.4   All-in-the-cloud

In this solution, an entire SWFMS is deployed inside the cloud and accessible via a web browser. A distinct feature of this solution is that no software installation is needed for a scientist and the SWFMS can fully take advantage of all the services provided in a cloud infrastructure. Moreover, the cloud-based SWFMS can provide highly scalable scientific workflows and task management as services, providing one kind of software-as-a-service (SaaS). One concern the user might have is the economic cost associated with the necessity of using a cloud on a daily basis, the dependency on the availability and reliability of the cloud, and the risk associated with vendor lock-in.

12.3.2   The Swift workflow management system

Swift is a system that bridges scientific workflows using parallel computing. It is a parallel programming tool for rapid and reliable specification, execution, and management of large-scale science and engineering workflows. Swift takes a structured approach to workflow specification, scheduling, and execution. It consists of a simple scripting language called SwiftScript for concise specification of complex parallel computations based on dataset typing and iterations [30] and dynamic dataset mappings for accessing large-scale datasets represented in diverse data formats. The runtime system provides an efficient workflow engine for scheduling and load balancing and it can interact with various resource management systems such as Portable Batch System (PBS) and Condor for task execution.

The Swift system architecture consists of four major components: Program Specification, Scheduling, Execution, and Provisioning, as illustrated in Figure 12.2. Computations are specified in SwiftScript, which has been shown to be simple yet powerful. SwiftScript programs are compiled into abstract computation plans, which are then scheduled for execution by the workflow engine onto provisioned resources. Resource provisioning in Swift is very flexible and tasks can be scheduled to execute on various resource providers, where the provider interface can be implemented as a local host, a cluster, a multisite grid, or the Amazon EC2 service.

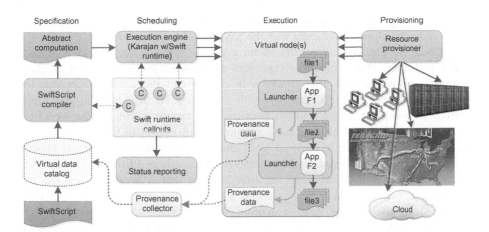

Figure 12.2 Swift system architecture.

The four major components of the Swift system can be easily mapped into the four layers in the reference architecture. The specification falls into the Presentation Layer, although SwiftScript focuses more on the parallel scripting aspect for user interaction than on graphical representation. The scheduling components correspond to the Workflow Management Layer, the execution components map to the Task Management Layer, and the Provisioning Layer can be thought of as mostly in the Operational Layer.

12.3.3 Integration challenges

For easy integration with a cloud platform, a Task-Management-Layer-in-the-cloud approach can be chosen by implementing a provider (such as an Amazon EC2) to Swift. Then, tasks in a Swift workflow can be submitted into Amazon EC2 and executed on Amazon EC2 VM instances. However, this approach would leave most of the workflow management and dynamic resource scaling outside the cloud. For application developers, we would like to free them from complicated cloud resource configuration and provisioning issues, and provide them with the convenience and transparency to scalable cloud resources. Therefore, we choose to take the Workflow-Management-Layer-in-the-cloud approach, which requires minimal configuration on the client side and supports easy deployment with virtualization techniques.

There are a couple of challenges associated with this integration approach. First, we need to port the SWFMS (in our case, Swift) into the cloud, which would usually involve wrapping up an SWFMS as a cloud service. In addition, to fully explore the capability and scalability of the cloud, the workflow engine may need to be reengineered to be able to interact directly with the various cloud services such as storage, resource allocation, task scheduling, and monitoring. On the client side, either a complete web-based user interface needs to be developed to allow users to specify and interact with the SWFMS, or a thin desktop client application needs to be developed to interact with the SWFMS cloud service.

Second, we need to address the resource provisioning issue. Although conceptually the cloud offers uncapped resources and a workflow can request as many resources as it requires, this comes with a cost and the presumption that the workflow engine can talk directly with the resource allocated in the cloud (which is usually not true without tweaking the configuration of the workflow engine). Considering these two factors, some existing solutions, such as Nimbus, would acquire a certain number of VMs and assemble them as a virtual cluster, onto which existing cluster management systems, such as PBS, can be deployed and used as a job submission/execution service that a workflow engine can directly interact with. We take a similar approach that creates a virtual cluster and deploys the Falkon [31] execution services onto the cluster for high-throughput task scheduling and execution. Falkon is a lightweight task execution service for optimized task throughput and resource efficiency delivered by a streamlined dispatcher, a dynamic resource provisioner, and the data diffusion mechanism [32] to cache datasets in local disk or memory and dispatch tasks according to data locality.

12.3.4   Integration architecture

We devise an end-to-end integration approach that addresses the previously mentioned challenges. We call it end-to-end because it covers all major aspects involved in the integration, including a client-side workflow submission tool, a cloud workflow service that accepts submissions, a CRM that accepts resource requests from the workflow service and dynamically instantiates a Falkon virtual cluster, and a cluster monitoring service that monitors the health of the acquired cloud resources.

12.3.4.1   The client submission tool

The client submission tool is a standalone Java application that provides an Integrated Development Environment (IDE) for workflow development and allows users to edit, compile, run, and submit SwiftScripts. Scientists and application developers can write their scripts in this environment and test run their workflows on a local host before they make final submissions to the Swift Cloud service to run in the cloud. It provides multiple submission options: execute immediately, execute at a fixed time point, or execute recurrently (per day, per week, etc.).

We integrate Swift with the OpenNebula cloud platform. We choose OpenNebula for our implementation because it has a flexible architecture, is easy to customize, and provides a set of tools and service interfaces that are handy for integration. Of course, other cloud platforms can be integrated in similar means. We show the system diagram of the integration in Figure 12.3.

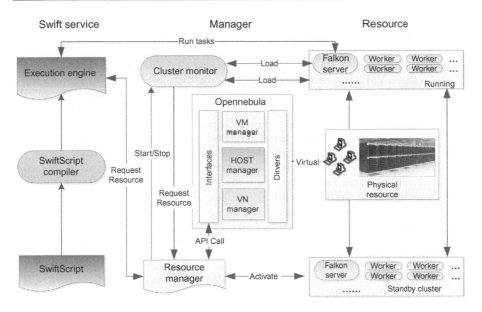

Figure 12.3 Integration architecture.

12.3.4.2   The Swift Cloud workflow service

One of the key components of the system is the Swift Cloud workflow service that it acts as an intermediary between the workflow client and the backend CRM. The service has a web interface for configuration of the service, the resource manager, and application environments. It also allows for workflow submission via the web interface, in addition to the client tool submission.

12.3.4.3   The CRM

The CRM accepts resource requests from the cloud workflow service and is in charge of interfacing with OpenNebula and provisioning Falkon virtual clusters dynamically to the workflow service. In addition, it also monitors the virtual clusters. The process to start a Falkon virtual cluster is as follows:

1. CRM provides a service interface to the workflow service: the latter makes a resource request to CRM.
2. CRM initializes and maintains a pool of VMs: the number of VMs in the pool can be set via a config file, the Ganglia is started on each VM to monitor CPU, memory, and IO.
3. Upon a resource request from the workflow service:
    a. CRM fetches a VM from the VM pool and starts the Falkon service in that VM.
    b. CRM fetches another VM, starts the Falkon worker in that VM, and makes that worker register to the Falkon service.
    c. CRM repeats step b until all Falkon workers are started and registered.
    d. If there are not enough VMs in the pool, then CRM will make a resource request to the underlying OpenNebula platform to create more VM instances.

4. CRM returns the end point reference of the Falkon server to the workflow service, and the workflow service can now dispatch tasks to the Falkon execution service.

5. CRM starts the Cluster Monitoring Service to monitor the health of the Falkon virtual cluster. The monitoring service checks the heartbeat from all the VMs in the virtual cluster, and will restart a VM if it goes down. If the restart fails, then, for a Falkon service VM, it will get a new VM, start Falkon service on it, and have all the workers register to the new service. For a Falkon worker VM, it will replace the worker and delete the failed VM.

6. Note that we also implement an optimization technique to speed up the Falkon virtual cluster creation. When a Falkon virtual cluster is decommissioned, we change its status to standby, and it can be reactivated. When CRM receives resource request from the workflow service, it checks if there is a standby Falkon cluster. If so, it will return the information of the Falkon service directly to the workflow service. It will also check the number of the Falkon workers already in the cluster.

   a. If the number is more than requested, then the surplus workers are deregistered and put into the VM pool.

   b. If the number is less than required, then VMs will be pulled from the VM pool to create more workers.

As for the management of VM images, VM instances, and VM network, CRM interacts with and relies on the underlying OpenNebula cloud platform. Our resource provisioning approach considers not only the dynamic creation and deployment of a virtual cluster with a ready-to-use execution service, but also efficient instantiation and reuse of the virtual cluster and the monitoring and recovery of the virtual cluster. We demonstrate the capability and efficiency of our integration using a small-scale experiment setup.

12.4 Experiment

In this section, we demonstrate and analyze our integration approach using a NASA MODIS image processing workflow. The NASA MODIS dataset [33] we use is a set of satellite aerial data blocks, with each block is of size around 5.5 MB, with digits indicating the geological feature of each point in that block, such as water, sand, green land, and urban area.

12.4.1 MODIS image processing workflow

The workflow (illustrated in Figure 12.4) takes a set of such blocks, obtains the size of the urban area in each of the blocks, analyzes and selects the top 12 blocks with the largest urban area, converts them into displayable format, and assembles them into a single PNG file.

12.4.2 Experiment configuration

We use six machines in the experiment, each configured with Intel Core i5 760 with four cores at 2.8 GHz, 4 GB memory, 500 GB HDD, and connected with

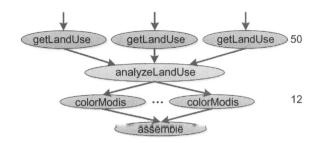

Figure 12.4 MODIS Image processing workflow.

Gigabit Ethernet LAN. The operating system is Ubuntu 10.04.1, with OpenNebula 2.2 installed. The configuration for each VM is one core, 1.5 GB memory, 20 GB HDD, and we use KVM as the hypervisor. One of the machines is used as the front-end, which hosts the workflow service, the CRM, and the monitoring service. The other five machines are used to instantiate VMs. Each physical machine can host up to 2 VMs, so at most 10 VMs can be instantiated in the environment.

12.4.3 Experiment results

In our experiment, we control the workload by changing the number of input data blocks, the resource required, and the submission type (serial submission or parallel submission). Therefore, there are three dependent variables. We design the experiment by making two of the dependent variables constant and changing the other. We run three types of experiments:

1. Serial submission
2. Parallel submission
3. Different number of input data blocks

   In all experiments, VMs are preinstantiated and put in the VM pool. The time to instantiate a VM is around 42 s and this doesn't change much for all the VMs created.

12.4.3.1 The serial submission experiment

In the serial submission experiment, we first measure the base line for server creation time, worker creation time, and worker registration time. We create a Falkon virtual cluster with one server with a varying number of workers, and we don't reuse the virtual cluster (Figure 12.5).

We can observe that the server creation time is quite stable and is around 4.7 s every time. Worker creation time is also stable, around 0.6 s each. For worker registration, the first one takes about 10 s, and the rest take about 1 s each.

For the rest of the serial submission, we submit a workflow after the previous one has finished to test virtual cluster recycling. We use 50 input data blocks to run the experiments.

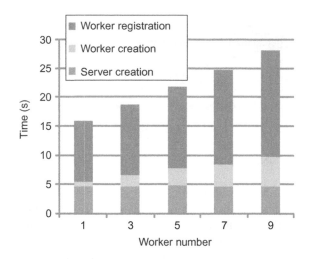

Figure 12.5 Base line for cluster creation.

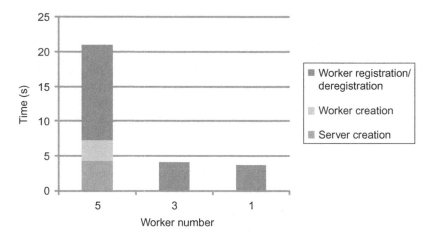

Figure 12.6 Serial submission, decreasing resource required.

In Figure 12.6, the resources required are one Falkon server with five workers, one server with three workers, and one server with one worker. In Figure 12.7, the resources required are in the reverse order of those in Figure 12.6.

From Figure 12.6, we can see that for the second and third submissions, the worker creation and server creation time are zero; only the surplus workers need to deregister themselves. In Figure 12.7, each time two extra Falkon workers need to be created and registered, and the time taken are roughly the same. These experiments show that the Falkon virtual cluster can be reused after it is created, and worker resources can be dynamically removed or added.

In Figure 12.8, we first request a virtual cluster with one server and nine workers. We then make five parallel requests for virtual clusters with one server and one

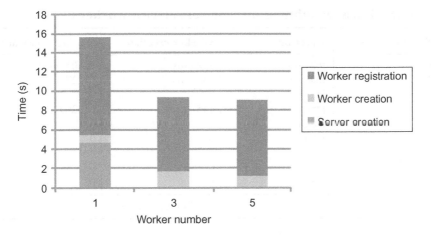

Figure 12.7 Serial submission, increasing resource required.

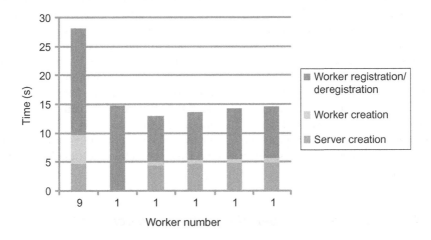

Figure 12.8 Serial submission, mixed resource required.

worker. We can observe that one of these requests is satisfied using the existing virtual cluster, whereas the other four are created on-demand. In this case, it takes some time to deregister all eight surplus workers, which makes the total time comparable to on-demand creation of the cluster.

12.4.3.2 The parallel submission experiment

In the parallel submission experiment, we submit multiple workflows at the same time to measure the maximum parallelism (the number of concurrent workflows that can be hosted in the cloud platform) in the environment.

First, we submit resource requests with one server and two workers, and the maximum parallelism is up to three. In Table 12.1, we give the results for

Table 12.1 Parallel submission, one server two workers

No. of clusters	Server unit	Worker creation	Worker registration
1	4624 ms	1584 ms	11305 ms
2	4696 ms	2367 ms	11227 ms
	445 ms	0	0
3	4454 ms	1457 ms	11329 ms
	488 ms	0	0
	548 ms	0	0
4	521 ms	0	0
	585 ms	0	0
	686 ms	0	0
	submission failed		

the experiment, in which we make resource requests for one, two, three, and four virtual clusters. The request of two virtual clusters can reuse the one released by the early request, and the time to initialize the cluster is significantly less than fresh creation (445 ms versus 4696 ms). It must create the second cluster on-demand. For the four virtual cluster request, because all VM resources are used up by the first three clusters, the fourth cluster creation will fail, as expected. When we change resource requests to one server and four workers, the maximum parallelism is two, and the request to create a third virtual cluster also fails. Because our VM pool has a maximum of ten VMs, it is easy to explain why this occurred. This experiment shows that our integrated system can maximize the cluster resources assigned to workflows to achieve efficient utilization of resources.

12.4.3.3   Different number of data blocks experiment

In this experiment, we change the number of input data blocks from 50 blocks to 25 blocks and measure the total execution time with varying number of workers in the virtual cluster.

In Figure 12.9, we can observe that, with the increase of the number of workers, the execution time decreases accordingly (i.e., execution efficiency improves). However, when using five workers to process the workflow, the system reaches efficiency peak. After that, the execution time goes up with more workers. This means that the improvement can't subsidize the management and registration overhead of the added worker. The time for server and worker creation, and worker registration remain unchanged when we change the input size (as shown in Figure 12.5). The experiment indicates that although our virtual resource provisioning overhead is well controlled, we do need to carefully determine the number of workers used in the virtual cluster to achieve resource utilization efficiency.

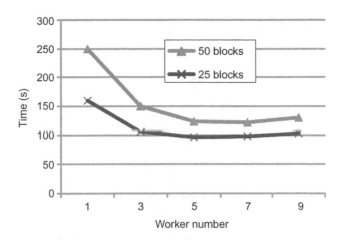

Figure 12.9 Different input size.

12.5 Experiment on Amazon EC2

In this section, we use Amazon EC2 as the resource provisioner and a Montage processing workflow to process 2MASS nebula graph. The region size of the 2MASS nebula graph is 0.5 and the image data are divided into 18 FITS images with size of 2.01 MB in each survey band (H, J, and Ks). As we do not integrate the CRM into Amazon EC2, we initialize the Falkon cluster manually.

12.5.1 Montage image processing workflow

Montage is a suite of software tools developed to generate large astronomical image mosaics by composing multiple small images. The workflow stages for generating the mosaic of three images are shown in Figure 12.10. The typical workflow process involves the following steps:

1. Image projection:
   a. Reproject each image into a common coordinate space (mProjectPP).
2. Background rectification:
   a. Calculate a list of overlapping images (mOverlaps).
   b. Perform image difference between each pair of overlapping images (mDiffFit).
   c. Fit difference images into a plane (mConcatFit).
   d. Background correction (mBackground).
3. Image co-addition (mAdd):
   a. Optionally divide a region into a grid of subregions and co-add images in each region into a mosaic.
   b. Co-add the processed images (or mosaics in subregions) into a final mosaic.

Finally, the mosaic is shrunk (mShrink) and converted into a JPEG image (mJPEG) for display.

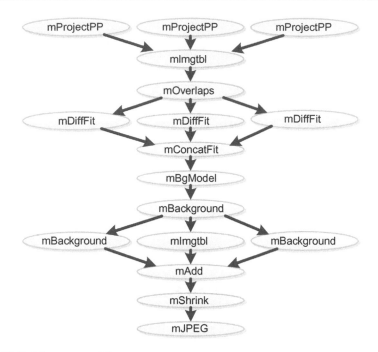

Figure 12.10 Montage workflow.

12.5.2 Experiment configuration

There are two Amazon instance types used in our experiment. The Falkon server and the Swift server use the same configuration: instance type is c1.medium with five CPU units, two CPU cores, and 1.7 GB memory. The Falkon worker is configured with instance type m1.small: one CPU unit, one CPU core, and 1.7 GB memory. All the instances use Ubuntu Server 11.10 as the operating system and are in the same security group.

12.5.3 Experiment results

In the experiment on Amazon EC2, we calculate the time cost to initialize the Falkon cluster and 2MASS nebula graph processing. In all experiments, instances are prelaunched using AMIs. The time to launch specified number of instances is shown in Figure 12.11. We can clearly see that the time increases with the instance number almost linearly. As the environment for launching instances in Amazon EC2 is uncontrollable, a few illogical data may appear that have already been excluded.

12.5.3.1 Falkon cluster initialization experiment

During the entire procedure of a Falkon cluster initialization, we first create the Falkon server and start the services on it. Then we create, register, and deregister workers concurrently.

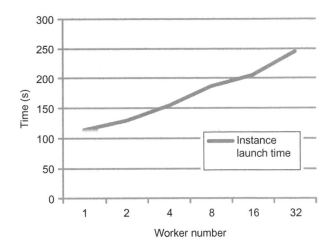

Figure 12.11 Cluster initialization.

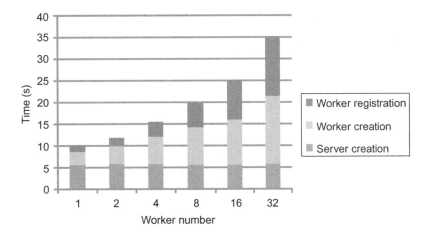

Figure 12.12 Cluster initialization.

In this experiment, we create a Falkon cluster with one server and a varying number of workers, and we don't reuse the cluster. We measure the server creation time, worker creation time, and worker registration time to compare with the experiment in OpenNebula. As we do not use a CRM in Amazon EC2, the worker creation/registration time is measured in different way compared to the results in the OpenNebula experiment. To calculate the worker creation/registration time, we use the end-time of the last worker finishes creating/registering minus the start-time of the first worker starts to create/register.

In Figure 12.12, we can observe the time cost to create a Falkon server and start services is around 5.5 s, which is very close to the server creation time in the OpenNebula experiment in Figure 12.5. Creation time for one single worker is stable, around 3.5 s each, and with worker number increasing, the average time to create a worker becomes lower—down to 0.5 s when the worker number reaches 32. Falkon server creation and Falkon worker creation time are affected by the performance and configuration of VMs. In addition, we have measured that the performance of Amazon instances is lower than the performance of local VMs with lower configuration parameter. To prove this, we initialize a local VM that is configured with one core and 1 GB memory and run a Falkon worker on it. The worker creation time is 1.1 s, much lower than 3.5 s. This also helps explain why the Falkon server creation time measured in the Amazon EC2 experiment is still longer, whereas the Falkon server configuration parameter seems much higher than the Falkon server we configured in OpenNebula experiment.

For worker registration, the time stays around 1.5 s each. Because the worker registration time is influenced by the network environment, we can determine why the time measured in the Amazon EC2 experiment varies from the results in OpenNebula experiment. In the OpenNebula experiment, the environment is deployed in Gigabit LAN. However, the network in the Amazon EC2 experiment, provided by Amazon, has a much smaller bandwidth. In addition, in the OpenNebula experiment, the first worker registration cost around 10 s, which is different from the result we measure here. Because the worker creation and registration is managed by the CRM and the first worker is in charge of notifying the server to start worker registration related mechanism, the 10 s consist of the resource scheduling time, command sending time, mechanism starting time, and first worker registration time. In our experiment in Amazon EC2, we do not use a CRM and the command to create workers was submitted manually. Therefore, we only measure the time to register one single worker, except the time cost in the preparation stage.

In this part, we measure the server creation, worker creation, and worker registration time of one Falkon cluster that consists of one server and 32 workers. Then we deregister the workers and measure the time it takes to deregister 16 workers→8 workers→4 workers→2 workers→1 worker. To calculate the worker deregistration time, we use the end-time of the last worker finishes deregistering minus the start-time of when the first worker starts to deregister.

In Figure 12.13, we can see that the deregistration time of one single worker is around 20 ms, which is quite short compared to the worker creation and registration time. Because of the relatively short deregistration time the network effect cannot be ignored. There exists several workers cost around 100 ms to deregister, which are regarded as dirty data and have been excluded. As we do not use a CRM, the communication procedure between the Falkon cluster and the CRM is skipped and the deregistration time in Amazon EC2 is much shorter than the time cost in OpenNebula (shown in Figure 12.6).

Finally, we measure the server creation, worker creation, and worker registration time of a Falkon cluster that consists of one server and one worker. Then, we expand the cluster scale exponentially by adding 1 worker→2 workers→4 workers→8 workers→16 workers into the cluster.

In Figure 12.14, we can note that the worker number increase exponentially, but the time cost rises almost linearly. The time cost to create and register one single worker is similar with the results in Figure 12.12.

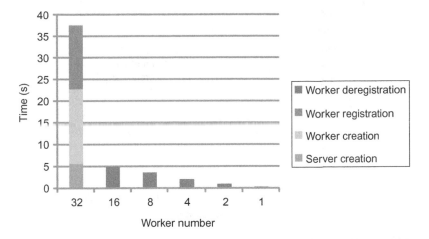

Figure 12.13 Decreasing Falkon workers.

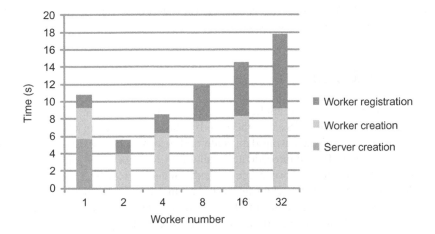

Figure 12.14 Increasing Falkon workers.

12.5.3.2 MASS nebula graph processing experiment

In this experiment, we submit a 2MASS nebula graph processing workflow to the Swift server, then Swift schedules and dispatches tasks to Falkon workers through the Falkon server. We change the number of workers in the Falkon cluster and measure the time cost of the entire procedure, except the cluster initialization.

In Figure 12.15, we can observe that, with the increase of the number of workers, the montage processing time decreases accordingly. After the worker number reaches eight, the time cost decreases slowly. If we consider both the montage processing time and cluster creation time, the total time may become larger with the increase of worker number. We can achieve the same conclusion as summarized

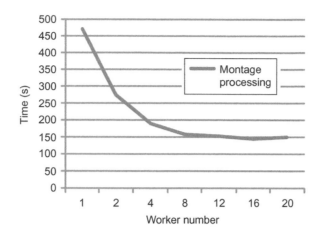

Figure 12.15 Montage processing.

from Figure 12.9. We should choose an appropriate cluster size based on the data size to achieve resource utilization efficiency.

12.6   Conclusions

As more and more scientific applications are migrating into the cloud, it is important to also migrate SWFMSs into the cloud to take advantage of cloud scalability and to handle the ever-increasing data scale and analysis complexity of such applications. The cloud offers unprecedented scalability to workflow systems and could potentially change the way we perceive and conduct scientific experiments. The scale and complexity of the scientific problems that can be handled can be greatly increased on the cloud, and the on-demand nature of resource allocation on the cloud will also help improve resource utilization and user experience. We presented our early effort in offering workflow management as a service by integrating the Swift workflow management system with the OpenNebula cloud platform, in which a cloud workflow management service, a cloud resource manager, and a cluster monitoring service are developed. We also conducted a set of experiments to showcase the functionality and efficiency of our approach.

For future work, we will leverage distributed storage for VM images and conduct large-scale experiments to find ways to improve VM instantiation, virtual cluster creation, and workflow execution.

Additionally, CRM is a very important module in charge of the management of VM images, VM instances, and VM network in the integration architecture. A CRM also receives resource requests and interacts with the underlying cloud platforms for resource provisioning. From the experiment in Amazon EC2 without a CRM, we can clearly see that virtual cluster reuse does not exist, which is not efficient. We will improve the CRM functionality to adapt to cloud platforms, such as

Amazon EC2, OpenStack, and CloudStack, which are gaining popularity in the science community. Then, we will develop a series of unified integration interfaces to integrate Swift with cloud platforms, which could be a reference to integrate other SWFMSs with cloud platforms.

References

[1] Hull D, Wolstencroft K, Stevens R, Goble C, Pocock M, Li P, et al. Taverna: a tool for building and running workflows of services. Nucleic Acids Res 2006;34:729−32 [iss. Web Server issue].

[2] Ludäscher B, Altintas I, Berkley C, Higgins D, Jaeger E, Jones M, et al. Scientific workflow management and the Kepler system. Concurr Comput Pract Exp 2006;18 (10):1039−65 [Special Issue: Workflow in Grid Systems].

[3] Freire J, Silva CT, Callahan SP, Santos E, Scheidegger CE, Vo HT. Managing rapidly-evolving scientific workflows, provenance and annotation of data, lecture notes in computer science, vol. 4145/2006, 10−18, 2006. Available from: http://dx.doi.org/10.1007/11890850_2.

[4] Deelman E, et al. Pegasus: a framework for mapping complex scientific workflows onto distributed systems. Sci Program 2005;13(3).

[5] Zhao Y, Hategan M, Clifford B, Foster I, Laszewski GV, Raicu I, et al. Swift: fast, reliable, loosely coupled parallel computation. IEEE Workshop on Scientific Workflows; 2007.

[6] Lin C, Lu S, Lai Z, Chebotko A, Fei X, Hua J, et al. Service-oriented architecture for VIEW: a visual scientific workflow management system. In: Proceedings of the IEEE 2008 international conference on Services Computing (SCC), Honolulu, HI; July 2008, p. 335−42.

[7] Rogers S. Big data is scaling BI and analytics, information management; September 1, 2011.

[8] Bell G, Hey T, Szalay A. Beyond the data deluge. Science 2009;323(5919):1297−8.

[9] Large Hadron Collider, <http://lhc.web.cern.ch>; 2012.

[10] <http://www.psc.edu/general/software/packages/genbank/>; 2012.

[11] Wilde M, Foster I, Iskra K, Beckman P, Zhang Z, Espinosa A, et al. Parallel scripting for applications at the petascale and beyond. IEEE Comput 2009; [Nov. 2009 Special Issue on Extreme Scale Computing].

[12] Foster I, Zhao Y, Raicu I, Lu S. Cloud computing and grid computing 360-Degree Compared. IEEE Grid Computing Environments (GCE08) 2008, co-located with IEEE/ACM Supercomputing; 2008.

[13] Hadoop, <http://hadoop.apache.org/>; 2012.

[14] OpenNebula, <http://www.OpenNebula.org>; 2012.

[15] Nurmi D, Wolski R, Grzegorczyk C, Obertelli G, Soman S, Youseff L, et al. The eucalyptus open-source cloud-computing platform. In: Proceedings of cloud computing and its applications; 2008.

[16] Keahey K, Freeman T. Contextualization: providing one-click virtual clusters in eScience. 2008. Indianapolis, IN; 2008.

[17] Openstack, <http://www.openstack.org>; 2012.

[18] Zhao Y, Fei X, Raicu I, Lu S. Opportunities and challenges in running scientific workflows on the cloud. IEEE international conference on Cyber-enabled distributed computing and knowledge discovery (CyberC); 2011.

[19] Palankar M, Iamnitchi A, Ripeanu M, Garfinkel S. Amazon S3 for science grids: a viable solution? In: Proceedings of the 2008 international workshop on data-aware distributed computing (DADC '08); 2008.

[20] Oliveira D, Ocaña K, Ogasawara E, Dias J, Baião F, Mattoso M. A performance evaluation of X-Ray crystallography scientific workflow using SciCumulus. IEEE CLOUD; 2011. p. 708−15.

[21] Deelman E, Singh G, Livny M, Berriman B, Good J. The cost of doing science on the cloud: the montage example. In: Proceedings of the 2008 ACM/IEEE conference on Supercomputing, SC '08. Piscataway, NJ; 2008. p. 50:1−50:12.

[22] Vecchiola C, Pandey S, Buyya R. High-performance cloud computing: a view of scientific applications. In: International symposium onparallel architectures, algorithms, and networks; 2009.

[23] Hoffa C, Mehta G, Freeman T, Deelman E, Keahey K, Berriman B, et al. On the use of cloud computing for scientific workflows. Third International workshop on Scientific Workflows and Business Workflow Standards in e-Science (SWBES). Indianapolis, IN; December 2008.

[24] Vöckler J-S, Juve G, Deelman E, Rynge M, Berriman GB. Experiences using cloud computing for a scientific workflow application. Invited Paper, ACM Workshop on Scientific Cloud Computing (ScienceCloud); 2011.

[25] Keahey K, Freeman T. Science clouds: early experiences in cloud computing for scientific applications, cloud computing and its applications 2008 (CCA-08), Chicago, IL; October 2008.

[26] Ramakrishnan L, Koelbel C, Kee Y-S, Wolski R, Nurmi D, Gannon D, et al. VGrADS: enabling e-Science workflows on grids and clouds with fault tolerance. In: Proceedings of the conference on high performance computing networking, storage and analysis (SC'09); 2009.

[27] Juve G, Deelman E. Wrangler: virtual cluster provisioning for the Cloud. In HPDC; 2011.

[28] Bresnahan J, Freeman T, LaBissoniere D, Keahey K. Managing appliance launches in infrastructure clouds, Teragrid 2011. Salt Lake City, UT; July 2011.

[29] Lin C, Lu S, Fei X, Chebotko A, Pai D, Lai Z, et al. A reference architecture for scientific workflow management systems and the VIEW SOA solution. IEEE Trans Serv Comput (TSC) 2009;2(1):79−92.

[30] Zhao Y, Dobson J, Foster I, Moreau L, Wilde M. A notation and system for expressing and executing cleanly typed workflows on Messy scientific data. SIGMOD Rec 2005;34(3).

[31] Raicu I, Zhao Y, Dumitrescu C, Foster I, Wilde M. Falkon: a Fast and Light-weight tasK executiON framework. Proceedings of the 2007 ACM/IEEE conference on Supercomputing. ACM; 2007, November. p. 43.

[32] Raicu I, Zhao Y, Foster I, Szalay A. Accelerating large-scale data exploration through data diffusion. International workshop on data-aware distributed computing 2008, co-locate with ACM/IEEE international symposium high performance distributed computing (HPDC); 2008.

[33] NASA MODIS dataset, <http://modis.gsfc.nasa.gov/>; 2012.

CPSIA information can be obtained at www.ICGtesting.com
Printed in the USA
LVOW01s1049181014

409405LV00005B/6/P